The Book-Collector

A General Survey of the Pursuit and of
those who have engaged in it at Home
and Abroad from the Earliest Period to
the Present Time

William Carew Hazlitt

Alpha Editions

This edition published in 2021

ISBN : 9789355390271

Design and Setting By
Alpha Editions
www.alphaedis.com
Email - info@alphaedis.com

Contents

PREFACE

SEVERAL monographs by contemporary scholars on the inexhaustible theme of Book-Collecting have made their appearance during the last twenty years. All such undertakings have more or less their independent value and merit from the fact that each is apt to reflect and preserve the special experiences and predilections of the immediate author; and so it happens in the present case. A succession of Essays on the same subject is bound to traverse the same ground, yet no two of them, perhaps, work from the same seeing point, and there may be beyond the topic substantially little in common between them and the rest of the literature, which has steadily accumulated round this attractive and fruitful subject for bookman and artist.

During a very long course of years I have had occasion to study books in all their branches, in almost all tongues, of almost all periods, personally and closely. No early English volumes, while I have been on the track, have, if I could help it, escaped my scrutiny; and I have not let them pass from my hands without noting every particular which seemed to me important and interesting in a historical, literary, biographical, and bibliographical respect. The result of these protracted and laborious investigations is partly manifest in my *Bibliographical Collections*, 1867-1903, extending to eight octavo volumes; but a good deal of matter remained, which could not be utilised in that series or in my other miscellaneous contributions to *belles lettres*.

So it happened that I found myself the possessor of a considerable body of information, covering the entire field of Book-Collecting in Great Britain and Ireland and on the European continent, and incidentally illustrating such cognate features as Printing Materials, Binding, and Inscriptions or Autographs, some enhancing the interest of an already interesting item, others conferring on an otherwise valueless one a peculiar claim to notice.

My collections insensibly assumed the proportions of the volume now submitted to the public; and in the process of seeing the sheets through the press certain supplementary Notes suggested themselves, and form an Appendix. It has been my endeavour to render the Index as complete a clue as possible to the whole of the matter within the covers.

As my thoughts carry me back to the time—it is fifty years—when I commenced my inquiries into literary antiquities, I see that I have lived to witness a new Hegira: New Ideas, New Tastes, New Authors. The American Market and the Shakespear movement[1] have turned everything and everybody upside down. But Time will prove the friend of some of us.

In the following pages I have avoided the repetition of particulars to be found in my *Four Generations of a Literary Family*, 1897, and in my *Confessions of a Collector*, 1897, so far as they concern the immediate subject-matter.

W. C. H.

BARNES COMMON, SURREY,

October 1904.

FOOTNOTES

[1] See the writer's *Shakespear, Himself and his Work: A Study from New Points of View*, second edition, revised, with important additions, and several facsimiles, 8vo, 1903.

CHAPTER I

The plan—The writer's practical career—Deficiency of a general knowledge of the subject—The Printed Book and the Manuscript independent branches of study—The rich and the poor collector—Their relative systems and advantages—Great results achieved by persons of moderate fortune—The Rev. Thomas Corser—Lamb and Coleridge—Human interest resident in collections formed by such men, and the genuine pleasure experienced by the owners—A case or two stated—The Chevalier D'Eon—The contrary practice—Comparatively early culture in the provinces and interchange of books—Lady collectors—Rarity of hereditary libraries—The alterations in the aspect of books—The Mill a fellow-labourer with the Press—A word about values and prices—Our social institutions answerable for the difference of feeling about book-collecting—Districts formerly rich in libraries—Distributing centres—Possibility of yet unexplored ground—The Universities and Inns of Court—Successful book-hunting in Scotland and Ireland—Present gravitation of all valuable books to London.

A MANUAL for the more immediate and especial use of English-speaking inquirers is bound to limit itself, in the first place, mainly to the literary products of the three kingdoms and the colonies; and, secondly, to a broad and general indication of the various paths which it is open to any one to pursue according to his tastes or possibilities, with clues to the best sources of intelligence and guidance. The English collector, where he crosses the border, as it were, and admits works of foreign origin into his bookcase, does not often do so on a large scale; but he may be naturally tempted to make exceptions in favour of certain *chefs-d'œuvre* irrespective of nationality. There are books and tracts which commend themselves by their typographical importance, by their direct bearing on maritime discovery, by their momentous relation to the fine arts, or by their link with some great personality. These stand out in relief from the normal category of foreign literature; they speak a language which should be intelligible to all.

It must be obvious that in a restricted space a writer has no scope for anecdote and gossip, if they are not actually out of place in a technical undertaking. Yet we have endeavoured to lay before our readers, in as legible a form as possible, a view of the subject and counsel as to the various methods and lines of Collecting.

Such an enterprise as we offer, in the face of several which have already appeared under various titles and auspices, may at first sight seem redundant; but perhaps it is not really the case. A book of this class is, as a rule, written by a scholar for scholars; that is all very well, and very charming the result is capable of proving. Or, again, the book is addressed by a bibliographer to bibliographers; and here there may be, with a vast deal that is highly instructive, a tendency to bare *technique*, which does not commend itself to many outside the professional or special lines. It was thought, under these circumstances, that a new volume, combining readability and a fair proportion of general interest with practical information and advice, was entitled to favourable consideration; and the peculiar training of the present writer during his whole life, at once as a *litterateur* and a practical bookman, encouraged the idea on his part that it might well be feasible for him to carry the plan into execution, and produce a view of a permanently interesting and important subject in all its branches and aspects, appealing not only to actual book-collectors, but to those who may naturally desire to learn to what the science and pursuit amount.

One of the best apologies for book-collecting, and even for the accumulation of fine books, is that offered by McCulloch in the preface to his own catalogue. The writer takes occasion to observe, among other points and arguments: "It is no doubt very easy to ridicule the taste for fine books and their accumulation in extensive libraries. But it is not more easy than to ridicule the taste for whatever is most desirable, as superior clothes, houses, furniture, and accommodation of every sort. A taste for improved or fine books is one of the least equivocal marks of the progress of civilisation, and it is as much to be preferred to a taste for those that are coarse and ill got up, as a taste for the pictures of Reynolds or Turner is to be preferred to a taste for the daubs that satisfy the vulgar. A man acts foolishly, if he spend more money on books or anything else than he can afford; but the folly will be increased, not diminished, by his spending it on mean and common rather than on fine and uncommon works. The latter when sold invariably bring a good price, more perhaps than was paid for them, whereas the former either bring nothing or next to nothing."

McCulloch's maternal grandfather was possibly the book-lover from whom the eminent political economist inherited his taste.

In common with the Manuscript Document and the Autograph Letter, the Written Book forms such a vast department of inquiry and study, that it would be undesirable, and indeed almost impracticable, in a volume of limited extent on book-collecting, to include the consideration of any collateral subject.

The broad facts regarding our national collections of MSS. are sufficiently well known, no less than the principal repositories in which they are to be found and consulted, and the individuals who have signalised themselves from time to time as owners of this class of property on various scales or on various principles. Nearly everybody with any claim to culture is familiar with the names of Cotton, Arundel, Harley, Lansdowne, Birch, Burney, Egerton, Hardwicke, and Stowe, in connection with precious assemblages of monuments in the National Library; Parker, Tanner, Fairfax, Ashmole and others at Oxford or Cambridge; Carew at Lambeth, and a succession of private enthusiasts in this direction, either independently or in conjunction with the printed side—Dering of Surrenden, Le Neve, Martin of Palgrave, Duke of Buckingham, Sir Thomas Phillipps, Libri, Lord Ashburnham, Heber, and Bright.

In the case of MSS. it is equally true with printed literature that the interest and value depend on circumstances, and are liable to changes and vicissitudes. They may be classified into countries, periods, and subjects, and their appreciation depends on their character even more than on their mere rarity. An unique MS. may possibly be quite worthless. A comparatively common one may command a good price. How numerous soever the ancient copies of Chaucer's *Canterbury Tales* might be, another coming into the open market would still be an object of keen competition; and where importance is coupled with scarcity or uniqueness, of course the latter feature lends a high additional weight to the matter, and multiplies inquirers.

We must, however, in justice to this branch of the topic and to our readers, refrain from further pursuit of the discussion of it, as its adequate treatment would absorb a monograph to the full extent as ample as the present, and such a Manual is in point of fact a desideratum—one, too, which the improved state of bibliographical knowledge would assist in rendering much more satisfactory than was formerly possible.

The *Rolls of Collectors* by the present writer afford a convenient view of the different classes of society in the now United Kingdom, which from the outset to the present day have created, during unequal periods of duration, more or less noteworthy centres of literary or bibliographical gatherings, from the Harley, Roxburghe, Heber, or Huth level to that of the owner— often not less to be admired or commended—of the humble shelf-ful of volumes. Here names occur associated with the most widely varied aims in respect to scope and compass, yet all in a certain measure participating in the credit of admitting to their homes products of intellectual industry and ingenuity beyond such matter as Family Bibles, Directories, Railway Guides, Charles Lamb's *Biblia-a-Biblia*, and sixpenny or threepenny editions of popular authors, which constitute the staple decorations of the average British middle-class household in this nonagenarian nineteenth century.

So early as the time of the later Stuarts, a movement seems to have commenced both in England and Scotland, not only in the chief centres, but in provincial towns, for the education of the middle class, and even of the higher grade of agriculturists, who sent their children to schools, and at the same time, in the absence of circulating libraries, improved their own minds by the exchange of books, as we perceive in contemporary diaries and correspondence; and Macaulay doubtless overcolours the ignorance and debasement of the bulk of society about the period of the Revolution of 1688, apparently in order to maintain a cue with which he had started. The Diary of John Richards, a farmer at Warmwell in Dorsetshire, 1697-1702, is an unimpeachable witness on the other side; it is printed in the *Retrospective Review*, 1853.

It was about the same date that we find even in Scotland a project for establishing throughout the country, in every parish, Reference or Lending Libraries, and some pamphlets on the subject have come down to us; but we hear nothing more about it. This was in 1699-1702, just when the indefatigable John Dunton was sending from the press his multifarious periodical news-books for the benefit of the more literary sort in South Britain.

The Circulating Library in the United Kingdom in its inception was intended more particularly for the better-to-do class, and even to-day its tariff is hardly compatible with very narrow resources. Perhaps the earliest effort to bring literature within the reach of the working-man was Charles Knight's scheme of "Book-Clubs for all Readers," mentioned in a letter to him of 1844 from Dickens.

A remarkable change in the fortunes and tactics of the collector has arisen from one in our social institutions. The book-hunter of times past, if he was a resident in the provinces, and worked on a more or less systematic and ambitious scale—nay, if he merely picked up articles from year to year which struck his fancy, relied, as he was able to do, on his country town. Thither gravitated, as a rule, the products of public and private sales from the surrounding neighbourhood within a fairly wide radius. If a library was placed in the market, the sale took place on the premises or at the nearest centre; there was no thought of sending anything short of a known collection up to London. The transit in the absence of railways was too inconvenient and costly. These conditions, which long survived better possibilities, naturally made certain headquarters throughout the kingdom a perfect Eldorado and Elysium, first of all for local enthusiasts miles round, and later on for metropolitan bargain-seekers, who made periodical tours in certain localities at present as barren as Arabia Petræa.

The principal points appear, so far as existing information goes, to have been in the North: Newcastle, York, Sheffield, Leeds; in the Midlands: Birmingham and Manchester; in the West: Plymouth, Exeter, and Bristol; in the South: Chichester; in the East: Norwich, Yarmouth, Colchester, Bury, and Ipswich. It was at Chichester that the poet Collins brought together a certain number of early books, some of the first rarity; his name is found, too, in the sale catalogues of the last century as a buyer of such; and the strange and regrettable fact is, that two or three items, which Thomas Warton actually saw in his hands, and of which there are no known duplicates, have not so far been recovered.

East Anglia during a prolonged period was peculiarly rich in holders and seekers of the Old Book, both manuscript and printed. It formerly abounded in monastic institutions, affluent county families, and literary archæologists. We may mention Lord Petre, the Hanmers of Mildenhall, the Herveys of Ickworth, the Bunburys of Bury, the Tollemaches, the Freres, the Fountaines, Sir John Fenn, Martin of Palgrave, Dawson Turner, and the Rev. John Mitford. It was the same, as we take elsewhere occasion to show, in the West of England, in the Midlands, in the Northern counties, and in the South of Scotland. The absence of ready communication with the metropolis and the relative insignificance of provincial centres kept libraries together. Their owners, while the agricultural interest was flourishing, had no motive for sale, and the inducement to part with such property was far less powerful, while the competition remained limited.

In Kent: Canterbury and Maidstone; in Surrey: Guildford, Croydon, Kingston, and even Richmond, may have helped to supply local requirements to a certain extent. But the Sydneys of Penshurst, the Oxindens of Barham, the Lee-Warlys, the Barretts of Lee, the Evelyns of Sayes-Court and Wootton, and others among the gentry of these and the adjacent shires, probably filled their shelves in principal measure from the London shops during their periodical visits to the metropolis for various purposes.

Even in later times the suburbs of London, and now and then such localities as Woolwich, Reading, Manchester, Shrewsbury, Salisbury, Wrexham, Conway, Keswick, and Dublin have yielded a prize or so, owing to the dispersion of some small library in the neighbourhood on the premises. Otherwise one may prospect the country towns all over the three kingdoms nowadays, and not see anything save new stock and penny-box ware. Even the provincial centres are, in general, sterile enough; but the rural districts are dried up. Every species of property seems to drift to London.

The Bristol houses, Kerslake, Jefferies, George, Lasbury, often came across rarities; but it is so no longer. The West has been threaded through. If there is a section of England where some good things may yet linger, it is, we should say, in Staffordshire, Lancashire, and Shropshire, to which might perhaps be added Worcestershire.

The seats of our two ancient Universities, and cathedral cities generally, have not yielded such ample fruit to the explorer, perhaps because there has always been a species of magnetic attraction, by which any spoils of the kind are drawn into the local libraries and museums. A graduate of Oxford or Cambridge, a canon of this or that church, a loyal dweller in Winchester or Lincoln, possesses or discovers a rare volume, and his impulse, if he does not keep it himself, is to bestow it on his place of residence or education. Whatever happens, the stranger coming to hunt in these preserves arrives only in time to learn that the stall or the shop has given up some unique desideratum a day or two before, and is referred to the librarian of the college, or to the buyer at such an address, if he desires to inspect it, which, if his aims are simply commercial, be sure he does not. The aggravation is already sufficient!

At the same time, the Universities and Inns of Court have been from time to time the homes of many famous book-collections. Robert Burton, Anthony Wood, John Selden, Sir David Dundas, Mr. Dyce, Dr. Bliss, Dr. Bandinel, Dr. Coxe, Mr. Bradshaw, are only a few select names.

In the same way there was a time, and not so distant, when Edinburgh, and even Dublin, yielded their proportion of finds, and the Duke of Roxburghe and General Swinton, David Laing and James Maidment, obtained no insignificant share of their extremely curious and valuable stores from their own ground. Now the Scotish amateur and bookseller equally look to the great metropolis for the supply of their wants, and the North Country libraries are sent up to London for sale. The capital of Scotland has lost its ancient prestige as a cover for this sort of sport, and is as unproductive as an ordinary English provincial town.

From an acquisitive standpoint the locality signifies no longer. The game is up. The three kingdoms have been well-nigh ransacked and exhausted. The country town is as bare as a bird's tail of anything but common-place stuff, bought in the London market, and (if any dweller in a distant city is simple enough to order it from the unsophisticated vendor) charged with a good profit and the freight up. Naturally the provincial dealer, if he stumbles on a gem or two in an accidental way, takes care that it is sold in no corner, unless it be at the corner of Wellington Street in the Strand. He considers that the value may be a matter of doubt, and he leaves it to gentlemen to decide between them how much it is worth. Do you blame him?

It is a frequently debated point whether at home in Great Britain the feeling for books, in the collector's sense, is not on the decline; and, indeed, the causes of such a change are not far to seek. The acute pressure of business among the wealthy mercantile class, which principally contributes to the ranks of book-buyers, and the decrease of resources for such luxuries among the nobility and clergy, might be sufficient to explain a shrinkage in the demand for the older and rarer literature in our own and other languages; but there is another and even more powerful agency at work which operates in the same direction, and is adverse to the investment of money in objects which do not appeal directly to the eye. The *bibliophile* discovers, when he has expended a small fortune (or perhaps a large one) in the formation of a library, that his friends evince no interest in it, have no desire to enter the room where the cases are kept, do not understand what they are told about this or that precious acquisition, and turn on their heel to look at the pictures, the antique furniture, or the china. This undoubtedly wide-spread sentiment strikes a very serious blow at a pursuit in which the enthusiast meets with slight sympathy or encouragement, unless it is at the hands of the dealers, naturally bound for their own sakes to keep him in heart by sympathy and flattery. Doubtless the present aspect of the question might have become ere now more serious, had it not been for the American market and the extension of the system of public and free libraries.

But, on the other hand, while enormous numbers of books are sold under the hammer year by year, there must be an approximately proportionate demand and an inexhaustible market, or the book trade could not keep pace with the auctioneers; and, moreover, we may be in a transitional state in some respects, and may be succeeded by those whose appetite for the older literature will be keener than it ever was.

The complaint of a superabundance of books of all kinds is not a new one. It goes back at least to the reign of Elizabeth and the age of Shakespeare, for in 1594, in a sermon preached at Paul's Cross, a divine says:—

"There is no ende of making Bookes, and much reading is a wearinesse to the flesh, and in our carelesse daies bookes may rather seeme to want readers, than readers to want bookes."

No one should be too positive whether it is to the rich or to the poor book-collector that the romantic element chiefly or more powerfully attaches itself. It has been our lot to enjoy the acquaintance of both classes, and we hesitate to pronounce any decided opinion. There is the unquestionable triumph of the man with a full purse or an inexhaustible banking account, who has merely to resolve upon a purchase or a series of purchases, and to write a cheque for the sum total. He is no sooner recognised by the members of the trade as a zealous enthusiast and a liberal paymaster, than offers arrive, and continue to arrive, from all sides. He is not asked to take any trouble; his library is an object of solicitude to everybody who has anything to sell; the order on his bankers is all that his humble servants desire. He finds himself, after the lapse of a decade or so, the master of a splendid collection, without having once known what it was to get disagreeably warm or anxious in the pursuit of a volume, to deliberate whether he could afford to buy it, or to submit to the ordeal of attending an auction, one of a motley throng in a fetid atmosphere. All these trials he has been spared; he has collected with kid gloves.

On the contrary, a good deal may be said in favour of the amateur of moderate fortune, who by personal judgment slowly accumulates an important and enviable assemblage of literary monuments, like the Rev. Thomas Corser, who spent £9000 during a lifetime on books, which realised £20,000, and would now bring thrice as much, and perhaps even more; and in that of men such as Charles Lamb and Samuel Taylor Coleridge, who had to pause before they laid out a few shillings in this way. The history of Lamb's books is more humanly interesting than the history of the Huth or Grenville library; as chattels or furniture they were worthless; they were generally the poorest copies imaginable; but if they did not cost money, they often cost thought; they sometimes involved a sacrifice, if the price was in the high altitude of a sovereign. In the case of Lamb, the sister's opinion was sought, and the matter lay ever so long in abeyance before the final decision was taken, and Lamb hastened to the shop, uncertain if he might not be too late, if the person whom he saw emerging as he entered might not have *his* book in his pocket. Here was payment in full for the prize; the coin handed to the vendor was nothing to it; Lamb had laid out more than the value in many a sleepless night and many an anxious calculation. Lamb, although he probably never bound a volume of his own in his life, or purchased one for the sake of its cover, could grow enthusiastic over his favourite *Duchess of Newcastle*, and declare that no casket was rich enough, no casing sufficiently durable, to honour and keep safe such a jewel.

Collectors of the abstract type looked, and still look, at the essence or soul— at the object pure and simple. A book is a book for a' that. It may be imperfect, soiled, wormed, cropped, shabbily bound—all those things belong to its years; let it suffice that there is just enough of the author to be got in glimpses here and there to enable the proprietor of him in type to judge his quality and power. That is what such men as Lamb wanted—all they wanted. A copy of Burton's *Anatomy*, of Wither's *Emblems*, or Browne's *Urn-Burial*, in the best and newest morocco, was apt to be a hinderance to their enjoyment of the beauties of the text, was almost bound to strike them as an intrusion and an impertinence—perchance as a sort of sacrilege—as though the maker of the cover was seeking to place himself on a level with the maker of the book. Nor are there wanting successive renewers of this school of collector—of men who have bought books and other literary property for their own sake, for their intrinsic worth, irrespectively of rarity and price. A relative of the writer devoted a long life—a very long one—to the acquisition of what struck him as being curious and interesting in its way and fell within his resources, which were never too ample; and in the end he succeeded in gathering together, without much technical knowledge of the subject, a fairly large assortment of volumes, not appealing for the most part to the severer taste of the more fastidious and wealthier amateur, but endeared to him at least, as Lamb's were, by the circumstances under which they came to his hands. Each one had its *historiette*. This gentleman represented, as I say, a type, and a very genuine and laudable one, too. I admired, almost envied him, not in his possession, but in his enjoyment of these treasures; they were to him as the apple of his eye. When I speak of him as a type, I mean that the same phenomenon still exists. In a letter of 1898 from the extreme North of England there is the ensuing passage, which strongly impressed my fancy: "Ever since I had a house of my own—nearly twenty years—I have been a collector of books on a humble scale. . . . Still, by being continually on the look-out for 'bargains,' I have managed to gather between three and four thousand volumes together, chiefly of a poetical nature." Now, to my apprehension, the present aspect of the matter touches a higher or deeper chord than that reached by the owner of the most splendid library in the universe; for all this Heliconian harvest signified personal search and personal sacrifice.

We do not always bear in mind that the rare books of to-day were the current literature not merely of, but long posterior to, the period of their appearance. They suffered two kinds and stages of deterioration and waste. While they remained in vogue among readers and students, they necessarily submitted to a succession of more or less indifferent owners, who regarded without much concern objects which it was in their power to replace without much difficulty. The worst day dawned, however, for our ancient literature, especially that of a fugitive or sentimental class, when it had ceased to be in demand for practical purposes, and was not yet ripe for the men, in whose eyes it could only possess archæological attractions. Independently of destruction by accidental fires, a century or two of neglect proved fatal to millions of volumes or other literary records in pamphlet or broadsheet form; and as tastes changed, the mill and the fire successively consumed the discarded favourites of bygone generations, just as at the present moment we pulp or burn from day to day cartloads of old science, and theology, and law, and fiction, and ever so much more, preparing to grow unique.

The Mill has been as busy as the Press all these centuries on which we look back. It has neither eyes nor ears, nor has it compassion; it unrelentingly grinds and consumes all that comes in its way; age after age it has reduced to dust what the men of the time refuse in the presence of something newer, and, as they hold, better. The printers of each generation, from those of Mainz downward, lent themselves, not unnaturally, not unwisely, to subjects in the first place (by way of experiment) which were not costly, and secondly to such as appealed to contemporary taste and patronage. We find under the former head Indulgences, Proclamations, Broadsides, Ballads; under the second, Church Service Books of all kinds, succeeded after a while by certain of the Classics. The impressions long remained limited; and continual use and subsequent neglect accomplished between them the task of creating the modern bibliographical and bibliomaniacal schools.

Even in Anglo-Saxon times the ferocity of warfare and the ravages of invasion on invasion, coupled with the scanty diffusion of literary taste, destroyed many of the monastic libraries. But, which is stranger and less excusable, even down to the second half of the seventeenth century, down to Aubrey's day, the greatest havoc continued to be made in this way alike among printed books and MSS., the latter being used for all sorts of utilitarian purposes—even as bungs for beer-barrels. In our own period it is immeasurably sadder and more astonishing to learn that, besides the losses arising from casual conflagrations to public and private libraries, the old vandalism is not extinct, and that nothing is sacred in its eyes, not even the priceless muniments of a cathedral church.

What must the aggregate have become, if such a process had not been steadily in operation all these centuries! And, even as it is, the dispersion of old libraries, like those of Johnson of Spalding and Skene of Skene, encourages the waste-paper dealer to believe that the end is not yet reached. The frequenter of the auction-rooms of London alone has perpetually under his eyes a mountain of illegible printed matter sufficient to overload the shoulders of Atlas.

Bibliomania has as many heads as the famed Briareus; but it seldom lifts more than two or three at once. Perhaps it would be impossible to name any variety of fancy which has not at some time entered into the pursuit which we are just now attempting to illustrate. The love of the book without regard to the binding, or of the binding irrespectively of the book; the fashion for works with woodcuts, of certain printers, of certain places, of certain dates; the establishment of a fixed rule as to a subject or a group of subjects, taken up collectively or in succession; a limitation as to price or as to size, for a candidate for admittance to some cabinets may not exceed so many inches in altitude; it must go back to the century which produced it, to be rewritten or reprinted, ere it may have a place.

It is said of the elder Wertheimer that, when some one expressed his astonishment at the price which he had given for an item, and even insinuated his want of wisdom, he retorted pleasantly that he might be a fool, but he thought that he knew greater ones than himself.

Do we not under existing conditions view with too uncharitable sentiments the marvellous good fortune of the book-hunters of the last century, at the very outset of a revival of the taste for our own vernacular literature? Does it not seem tantalising to hear that Warton the historian could pick up for sixpence a volume containing *Venus and Adonis*, 1596, and seven other precious *morçeaux*, off a broker's counter in Salisbury, when the British Museum gave at the Daniel sale £336 for the Shakespeare alone? What a thrill passes through the veins, as we read of Rodd the bookseller meeting at a marine store-shop on Saffron Hill, somewhere about the thirties, with a volume of Elizabethan tracts, and having it weighed out to him at threepence three-farthings! Our space is far more limited than such anecdotes; but they all strike us as pointing the same moral. If one happens on a Caxton or a quarto Shakespeare to-day for a trifle, it is the isolated ignorance of the possessor which befriends one. But till the market came for these things, the price for what very few wanted was naturally low; and an acquirer like George Steevens, Edward Capell, or Edmond Malone was scarcely apt to feel the keen gratification on meeting with some unique find that a man would now do, seeing that its rarity was yet unascertained, and even had it been so, was not likely to awaken much sensation.

Low prices do not alone establish cheapness. Cheap books are those which are obtained by accident under the current value. In the time of the later Stuarts, Narcissus Luttrell found from one penny to sixpence sufficient to satisfy the shopkeepers with whom he dealt for some of the most precious volumes in our language; and a shilling commanded a Caxton. The Huths of those days could not lay out their money in these things; they had to take up the ancient typography in the form of the classics, or large-paper copies of contemporary historians, or the publications of Hearne.

We do not know that the celebrated Chevalier D'Eon was singular in his views as a collector in the last century. He bought in chief measure, if we may judge from a document before us, what we should now term nondescripts, and in the aggregate gave a very handsome price at a London auction in 1771 for an assemblage of items at present procurable, if any one wanted them, at a far lower rate. There is not a lot throughout which would recommend itself to modern taste, save the *Cuisinier François*, and perhaps that was not in the old morocco livery considered by judges as *de rigueur*. We append the auctioneer's account entire, because it exhibits a fair example of the class of book which not only Frenchmen, but ourselves, sought at that time more than those for which we have long learned to compete, and which were then offered under the hammer by the bundle, if not by the basketful. For £8, 4s., a hundred and twenty-five years ago, how many quarto Shakespears could one have acquired?

THE CHEVALIER D'EON,
Bought of Baker & Leigh.

£ s. d.

Catalogus Librorum MSS. Angl. et Hibern	0	7	6
Index Librorum Bibliothecæ Barberinæ, 2 vols.	0	10	6
Reading Catal. Lib. in Collegio Sionensi	0	4	0
Le Long, Bibliothèque Hist. de la France	0	9	0
Voyage Literaire de deux Religieux Benedictins	0	5	0
Histoire de Demelez de la Cour de France	0	2	6
Memoires sur le Rang entre les Souv. de l'Europe, &c.	0	2	6
Discours Politiques sur Tacite, par Josseval	0	2	0
Dictionnaire Mathematique, par Ozanam	0	5	0
Dictionnaire Practique du Bon Menager de Campagne, par Liger, 2 vols.	0	6	0
Leland agt. Bolingbroke's Study of History	0	2	0
Mutel's Causes of the Corruption of Christians	0	1	0
Bindon on Commerce	0	2	6
Essay on Money, Trade, War, Banks, &c.	0	1	0
England's Gazetteer, 3 vols.	0	7	6
Halifax's Advice to a Daughter	0	1	0
Tresor de la Pratique de Medecine, 3 vols.	0	4	0
Seneque de la Consolation de la Mort	0	1	0
Tacite (la Morale de) par Houssaie	0	1	6
Tite Live reduit en Maximes	0	1	0
Gracien l'Homme Universel	0	1	6
L'Ecole de l'Homme	0	2	6
Memoire pour diminuer le nombre de Preces	0	1	6
Receuil des Edits	0	1	6

Le Secret des Cours, par Walsingham	0	1	6
Receuil de Maximes pour Institut. du Roy	0	1	0
Callieres de la Science du Monde	0	1	0
Traités des Interests des Princes' & Souverains de l'Europe	0	1	0
Sciences des Princes, par Naudé, 3 vols.	0	5	0
Etat present du Royaume de Danemarc	0	2	0
Memoires de l'Empire Russien	0	1	6
Memoires & Negociations Secrettes de diverses Cours de l'Europe par M. la Torre, 5 vols.	0	7	6
Memoires pour Servir a l'Histoire de Corse	0	1	6
Memoires Militaires sur les Anciens, 2 vols.	0	2	0
Histoire Generale de Suisse	0	2	0
Memoire du Card. Richelieu, 5 vols.	0	5	0
La Vie du Card. Richelieu, 2 vols.	0	4	0
La Vie de Mons. Colbert	0	1	6
Voyage de Grece, Egypte, &c.	0	2	0
Voyage du Mont du Levant	0	1	6
Lettres du Card. Richelieu	0	1	0
Lettres d'un Turque a Paris	0	1	6
Lettres Persanes, par Montesquieu	0	3	0
Le Passe Tems Agreable	0	1	6
Essai Politique sur le Commerce	0	2	0
Theorie de l'Impot	0	2	0
Histoire du Systeme des Finances, 1719 & 1720, 6 vols.	0	6	0
Histoire du Commerce, par Huet	0	2	0

Le Vrai Cuisinier François	0	1	6
Dictionnaire Neologique	0	2	0
Relations de quelques Religieux, 6 vols.	0	10	6
Reflexions sur l'Edit	0	1	0
Several lots of Pamphlets, 1s. each	0	4	0
Five Pamphlets, at 6d. each	0	2	6
	£8	4	0

Jan. 12th, 1771.

Recd. the contents

For Baker and Self,

GEO. LEIGH.

The neglect of our early literature continued, as we have said, down to the second half of the eighteenth century. Prior to that time, all the information at our command tends to show that collectors almost uniformly restricted themselves to the books current in or about their own time, as we find even Pepys asking Bagford to secure for him, not Caxtons or Elizabethan books, but items which we should now regard with comparative or absolute indifference. While some insignificant trifle, which had happened to go out of print, was sought with avidity, while editions of the classics and Continental writers, long since converted to waste paper, were objects of keen rivalry, the most precious examples of ancient English and Scotish typography and poetry were obtainable for pence.

A very interesting side to the subject before us is the share claimable in it by the fair sex. In our two *Rolls of Book-Collectors* we have included the names of several ladies, who in the seventeenth and eighteenth centuries, as well as in the earlier part of the present, established a title to rank among possessors of libraries in a larger or smaller measure. Two of the most prominent names are probably those of Miss Richardson Currer, of Eshton Hall, Yorkshire, and Mrs. Rylands of Manchester, the latter not only the acquirer of the Althorp treasures, but of a most valuable body of books, ancient and modern, in augmentation of them. This feature in the annals of collecting is the more to be borne in mind, in that it has in recent days declined almost to disappearance, and may be said to be limited to a few gentlewomen, who pursue special studies, like the Hon. Alicia Amherst and Mrs. Earle, and bring together for use or reference the works illustrative of them.

A study of the writer's *Rolls of Book-Collectors*, which embrace over two thousand names, will satisfy any one that the hereditary or transmitted collections in this country are very few, if we limit ourselves to libraries of note, and do not compensate for the long catalogue of old libraries which have been dispersed even in our own time. Are there really more than the Miller and the Huth, unless we add the Spencer or Althorp, kept intact and amplified, yet in the hands of a stranger? Book-collecting by individuals is, then, mainly a personal affair, which begins and ends with a life. The continuance even of the two libraries above mentioned in private hands cannot be regarded as otherwise than precarious and terminable; the fourth succession of Miller has just expired in an unexpected manner, and the destiny of the Britwell treasures is problematical. Rumour has long since pointed to the Advocates' Library at Edinburgh as the ultimate reversioner.

In a volume of moderate compass, professedly addressing itself in a special manner to English collectors, the consideration of foreign literature must of necessity be a secondary and incidental feature and element, although it may be quite true that our countrymen and countrywomen look so frequently aside, as it were, from the literary productions of their own soil to study those of other lands. In Great Britain we may be said to be much more cosmopolitan in our book-collecting tastes than many of our contemporaries on the Continent of Europe, Germany perhaps excepted. In France, Spain, Portugal, Italy, and elsewhere, the demand is almost exclusively for native authors; but the Germans, Americans, and ourselves take a pride, and a just one, in being more catholic and broad: we see the advantage, no doubt, and no doubt we reap the fruit, of such a policy. At the same time, in a monograph of limited scope it is obviously impossible to embrace even a general view of the enormously wide range which is before any one who crosses over from his own country to add to his English possessions even a select collection of books in foreign languages; and we have confined our efforts in this direction to an indication of such typical or special works (principally French) as are usually sought by people in these islands, who resort more or less to the Continental market. Even prominent Anglo-French amateurs like Mr. R. S. Turner and Lord Ashburton are found keeping within certain classes of literature, and certain copies recommendable by their *provenance*, binding, or graphic peculiarities.

CHAPTER II

Spoliation of public libraries in past times—Denouncers of the robbers of books—Schedule of public libraries in the United Kingdom—View of the chief features of some of these—Cathedral libraries—Public libraries on the Continent and in America—Early English books in foreign collections—Difference in the constitution of public collections—Private libraries—Their classification—The writer's *Rolls of Collectors*—The Harleian Library—The idea borrowed from abroad—Formation of a new English School of Collecting—The Roxburghe sale in 1812—Richard Heber and his vast library—His services to literature—His scholarship—The Britwell Library.

IT hardly falls within the province of a manual for the book-collector to dwell on the character and relative merits of the purely public libraries at home and abroad, or even on the bibliographical possessions of private personages which are not available for purchase. Recent experience, however, teaches us that we are not entitled to count any longer on the intact preservation of the books of any individual or family, as the sale by auction has almost become fashionable. At any rate, there can be no harm in introducing a few remarks on this aspect and branch of our subject, particularly seeing that the effect of throwing on the market thousands of rare books, which were once thought to be hopelessly unattainable, has contributed to improve the prospects and opportunities of purchasers.

The spoliation of public libraries at home and abroad is an aspect of the question or subject neither very agreeable nor very flattering. In England and other parts of the Empire, within the last century, numerous examples have occurred where valuable or unique books have been stolen or mutilated. The national collection in Great Russell Street has perhaps suffered the least, and whatever may be said about the system on which it was formerly conducted and managed, sufficient care seems always to have been exercised to guard against depredators of various kinds. So far as is publicly known, petty thefts of articles more or less easily replaceable are all that we have to regret. It is notorious that the Bodleian has lost several important volumes, and no one will probably ever arrive at any definite information of the extent to which the libraries at Cambridge and the other minor collections at the sister Universities of Oxford, Edinburgh, and Dublin have been pillaged and impoverished.

It has been the same all over the Continent. The Bibliothèque Nationale at Paris, and many of the leading provincial libraries of France, have been robbed wholesale in former times, and in some cases annihilated. One has only to read the observations and evidence of M. Achille Jubinal accompanying a (then) inedited letter of Montaigne (8vo, Paris, 1850), to form an idea of the ravages which have been made through neglect of officials and dishonesty of visitors; and what must the fact be in Italy, Spain, Portugal, and elsewhere? The denunciations against robbers of books and libraries date, however, from the remotest period, and were at first highly necessary as a means of safeguarding the treasures of monasteries and churches. Isaac Taylor, in his *History of the Transmission of Ancient Books to Modern Times*, 1875, p. 246, prints an anathema of this kind: "Whosoever removeth this volume from this same mentioned convent, may the anger of the Lord overtake him in this world, and in the next to all eternity. Amen." Let the energetic explorers who have transferred so many hundreds of such MSS. to the Vatican and the British Museum look to it; and what are His Holiness and the Trustees in Great Russell Street but palpable accessories after, if not before, the fact! A common peril hangs over them all.

A visit to a library such as the British Museum or the Bodleian, or even to those of some of the Colleges at Oxford and Cambridge, is apt to instil a feeling of reverential affection for the founders and benefactors of such institutions; the existing functionaries seem to withdraw into middle distance, and one enters into communion with the spirits of the departed.

From the private collector's point of view these great public libraries are mainly serviceable for purposes of reference and comparative study. These storehouses of bibliographical and literary wealth may be classified into—

(i) National or quasi-National Collections:—

- The British Museum
- Guildhall Library
- South Kensington Museum (Dyce and Forster and General Fine Art Collections)
- Society of Antiquaries
- Dr. William's Library, Gordon Square
- Chetham Library, Manchester
- Spencer-Rylands Library, Manchester
- Bodleian
- University Library, Cambridge
- University Library, Edinburgh

- Advocates' Library, Edinburgh

- Signet Library, Edinburgh

- Hunterian Library, Glasgow

- Trinity College, Dublin

The British Museum readily divides itself, of course very unequally, into the Printed Book and Manuscript Departments, and each of these has been periodically enriched by large donations or purchases *en bloc*, the former more especially by the gift of the Grenville books, and the latter by the Cottonian, Harleian, Lansdowne, Stowe, and Hardwicke MSS. The Bodleian would fall far short of what it is, had it not been for the bequests of Tanner, Selden, Burton, Crynes, Gough, Malone, and Douce, and so with the University Library at Cambridge, which owes so much to Bishop Moore's books, and Trinity, Dublin, to Archbishop Marsh's.

(ii) College Libraries:—

- Sion College

- Dulwich College

- Eton College

- Winchester College

- Stonyhurst College

- St. Cuthbert's College, Ushaw

- Cambridge Colleges

- Oxford Colleges

Sion College preserves a few items of the rarest and most precious class— Shakespeare's *Lucrece*, 1594, Barnfield's *Affectionate Shepherd*, 1594, the *Phœnix Nest*, 1593, Drayton's *Matilda*, 1594, and others; but a few specified in the old catalogue have disappeared. Many of the most valuable volumes bequeathed by Edward Alleyn to Dulwich are now among Garrick's books in the British Museum, or among Malone's at Oxford, *by conveyance*; but a few yet remain. Eton College Library contains a small number of early printed books (including Caxton's *Book of Good Manners*) and the unique copy of Udall's *Ralph Roister Doister*. At Winchester they have a volume or two of very rare poetical tracts of Elizabeth's and James I.'s time. Stonyhurst is solely remarkable for MSS. and printed works of Robert Southwell and other Romish writers.

Of the subordinate libraries at Oxford and Cambridge the treasures are innumerable. Those which belong to the printed department are very fully registered in special catalogues and by Hazlitt, except, perhaps, the very recent legacy to Trinity College, Cambridge, of the library of the late Mr. Samuel Sandars, rich in early English typography, and the result of life-long researches.

Outside these fall the Royal Library at Windsor, which includes the unique perfect Æsop, and one of the two books on vellum (the *Doctrinal of Sapience*) printed by Caxton; the Archiepiscopal one at Lambeth, rich in rare early printed books and MSS., and the Chetham and Rylands foundations at Manchester, the latter comprehending the Althorp treasures *en bloc*. Humphrey Chetham also established the Church Libraries at Turton and Gorton, bibliographical notices of which have been printed by Mr. Gilbert French, 4to, 1856; and a few strays from the Chetham collection will be incidentally mentioned hereafter.

A reference to the writer's *Collections*, where such facts are not matters of familiar knowledge, will show that the majority of this section is more remarkable for the possession of a few rarities, or even unique items, than for a systematic representation of classes and periods. Yet some are very strong in specialities: Christ Church, Oxford, in music; Magdalen, Cambridge, in early English books (Pepys's); Corpus, Cambridge, in MSS. (Archbishop Parker's); the Bodleian, in Shakespeariana, early popular books, Elizabethan poetry, &c. (Malone's, Douce's, Selden's, Burton's), and so forth.

(iii) Cathedral Libraries:—

- St. Paul's, London

- Canterbury (Christ Church)

- York Minster and Chapter

- Peterborough

- Lichfield

- Lincoln

- Hereford

At Lincoln there was formerly the precious Honeywood bequest, improperly sold to Dibdin for 500 guineas; but the library still contains about 5000 volumes, to which the Dean and Chapter make additions from time to time; and there is a paid custodian, who is one of the minor canons. York Minster and Chapter are rich in early typography and Yorkshire books. The Cathedral library is under the charge of a canon as librarian and a vicar-choral as sub-librarian, who receive no salary. It is open to the public on three days in summer and on two days in winter in each week. There is no fund for the support or improvement of the library, except the interest of £400 and a few voluntary subscriptions. Hereford possesses a remarkable assemblage of chained volumes. To the present group most properly appertains the library at Westminster Abbey, founded by Lord-Keeper Williams, while he was Dean of Westminster.

(iv) Public Libraries on the Continent or in America:—

- Bibliothèque Nationale, Paris
- French Institute (the gift of the late Duc d'Aumale), Chantilly
- Vatican Library, Rome
- Royal Library, Naples
- Medicean Library, Florence
- St. Mark's Library, Venice
- Royal Library, Turin
- Imperial Library, Vienna
- Imperial Library, St. Petersburg
- Royal Library, Berlin
- Library of Electors and Kings of Bavaria, Münich
- Library of the Dukes and Kings of Saxony, Wölfenbüttel
- Landerbibliothek, Cassel
- Public Library, Hamburg
- Public Library, Göttingen
- Public Library, Zürich
- Archiepiscopal Library, Eichstadt
- Archiepiscopal Library, Salzburg
- Archiepiscopal Library, Worms, &c.
- Plantin Museum, Antwerp
- University Library, Upsala
- Royal Library, Copenhagen

- Lenox and Carter Brown Libraries, New York

The two last named, as it may be at once concluded, are principally English and Anglo-American in their character. Our collectors do not, as we are aware, by any means restrict themselves to the literature of the mother country so exclusively as their Transatlantic contemporaries; and for them therefore it becomes of importance and interest to acquire through catalogues a familiarity with the contents of the leading assemblages of foreign and classical literature in Continental hands. But there are very few of the great public libraries abroad which have not casually or otherwise acquired English books, and those of the rarest description. At Göttingen they have, from an auction at Lüneburg in 1767, the *C. Merry Tales* of 1526; at Cassel, Marlowe's *Edward II.*, 1594; and at Hamburg the Elizabethan edition of *Blanchardine and Eglantine*, 1597, all unique or most rare; and this is only by way of instance or sample. The Huth copy of Shakespeare's *Sonnets*, 1609, was obtained from Zürich.

The private amateur does well if he keeps before him the salient features connected with his pursuit from this point of view. It is to be deeply regretted that the Government of the Netherlands did not take steps to preserve intact the Enscheden collection at Haarlem, in the same manner that that of Belgium did the Plantin heirlooms.

The late Mr. Quaritch narrated an amusing and characteristic anecdote, commemorative of his participation in the Enscheden sale, where the agent of the British Museum waited till the morning to bid at the table for the *Troy-Book*, printed by Wynkyn de Worde in 1502, and he bought it privately over-night of the auctioneer.

There is, it must be noted, a fundamental difference in the constitution of public libraries in Great Britain and America as compared with those on the Continent. The latter, if they do not restrict themselves, in principal measure, to the literature of their own country, or at least tongue, very seldom go far outside those limits otherwise than by accident or for works of reference. On the contrary, the English and American collections are cosmopolitan, like those who have formed them. At the British Museum a volume in Icelandic, Chinese, Hawaian, or any other character is welcomed nearly as much as one in the vernacular. In Germany, at all events at Berlin and Vienna, English books of importance are recognised. But at the Bibliothèque in Paris it is not so. The French collect only the classics and their own literature, just as they ignore in coins all but the Greek and Roman and national series.

Within their own lines, however, it is wonderful, looking at all the political convulsions which the country and capital have undergone, what vast treasures remain in France—treasures of all epochs and in every class, from the rise to the fall of the monarchy, from volumes written for the Carolingian, if not Merovingian kings, to volumes bound for Marie Antoinette.

Some interesting and instructive notices of our own public libraries, and of a few private collections of former times, may be found in the later volumes of the *Retrospective Review*.

The two *Rolls of Collectors* before mentioned are capable of making a not inconsiderable volume; but they are classifiable in groups and periods, and certain individuals may be taken as the central figures in the successive onward movements. Our immediate concern is with printed monuments, and consequently we do not hearken back beyond the men who witnessed the introduction of typography. Nor does there appear, while the purchasing power of money for literary possessions or the book-closet was high, to have been any *esprit de corps* or emulation tending to constitute schools or *côteries*, and to raise certain books or series to an artificial standard. Men at first acquired at random what happened to fall in their way; booksellers there were few or (except at London or in the Universities) next to none; and auctions were long unknown. Except for topography and the classics, there was, down to the middle of the eighteenth century, no active competition. The bulk of the Harleian Library was probably obtained without extravagant outlay, though not without labour and time; not those divisions which we should now prize would be the most expensive, unless we include the manuscripts for which Lord Oxford had even then to pay a price.

We have drawn the line where it appears that the principle of forming libraries, in the modern sense of the word, commenced in this country. Down to the Harleian epoch, when the Continental system began to influence us, the shelf of books which we observe in many old prints was the limit of nearly all collectors: not necessarily of their resources, but of their views and of the feeling of the time. Men acquired a handful or so of volumes, which came into their hands by gift or otherwise; from the absence or paucity of public institutions there were few individuals of any culture whatever without a few books besides the family Bible and *Pilgrim's Progress*; but such a colossal accumulation as was formed under the auspices of the second Lord Oxford, and still more that of Richard Heber, was as undreamt of as the vast and multifarious contents of the building in Great Russell Street as it now exists. A study of early correspondence and other sources of original information on the present point will be found to corroborate such a view of the average private collection in these islands anterior to the last century.

It was not till many years after the dispersion of that noble Harleian memorial of generous ardour among the public and private collections of England and the Continent (Dr. Johnson in his letter to Sir F. Barnard, 1768, says that many books passed direct into the *Bibliothèque du Roi* at Paris), that the Shakespeare revival led to an inquiry, on the one hand, into the literature connected with the Elizabethan period, and on the other to a partial discovery of how much of it had perished. That epoch may be regarded as the true Hegira from which we have to date the modern annals of collecting; the antecedent time was in a sense pre-historic, for the most precious remains of our national literature were unheeded and uncalendared; the means of forming a comprehensive estimate of the printed stores in actual existence were yet latent or unknown, and the almost undivided attention of students and purchasers was directed to the ancient classics and foreign typography. It must be conceded, we think, that whatever the importance of those branches of inquiry may be, the cause of British letters is more closely and permanently bound up with our own classics and the products of our own soil; and we repeat that the movement which first gave a stimulus to a sort of revolt from the Continental school and to the formation of a native one was the persuasion, on the part of a few scholars, that something more was to be done towards popularising the plays of Shakespeare and his more eminent contemporaries, and elucidating their writings by the help of those who lived amid the same scenes and habits of thought and under the same institutions.

Leigh Hunt used to speak to me of having attended the great Roxburghe sale in 1812 just for the sake of gaining an idea of what such an affair was. It was, no doubt, a fine collection which the noble owner and his predecessors (particularly John, Earl of Roxburghe in the time of Queen Anne) had acquired, mainly in the preceding century, at very moderate prices; and the result must have been highly satisfactory to the estate. But many things have happened since then; the Heber Library, the most extensive, most valuable, and most ill-fated in its realisation: the grandest and proudest bibliographical monument of the nineteenth or any other century, has been completed and scattered; and yet to-day, if the general reader were asked, he would probably be of the belief that the first rank was due to the earlier personage and collection. There is somehow a prestige about the Roxburghe sale which time seems incapable of weakening; yet in comparison with its successor it was a mere handful; and in fact the accumulations even of Harley, the second Earl of Oxford, vast and precious as they may have been, were not equal in magnitude or in value to those of Heber, of whom the most surprising and most interesting trait is his conversance with the interiors of so many of his treasures; nor should we ever forget his generosity in lending them to literary workers. The Rev. Alexander Dyce, who so ably edited our elder dramatists and poets, could never have accomplished his projects, if Heber had not come to his assistance with the rare, or even unique, original editions.

We have taken elsewhere an opportunity of recording the probable obligation under which we all lie to Heber for his offices in prevailing on the Government under the Regency to arrange the so-called gift to the country of the library of George III. What an inestimable boon and advantage it would have been, had he left us his own magnificent gatherings, with the liberty of exchanging duplicates! To how many a subsequent collection would such a step have been the deathblow or rather an insuperable bar! The Britwell and Huth libraries would have been robbed of half their gems, and the Daniel sale could not have proved the singular *coup* and sensation which it was, had the Heber element been absent.

The flyleaves of an enormous proportion of Heber's books are found enriched by his scholarly and often very interesting memoranda; they usually bear a stamp with BIBLIOTHECA HEBERIANA, but never an *ex libris*. That distinction the accomplished owner resigned to minor luminaries. The notes are always pertinent and occasionally numerous; and the pages of the sale catalogue, of which we have no fewer than thirteen parts, are lifted above mechanical common-place by the curious and varied matter interspersed from this source, as well as to a certain extent from the pen of John Payne Collier, who edited the early poetical and dramatic portions, and attended the auction to secure some of the rarest old plays for his friend the Duke of Devonshire.

Heber had, in the course of a not very prolonged life (he died at sixty), absorbed by degrees mainly all that fell within his reach, both at home and abroad; and he acquired much which never came to England, but was warehoused at Antwerp or elsewhere on the Continent, pending future arrangements, which he did not live to make. The library is said to have cost £150,000, and to have fetched about a third of that sum. As the owner had built it up from the ruins of others, so some more recent collectors found there their opportunity.

A good deal of interesting information about this once conspicuous figure in book-collecting circles may be found in Dibdin's *Reminiscences*. Heber seems to have inherited some shares in Elliott's brewery at Pimlico, and a residence within the precincts. How far this fortune contributed to enable him to devote so large an amount to the purchase of books and MSS., we hardly know; it was said that he derived advantage from the slave trade, but perhaps this was a calumny. At any rate, there was trouble which saddened his later years.

Mr. William Henry Miller of Craigentinny bought nearly the whole of the early English poetry, and made the Britwell Library what it was and is; and George Daniel of Canonbury carried off, at what might have then seemed exorbitant prices, the Shakespeare quartos, to have the enjoyment of them for thirty years, and then leave them as a valuable inheritance to his family; for his death just occurred, when Henry Huth had begun to compete more courageously for this class of books, and when the National Library was in a better position to offer tall figures for really vital acquisitions. It was in 1864, and the struggle for the quartos and a few other prizes was principally between the British Museum, Mr. Huth, and Sir William Tite.

At the present moment the Britwell collection is probably, on the whole, the finest private library in the kingdom; the founder of it was a solicitor in Edinburgh, whose name already meets the eye as a purchaser in 1819, when the Marquis of Blandford's books were sold at White-Knight's, and it passed by bequest to the Christy family, in whose hands it now remains.

Had it not been for Heber and for the bibliophobia which prevailed, when his possessions came to the hammer in 1834, it is doubtful whether Miller of Craigentinny could have achieved the extraordinary *coup*, which he did by transferring to his own shelves at one swoop the harvest of a lifetime—a lifetime almost dedicated to a single object.

CHAPTER III

The Huth Library—Special familiarity of the writer with it—Seven influential collectors of our time—The great dispersions of old-established libraries—Althorp—Ashburnham—Johnson of Spalding—List of the other leading collections, which no longer exist.

DURING a long series of years it was my special good fortune to see nearly every week the late Mr. Henry Huth, and to learn from him many particulars of the sources from which he had derived some of his fine and rare books. We made Mr. Huth's acquaintance not long after the enrichment of his library by the sale of George Daniel's collection in 1864; and that, with his very important acquisitions when Mr. Corser died, and his early English poetry came into the market soon after, constituted the backbone or stamina of the new-comer. Mr. Huth did not collect on a large scale during a great length of time; he made his library, or had it made for him, chiefly between 1854, when he bought his first folio Shakespeare at Dunn-Gardner's auction, and 1870. Once or twice his health and spirits failed, and he was always more or less desultory and capricious. We saw him one afternoon, when he shyly mentioned that he had at last taken courage to order home the Mazarin Bible, which Mr. Quaritch had kept two years after giving £2625 for it at the Perkins sale, and then sold to Mr. Huth for £25 profit. He did not show the book to us, for he had not opened the parcel, and confessed that he was rather ashamed of himself. A very curious circumstance was that one of the Rothschilds, who had been nibbling at the copy, called at Quaritch's a day or so later, and was of course vexed to find that he had been anticipated. Huth necessarily bought in every case, like Addington and Locker, at the top of the market, for he waited till the books were shown or sent to him; he never searched for them. Condition governed his choice a good deal; he was fond of Spanish books, his mother having been a Spaniard, and of early German ones, being a German on his father's side. He took the classics and Americana rather hesitatingly, and there is no doubt that the old English literature interested him most powerfully, as it was most fully represented on his shelves. The folio volume of black-letter ballads, knocked down to his agent at the Daniel sale for £750, was regarded by him with special tenderness; but we think that its real history was unknown to him. He was not aware that it was only a selection by Daniel from a much larger number obtained by Thorpe the bookseller from a private source, suspected to have been a person in the employment of the Tollemaches of Helmingham Hall, near Ipswich. Thorpe parted with the bulk to Mr. Heber for £200, and the latter, in sending the vendor the money, declared how conscious he was of his extravagance, and asked whether he had been so fortunate as to secure "the inheritance of the Stationers' Company!"

A far more extensive collection, though of later date, came some years afterward into Mr. Huth's possession; it consisted of three hundred and thirty-four sheet ballads of the Stuart period, which had formed part of a larger lot bought at a house-sale in the West of England for fifty shillings. Some went to the British Museum, some elsewhere; Mr. Huth's share cost him £500!

The Huth catalogue is a disappointing production, owing to the circumstance that a good deal of useful information was suppressed, and the opportunity was not taken, where expense was the least object, to furnish an exhaustive account of the books. It is singular that the Grenville and Chatsworth catalogues were spoiled much in the same way, and that Lord Ashburnham's own privately printed account of his books is a thousandfold inferior to the auctioneer's one.

The Duke of Roxburghe, Mr. Heber, Mr. Grenville, Mr. Daniel, Lord Spencer, Mr. Miller and Mr. Huth were seven personages who exercised on the printed book-market in their time (to say nothing of MSS.) a very notable influence, particularly Heber. One might add the names of Mr. Jolley, Mr. Bright, and Mr. Corser, who severally between 1810 and 1870 made their competition sensible and raised the standard of prices for many classes of old English books. It was said in 1845, when the Bright Library was dispersed, that the advance in realised values led some collectors to relinquish the pursuit. The formation, not only of such a library as that of Heber or Harley, but that of Corser or Daniel or Bright, will be in the future a sheer impossibility from the absence of the means of acquiring in many branches so large a proportion of the rarer *desiderata*. To gather together a collection of books on an extensive scale may always remain feasible; but the probability seems to be that assemblages of literary property outside mere works of reference will show a tendency to distribute themselves over a more numerous body of owners, including the public repository, which year by year removes a certain body of rare books of all kinds beyond the reach of competition. The Bright episode was to a considerable extent a duel between Mr. Corser and the British Museum. But Mr. Miller and Lord Ashburnham, and (it may be added) Mr. Henry Cunliffe of the Albany, were also in the field; and two years prior, Maitland in his *Account of the Early Printed Books at Lambeth*, 1843, already takes occasion to animadvert on what he terms the puerile competition for rarities, which had then set in.

Miss Richardson Currer, of Eshton Hall, Craven, Yorkshire, whose extensive and valuable library came to the hammer in 1864, was one of the most distinguished lady-collectors of the century. There is a privately printed catalogue of the books, of which two editions appeared in 1820 and 1833. Miss Currer was a competitor side by side with those already named for a certain proportion of the literary treasures which were in the market in her time. The late Lady Charlotte Schreiber confined herself to a few subjects, of which playing-cards were one; but both these personages have been eclipsed in our immediate day by Mrs. Rylands, who conceived, as a tribute to the memory of a deceased husband, the princely design of founding on the theatre of his commercial success a grand literary monument, of which the Spencer books should be the nucleus and central feature.

One of the greatest surprises of our time in a bookish way was not the sale of the library at Althorp, which had been rumoured as a contingency many years before it occurred, but its transfer by the purchaser to Manchester. We were all rather sorry to learn that the climax had at length been reached; the sacrifice was doubtless a painful one on more than one account; but it was presumably unavoidable, and the noble owner was encouraged by numerous precedents: the fashion for selling had quite set in then. I visited Althorp in 1868 for the purpose of examining some of its treasures. I remember the room, and the corner of it where the largest private collection of Caxtons in the world was kept, and the glass case which enshrined quite a number of Elizabethan rarities. His Lordship mounted a ladder to get me one or two of his Aldines printed on vellum. He showed me a delightful old volume of tracts, bound in a vellum wrapper, some absolutely unique, which his grandfather had bought, and a copy of the romance of *Richard Cœur de Lion*, 1509, which came out of a poor cottage in Lincolnshire. That former Lord Spencer once did a *gentlemanly* act in handing Payne the bookseller a *bonus* of £50, on finding that a volume he had had from him was a Caxton. Alas! the spell is broken. Althorp was its library, and that has left it for ever! *Sic transit gloria.*

In the wake of the Spencer books have followed those of the late Earl of Ashburnham, whose representative had previously disposed of his father's coins and of some of the MSS. The remainder of the latter still await dispersion or a purchaser *en bloc*.

The Ashburnham printed books included a considerable number of Caxtons and Wynkyn de Wordes, the *St. Albans Chronicle* and *Book of Hunting*, &c., printed at the same place, and many distinguished rarities in the foreign series of ancient typography; but first and foremost the Perkins copy of the Gutenberg or Mazarin Bible on vellum, which realised £4000, being £600 in excess of the figure given by the buyer. There was also the Bible of 1462 on vellum, which fetched £1500.

But the prevalent characteristic of the collection was an ostensible indifference on the part of the nobleman who formed it to condition. There were several fine books and interesting examples of binding; but the absence of any definite plan and of judgment was conspicuous throughout. Circumstances aided the immediate proprietor in his project for converting the property into cash, and the prices reached were, in the cases of the early printed volumes by Caxton and others, simply unprecedented, looking at the sorry state of the copies offered. The catalogue (sooth to speak) was not very carefully or scientifically prepared, and when the important lots were put on the table, the company had, as a rule, some serious deduction to make from the account printed by the auctioneers. The noble vendor did not see anything unbecoming in attendance to note the prices of lots during the earlier stages, and did not disguise his gratification when a book brought a heavy profit. Yet twenty years ago it was almost accounted a disgrace for an ancient family even to part with its heirlooms. In those cases, when want of the money cannot and is not pleaded, the proceeding seems all the stranger and the more discreditable. The late Lord bought at the right time, and his son sold at the right time. The prices realised were not merely high, but outrageous. Yet, after all, prices are a figure of speech and a relative term. To a wealthy Manchester manufacturer a thousand pounds are nothing more than four figures on a piece of paper instead of one or two, and the sole difference between £1000 and £2000 is the substitution of one numeral for another.

It was known, in a few cases, what the noble owner had given for the articles. His *Jason*, printed by Caxton, cost £87 *plus* commission, and produced £2100. The *Merlin* of 1498 was bought for 30 guineas, and realised £760. A little French volume by Jean Maugin, *Les Amours de Cupidon et de Psiche*, 1546, was carried to £60, having been acquired for half-a-crown. Certain other antecedent quotations were left far behind, as in the *Canterbury Tales* of 1498, which at Dunn-Gardner's sale in 1854 brought £245, and now went up to £1000, and in the Antonius Andreas of 1486, which was thought worth £231, as probably the earliest volume issued in the City of London.

There was a notable drop in the biddings for the imperfect copies of Chaucer from Caxton's press, and a host of items went for next to nothing, which in an inferior sale would have realised far more. It is ever so; and of course there was half a century's interest on the outlay. Still what an intense pleasure beyond money it had afforded the nobleman who formed it! And let us think, again, to how long a succession of holders the same beautiful or rare book has been a friend and a companion, a source of delight and pride!

It was remarked in the room that the present Earl had enlarged his father's possessions only to the extent of ONE VOLUME (No. 2748), for which he gave £4, and which yielded him £7. He had no right to complain so far.

Concurrently with the Ashburnham episode in 1897, there came upon us all, like a shell, the extraordinary report, which proved too true, not only that the representative of Johnson of Spalding had determined to part with the valuable library preserved in the house since at least the time of the Stuarts, if not of the Tudors, but that Mrs. Johnson had actually called in a local clergyman to select what books he deemed worthy of being sent up to London for sale, and had committed the residue to a local auctioneer. *The catalogues were partly distributed before the books were added,* and very few booksellers were even aware of the matter, till the sale was over. Not more than three or so, and a few private persons, were present; the volumes were made up in parcels and only one mentioned, and the bidding did not exceed two or three shillings a lot. Supposing 2000 items, comprised in 100 bundles at 3s. each; the grand total would be £15! Blades quotes the library as containing seven Caxtons, and the late Mr. Henry Bradshaw thought it worth while to pay a visit to Spalding to make notes, which he very kindly communicated to us. One of the purchasers at the sale offered me two of his minor acquisitions for £30. Although the library included a proportion of desirable articles, many of the books were esteemed so worthless that the acquirers removed the *ex libris,* and left the rest behind them!

Some of the Caxtons in the public library at Cambridge have belonged to the Johnson family, and are supposed to have been formerly presented to it by those of Spalding. They were acquired in the earlier half of the reign of Henry VIII. by Martin Johnson at the then current prices—from sixpence to a shilling or so; and a stray or two from the same collection, long prior to the dispersion of 1897, has occurred in the auction-rooms. I have to mention in particular the *Spalding Chartulary,* sold in 1871. But a few still remained on the old ground, and fortunately five were bound up together in one volume, which was not comprised in the wretched *fiasco* and anti-climax. This precious collection was offered to Mr. Jacobus Weale, while he was still curator at South Kensington, for £20, and declined, because, as an officer of a public institution, he could not accept it at that price, and was unable to pay the real value. Two, *Curia Sapientiæ,* by Lydgate, and *Parvus et Magnus Cato,* have since been acquired by the British Museum, with five excessively rare specimens of the press of Wynkyn de Worde. The National Library did not require the *Reynard the Fox* or the *Game of the Chess.*

The Spalding case was as unique as some of the books themselves. The owner seems to have been grossly ignorant of their value, as well as wholly indifferent to the property as heirlooms.

Except as a matter of record and history, the collector need not so greatly concern himself with all those libraries which have been scattered, and yet he finds it desirable to refer to the catalogues, if they were publicly sold, in order to trace books from one hand to another, till they return into the market and find a new owner—perhaps himself. One might fill a volume with a list of all the sales which the last forty years have witnessed; but, taking the principal names, let us enumerate:—

Addington	Ireland
Ashburnham	Johnson of Spalding
Auchinleck (Boswell)	Laing
Bandinel	Maidment
Beckford	Makellar of Edinburgh
Blew	Middle Hill
Bliss	Mitford
Bolton Corney	Offor
Collier	Osterley Park
Corser	Ouvry
Cosens	Rimbault
Crossley	Sir David Dundas
Dunn-Gardner	Sir John Fenn
Fountaine	Sir John Simeon
Fraser of Lovat	Singer
Frere	Stourhead
Fry	Sunderland
Gibson-Craig	Surrenden
Halliwell-Phillipps	Syston Park
Hamilton Palace	Way
Hartley	William Morris (residue after private sale)
Henry Cunliffe	Wolfreston
Inglis	

Within these broad lines, which do not include libraries privately acquired by institutions, such as the Dyce, Forster, and Sandars, or by the trade, which is an almost daily incidence, are comprehended a preponderant share of all the important books which have come to the front since the earliest period, of which there is an authentic register.

For we have to recollect that many of the persons whose possessions were dispersed only in our time were buyers a century or more ago, and had from Osborne, at what still appear to our weak minds provokingly low prices, his Harleian bargains. By the way, he kept them a tolerably long time. Did some one help him to find the money, or did he pay it by instalments? Seriously speaking, it was rather a white elephant. One of the most notorious private transactions in the way of sales of books *en bloc* was that by the Royal Society in 1873 of the printed portion of the Pirkheimer Library, presented to it by Henry Howard, Duke of Norfolk, the first president, and originally purchased by his ancestor, the celebrated Earl of Arundel, in 1636.

The dispersion of the Harleian Library doubtless gave an impetus to the revival in the eighteenth century of a taste for book-collecting; but of course a large proportion of the purchases from Osborne himself was on the part of buyers who parted with their acquisitions, and of whom we have no further record. But the Osterley Park and Ham House collections, the latter still intact, owed many indeed of their greatest treasures to this source. In 1768 Dr. Johnson, who had had a leading hand in the compilation of the Harleian Catalogue, and had so gained a considerable experience of the bearings of the matter, as they were then understood, addressed a long and interesting letter to the King's Librarian on the subject of the public collections of Europe and other bibliographical particulars.

Of the libraries above mentioned, the Sunderland, Syston Park (Sir John Thorold), and Hamilton-Beckford collections owed their chief importance to early typography, *editiones principes* of the classics, and bindings. Among the Blenheim books were a few miscellaneous rarities in the English class. Of Beckford's volumes many contained his MSS. notes.

The Surrenden (Dering family), Stourhead (Sir Richard Colt-Hoare), and Hartley libraries were historical and topographical. In the Inglis, Dunn-Gardner, and Osterley Park (Earl of Jersey) catalogues we encounter, among a good deal that is more or less commonplace, the rarest ancient typography, poetry, and romances.

We next approach the larger and more important Private Collections of books, which are more or less of a permanent and hereditary character, and which we have to content ourselves with admiring at a distance or otherwise according to circumstances. We cannot enumerate the holders of a few volumes or so up and down the country. The names of which we think are

Devonshire, Bute, Bath, Dysart, Bridgewater (Earl of Ellesmere), Britwell, Huth, Aldenham (H. H. Gibbs), and Acton (or Carnegie). The Duke of Fife is believed to possess some curious books inherited from Skene of Skene. The Duke of Northumberland owns a few, and a few are in the possession of Lord Robartes at Llanhydrock, near Bodmin, Lord Aldenham, and Mr. Wynn of Peniarth. All these centres affect the book-collector in one of two ways: in showing him what exists, and in showing him now and then what he is never likely to obtain. For in these repositories there are actually certain things which have never been offered for sale, and of which the most indefatigable research has failed to bring to light other examples. Such is not the case, however, with Lord Acton's library at Aldenham Park, near Bridgnorth. That is a collection made by a scholar for scholars; it is wonderfully extensive and complete in its way, and it were much to be desired that it should be preserved intact. It commercial value is, relatively to its extent, inconsiderable.

The collections at Chatsworth and Devonshire House (including the books of Henry Cavendish and many of those of Thomas Hobbes) principally consist of early printed literature, English and foreign, and old plays; of the latter the Kemble dramatic library formed the *nucleus*, Payne Collier filling up at the Heber and other sales many important *lacunæ*. The late Duke ill-advisedly engaged a foreign gentleman to compile his catalogue, and the result is most unfortunate. Besides the Henry Cavendish and Hobbes elements, a few very valuable items came from the old library at Bolton Abbey, Yorkshire.

The Althorp heirlooms, now removed to Manchester, have been familiarised by the catalogues of them printed by Dibdin; but there are hundreds of precious volumes which he has overlooked, and of which some account is given in the present writer's *Collections* from the books themselves. An idea of the Dysart and Britwell libraries is to be gathered from Blades's *Caxton*, Dibdin's *Ames*, and Hazlitt's *Collections*. Of the possessions in this way of the Marquises of Bath and Bute we gain only casual glimpses from the same sources. Payne Collier and Hazlitt have made the Bridgewater House library fairly well known. The Huth one is elsewhere referred to, and of Lord Acton's a sale catalogue of a portion was prepared some years since, as well as a bibliographical account; but the former was suppressed, and the latter remains incomplete and in MS.

Of Lord Aldenham's collection (Early English Literature, Bibles, Classics, MSS., &c.) there is a privately printed catalogue, 1888, and there is also one of the late Mr. Locker-Lampson's literary treasures.

CHAPTER IV

Classification of collections—Origin of the taste for books—Schedule of topics or branches of inquiry—Each separately considered and the authorities cited—Ancient typography—British history and topography—Liturgies—Books of Hours—The *Imitatio Christi*—*Pilgrim's Progress*—Books of Emblems—Books of Characters—Books printed before the Great Fire, at Oxford, during the Civil War and Interregnum, &c.—Monastic and patristic writers—English devotional and other books printed abroad—Froschover's Zürich Bible of 1550—Other Bibles—The French Bible of 1523-28—Minor specialisms.

AS books, in a manuscript or printed shape, are far more numerous and varied than any other species of property, and are also more largely sought for purposes of direct study and instruction, there exists the greater difficulty in attempting to advise collectors as to the line which it is best, wisest, or safest to embrace.

The class of persons who engage in this attractive pursuit are:—

(i) Pure amateurs, without any eye to the financial question.

(ii) Specialists of more than a single kind.

(iii) Students.

(iv) Speculators.

(v) Miscellaneous or casual buyers.

The normal amateur starts, in general, without any well-defined scheme before him. He has seen in the hands of a friend, perhaps, a curious book; and the notion takes possession of him, rather stealthily, yet rather languidly too, that it might be a "nice" thing to have oneself—that or such another. The spirit of collecting, like a delicate germ, is at first easily extinguished; but an incident as trivial and fortuitous as the one just suggested has ere now constituted the *nucleus* and starting-point of a large library. It may, indeed, be a favourable symptom and augury when a man begins circumspectly and deliberately; he is more apt, other circumstances favouring, to prosecute his scheme to the end, and to prove a valuable friend to the trade.

We have mentioned that the Specialist may be of more than one sort. He may, in short, be of ten thousand sorts; and the Student, after all, may be bracketed with him; for both equally devote their exclusive attention to a prescribed class of works or branch of inquiry for a more or less definite term.

The subjects which principally engage the notice of specialists are:—

Ancient Typography (including Xylographic works).

Roman Catholic books.

English books printed abroad.

English, Scotish, and Irish History.

Voyages and Travels.

Irish Literature.

English Topography.

Scotish Literature.

English Genealogy and Family History.

Early illustrated books.

Modern illustrated books.

Liturgies and Prayer-Books.

French illustrated books.

Books of Hours.

Books of Emblems.

Bibles.

Books of Engravings.

Editions of the *Pilgrim's Progress*.

Early English Poetry.

Early Romances.

Occult Literature.

Early Music.

Folk-lore.

Spanish Romances.

Tobacco.

Italian Romances.

Educational books.

Dantesque Literature.

Caricatures in book form.

Cromwell Literature.

Miracles and phenomena.

Civil War and Commonwealth tracts.

Broadsides.

Editions of the *Imitatio Christi*.

Chap-books.

There is probably not much of consequence to be suggested outside this calendar from which an intending collector may make his choice. Each of the topics indicated is, for the most part, susceptible of being subdivided and subdivided again.

Ancient Typography is not only a large, but a difficult and costly field. It is, notwithstanding, a not unusual circumstance for a beginner, and not a rich one, to start by making himself master of a few examples of our first printers; and this arises from the fact that among the remains in such a line of collecting are pieces of no high interest or character, and copies whose condition does not attract the riper connoisseur. At the same time it arises from the feeling of the period which witnessed the dawn of the art, that a heavy percentage of the output of the printers of all countries amounts to little more than typographical curiosities, which may be substantially possessed in the form of an example of moderate cost. The novice generally selects books and tracts of foreign origin, and of a theological or technical complexion. Perhaps he goes further—even so far as to discard his earlier purchases; perhaps he does not. It is a matter of taste and money. If he does not seek the finest and rarest specimens, especially in the English series, it is not too much to say that £500 spread over a career would suffice to procure one a fair representation in which Fust and Schoeffer, Gutenberg, Mentelin, and Caxton might appear in the form of a leaf—possibly a damaged one. Yet there would be a chronological view in actual originals of the art of printing from the commencement in all countries. We go for our facts on this subject to Panzer, Hain, Brunet, the British Museum Catalogue, &c.

British History and *Topography* are alike departments which can scarcely be regarded as specialities without questionable fitness. For when we survey the catalogues of those who have professedly restricted their aim to these two ranges, and reflect that all such collections are, by the light of bibliographical authorities, more or less tentative and imperfect, we are brought to the conclusion that there would be, in a thoroughly exhaustive treatment of the matter, less left outside than could be found within. Of the divisions which present themselves above so much is capable of being drawn into the two other series. Numerically an assemblage of ancient and modern books in these classes would be by possibility immense. But the attendant outlay, unless certain signal rarities were included, or it was deemed necessary to comprise all the poetical relics with a historical or a topographical side, ought not to be relatively so high as that on the preceding category, particularly if the acquirer were satisfied here and there with trustworthy reproductions of three-and-four-figure items. From £1000 to £1500 will go a long way in supplying a collection with that qualifying proviso; without it, four times the amount would barely cover you. The Hartley and Phillipps catalogues should be consulted, as well as Upcott and other older authorities.

Liturgies form one of the tastes and objects of pursuit of persons who have left behind them the fancies of their novitiate, and possess the means of purchasing a description of literature which is abnormally costly, and might prove more so, were the buyers more numerous. The editions of the Prayer-

Book fall under this section, and are almost innumerable, being tantamount to *Annuals*, and of many years we possess more than one issue.

The printed *Books of Hours* might, from their extent, as regards subordinate variations arising from the different uses and occasional changes in portions of the ritual, constitute in themselves a life's study and absorb a fortune. There is great disparity in their typographical and artistic execution, no less than in their commercial value. A tolerably full description of the series occurs in Brunet, Lowndes, Maskell, the British Museum Catalogue, and in those of the principal collectors on these lines. Of those adapted to English or Scotish uses there is an account in Hazlitt's *Collections*; but we may look in the early future for an exhaustive monograph from the pen of Mr. Jacobus Weale.

The British Museum is singularly rich in editions in all languages of the *Imitatio Christi*, having enjoyed the recent opportunity of supplying wants from an enormous collection sold by public auction *en bloc*. The Offor Catalogue is considered an authority on the *Pilgrim's Progress* and other works of Bunyan; but the National Library contains a large proportion of these books, and the Huth Catalogue and Hazlitt's *Collections* must not be overlooked.

The authorities just cited, the Corser Catalogue, and the publications of the Holbein Society, will prove useful guides to any one desirous of studying the EMBLEM Series, which was some time since in marked request, but has sustained the customary relapse, and is what booksellers term rather *slow* just now. Our own literature is not particularly wealthy in these productions; there is nothing of consequence beyond Whitney, Peacham, *The Mirror of Majesty*, 1618, Wither, Quarles, and Harvey (*School of the Heart*). But if the collector goes outside the national frontier, he meets with works of this class in even bewildering abundance in regard to number, variety of type and treatment, and degree of artistic and literary merit. Moreover, among the works of this species just enumerated as of national origin, four of the six were more or less heavily indebted to the Continent; the Whitney was printed at Leyden, and Wither, Quarles, and Harvey did little more than write English letterpress to sets of foreign plates.

Books of Characters, of which perhaps Earle's *Microcosmography*, 1628, is the most familiar, have attracted attention from more than one of our book-fanciers; they constitute a somewhat extensive series, and we gain a fair *aperçu* of it in the catalogue of the library of DR. BLISS, of St. Mary's Hall, Oxford, 1858. It was Bliss who reprinted Earle in 1811, and inserted a bibliography of publications on similar lines.

The above-mentioned gentleman also lent himself to two other paths of collecting: one suggested by local associations, and consisting of works printed at Oxford, the second dealing with those which appeared just prior to the Great Fire of London in 1666.

One of Bliss's Oxford friends, DR. BANDINEL, Bodley's librarian, made it his speciality to bring together as many of the fugitive publications as possible relative to the Civil War Period and the Commonwealth, and MR. JOHN FORSTER did the same. The Bandinel Catalogue, 1861, is an excellent guide on this ground, although it is almost unnecessary to state that it is very incomplete. The best and most exhaustive assemblage of the literature of the Troubles and Interregnum (1640-59) is the descriptive list of the King's pamphlets in the British Museum formed by Thomason the stationer.

The interest and profit attendant on the study of the monastic and patristic writers, who may be said to be less strictly national and more cosmopolitan than those of later schools, are, as a rule, casual and slender for the merely literary consulter or peruser, supposing the rather extreme case, where such a person is sufficiently courageous and robust to engage in anything approaching a serious examination of these families of books. The authors were true enthusiasts, labouring to their lives' last thread in some obscure cell or dim closet, where pride of authorship, as we may feel and enjoy it, there was none, when beyond the walls of a convent or those of a native town their names were unknown, their personality unrecognised. Except to the theologian or ritualist how repellent and illegible this mass of printed and manuscript matter must ever seem! How deficient in human sympathy and pertinence! These treatises, so erudite, so prolix, and so multifarious, were composed by men (Universal, Irrefragable, or Seraphic Doctors), and after a certain date by women too (Angelical Sisters), who had no knowledge of the world, of society, of human nature, or of real philosophy. Yet they were, and long remained, the class of literature most cultivated, most studied, and most multiplied; and to this hour, notwithstanding the destruction of millions of them, they abound in our national, cathedral, and college libraries, and in private collections dedicated to that particular side of inquiry and learning. In the booksellers' catalogues we sometimes meet with examples, which are recommended to the curious buyer by their illustrations of conventual life, and their exposure of those vices which a state of celibacy is calculated to promote in both sexes. The chained book is not an uncommon feature in the ancient ecclesiastical repositories, and even in certain churches; and apart from the Scriptures, it almost invariably enters into the department of early divinity or polemics.

Whatever may be thought of this branch of the theological library, there is an undoubted market for it, or some portions of it, as stocks are kept both here and abroad, although on a more restricted scale, perhaps, than formerly. It is extremely probable that, if any one who was learned enough and dexterous enough should make a decoction of all the uncountable folios which exist up and down the globe, the result might be a single volume of not very ample dimensions, affording its share of insight and edification.

The call on the part of a narrow coterie of churchmen for the Catholic literature of the sixteenth and succeeding centuries, more especially the books produced at Continental presses, necessarily resulted in the rapid inflation of the value, while it brought to light from numberless recesses a vast assemblage of works previously undescribed and unknown. Many of these works were produced at obscure localities in France and the Netherlands; but Paris, Douay, Brussels, Antwerp, Mecklin, Tournai, Bruges, Ghent, Breda, are responsible for a majority. Besides the purely religious publications, quite a large number of secular books, and those of permanent and striking interest, owed their origin to the same region, particularly to Amsterdam, the Hague, Middelburg, Dort. The source of all this foreign production was mainly either the employment of Englishmen and Scots abroad on military service, or their residence there in exile or for other purposes. Italy, Switzerland, Germany, and even Poland, lent their presses to the British author; the scarce tracts by James Crichton (the Admirable) proceeded from Milan or Venice. We know what important centres for English controversial divinity and political pamphleteering were Geneva, Basle, and Zürich, and the last-named place is particularly associated with the name of Christopher Fröschover, printer of the Bible of 1550. A distinct feature in this vast body of Continental typography connected with us is the curious and often unique light which it incidentally throws on the lives of our countrymen and countrywomen, segregated by their employments or opinions from their compatriots at home, and obliged to resort to printers ignorant of the language which they committed to type. A tolerably exhaustive estimate may be found of this branch of the subject by a reference to the *General Index* of Hazlitt's COLLECTIONS (1867-91).

To the Duke of Sussex's Catalogue, and those of Lea Wilson, George Offor, Francis Fry, William Maskell, W. J. Loftie, W. J. Blew, Farmer-Atkinson, Lord Ashburnham, and the Rev. W. Makellar of Edinburgh, we must go for the means of bibliographically estimating the editions of the Scriptures and the Prayer-Book; and the Huth and Caxton Exhibition Catalogues should be consulted. The ordinary English and American collector seldom goes beyond English, French, German, and Latin Bibles. Of all these, not even excepting the Fust and Gutenberg or Mazarin, the original impression of the Scriptures in French, published at Paris and Antwerp in six volumes between 1523 and 1528, is by far the rarest; and the next place or rank is perhaps due to the German one, printed at Zürich in the same number of volumes, 1527-29, of which an imperfect copy is in the Huth Library. The Mazarin Bible has grown rather commoner of late years. It is certainly much more so than Coverdale's English one of 1535 in a perfect state, or Tyndale's New Testament of 1526.

It is a point about it not generally known, that the extant copies on vellum and on paper differ.

For History, Genealogy, Topography, and well-nigh all other branches of human science, the student finds himself referred to the Middle-Hill Library, now in course of gradual dispersion; but this is far richer in the manuscript than in the printed book department. He may also profitably consult the catalogues of Mr. Hartley and Mr. Tyrrell (City Remembrancer), of whom the second collected largely on London.

Mr. Bolton Corney, Mr. Grenville, and Mr. Jadis made voyages and travels, books relating to America, and the first-named literary *adversaria*, distinct features in their enormous aggregate of volumes.

Information on early English poetry and the drama may be sought in the catalogues of Sykes, Perry, Caldecott, Heber, Chalmers, Jolley, Wolfreston, Way, Daniel, Corser, Collier, Frere, Bliss, Bright, Mitford, Ouvry, Bandinel, Halliwell-Phillipps, and of course Huth.

Mr. Brook Pulham concentrated his attention on the writings of George Wither, Mr. Bragge on works illustrative of Smokers and Tobacco, and Major Irwin on the occult and supernatural.

Mr. Henry Pyne during a long series of years made an extensive collection, restricted to English books dated prior to the year 1600, and as a rule, it must be added, to the commoner class of publications.

CHAPTER V

Voyages and travels—Their strong American interest—Maryland and Pennsylvania—New Plymouth—Sir John Mandeville—Columbus and Vespucci—Early medical literature—Harvey and the circulation of the blood—Occult literature—Phenomena—Technical works—The paddle-wheel—Books printed in a special manner—Chapbooks—Garlands—Ballads—Broadsides—Street advertisements—General or miscellaneous collections—Omnivorous buyers—Richard Heber, Sir Thomas Phillipps, James Crossley—A moral deduced—Most interesting types of collector—Advantages connected with restriction to personal tastes or wants—Dangers of emulation and servility—Mr. Quaritch's *Dictionary of Collectors*—Various sorts of genuine collector.

VOYAGES and Travels have always engaged a large share of attention and study, and comprise the central and very interesting feature of almost the entire body of early Americana, dealing with the discovery and colonisation of that continent. This part of the subject before us has received, owing to recent political occurrences, a further development in the direction of Africa. To the purely American collector, who of course takes in Canada, his own literary heirlooms are unexceptionally material; and if he works on a comprehensive principle, he admits every item relevant to the series, however costly and however individually trivial. An Englishman, as a rule, is content with typical or representative examples. The late Mr. Huth long remained unpersuaded that books of this character were *desiderata*.

There can be no doubt, however—and Mr. Huth concurred so far from the outset—that there are certain Anglo-American works which are, so to speak, indispensable to a library of any pretensions. For instance, it must not be without such capital productions as those written or published in elucidation of the history of the New World by Drake, Cavendish, Hakluyt, and Purchas; or such, again, as contribute to throw light on the settlement of New England and the progress of the Pilgrim Fathers. This group of literature has grown within the last twenty years almost unattainable by the less opulent bibliophile; its commercial value has risen to four times that to which the previous generation was accustomed. The most signal feature in the whole series is, however, out of the pale of commerce. The precious manuscript found at Fulham Palace in 1896, giving a detailed account of the settlement of New Plymouth, has by a graceful international act been restored, as it were, to its fittest home, although many of us in Old England would have, no doubt, preferred to see it deposited in Great Russell Street.

There is another source of association with the mother country which commends to the notice of many, not exclusively American in their tastes or objects, the literary memorials of Maryland and Pennsylvania, so intimately associated with the English families of Calvert and Penn. There is no rarer volume among the first Anglo-American monuments than Hariot's *Virginia*, 1588, which is worth from £100 to £120.

Among the favourite books of travel are Sir John Mandeville's *Voyages*, of which there are ancient editions in English, French, Italian, and German, and which is being constantly reproduced with the quaint illustrations. The narratives of Pinto, "prince of liars," and Bruce are gaining increased credit and confidence. Leo's *Description of Africa*, in the English version of 1600, has a map already showing the source of the Nile in an inland lake. The labours of the Hakluyt and Geographical Societies have conferred respectively great benefits on the cause of discovery and verification.

In the famous *Letter of Columbus*, 1493, in its various forms, the *Mundus Novus* and *Paesi Retrovate* (1507) of Vespucci, and a few other leading publications, there is a recognised interest regardless of the countries of origin.

We owe to the entrance into the lists of sundry members of the medical profession a temporary emergence from oblivion and respite from the waste-basket of what the booksellers describe in their catalogues as "Rare Early Medical." There is no doubt that among these obsolete publications may be detected many curious points and many evidences of former acquaintance with supposed latter-day inventions or ideas. A prominent feature in the series is Harvey's Latin treatise on the circulation of the blood, of which he was the (rather late British) discoverer. But, on the whole, the group of early works dealing with medicine and surgery is of questionable interest outside the purely practical range as a comparative study, and those which treat of anatomy and other cognate topics are in the last degree gruesome. They are the antipodes to the *belles lettres*.

Occult Literature is susceptible of a division into several classes or sections: Religious Cults, Necromancy, Magic, Second Sight, Divination, Astrology, Palmistry, of which all have their special literatures and bibliographies. Major Irwin recently sold an extensive series of works on these and kindred topics. Cornelius Agrippa, Ashmole, Bulwer, Lilly, Partridge, Gadbury are among the foremost names of older writers in the present categories. But for the faiths and worships of antiquity which may be ranked in the first order of importance and solid interest, we chiefly depend on modern books, such as Payne, Knight, Inman, Davies, Forlong; and there is quite a small library on that branch which touches on theosophy and similar speculations—all having a common source in the grand principle of Agnosticism. Further information will be found collected on this and the topics which we notice below in Hazlitt's *Popular Antiquities*, 1870.

For those who are interested in Portents, Phenomena, *Lusus Naturæ*, Murders, Earthquakes, Fires, there is the catalogue of MR. NASSAU, 1824. The British Museum has in recent times grown more complete in the same direction. The founders and earlier curators of the institution appear to have regarded such *nugæ* as beneath the dignity of a national library; but in fact the information which they, and possibly they alone, convey, is frequently of historical, biographical, or topographical relevance.

There has been a rather marked tendency to a rise in the value of a section of technical publications which deals with the earliest notices in English literature of such subjects as Electricity, the Microscope, the Steam-Engine, the Paddle-Wheel, and the Telephone, and the books identified with these subjects are now commanding very high prices. An uncut copy of Thomas Savery's *Navigation Improved*, 1698, where the principle of the paddle-wheel is discussed, fetched at Sotheby's in June 1896, £16, 15s.

This is a somewhat fresh departure, but it is not an unsound or unreasonable one, and the series is limited. An almost invariable incidence of these artificial figures is to draw out other copies, and then the barometer falls.

The name of MR. EYTON is identified with copies of books printed on vellum or on some special paper, not unfrequently for his own use or pleasure; and this gentleman's catalogue is serviceable to such as desire to follow his precedent, of which the modern *Edition de Luxe* is an outgrowth. Eyton would have proved an invaluable friend to Japanese vellum, had he belonged to a later decade of the century.

The CHAP-BOOK, which dates from the reign of Elizabeth, and was sold for a silver penny of her Highness, becomes less rare under the Stuarts, and common to excess at a later period down to our own days. A large proportion of this species of literature consists of abridgments of larger works or of new versions on a scale suited to the penny History and Garland. Pepys was rather smitten with those which appeared in and about his own time, and at Magdalen, Cambridge, with the rest of his library, a considerable number of them is bound up in volumes, lettered *Penny Merriments* and *Penny Godlinesses* respectively. The Huth Collection possesses many which were formerly in the Heber and Daniel libraries. All these productions share the common attributes of very coarse paper, very rough cuts, and very poor type. They are interesting as eminently *folk-books*—books printed for the multitude, and now, especially when the article happens to be of unusual importance and rarity, worth several times their weight in gold. Two catalogues of Chap-Books and Popular Histories were edited by Mr. Halliwell for the Percy Society in 1848-49.

In the present writer's bibliographical works, to which there is a General Index, will be found an account of all that have come into the market between 1866 and 1892. Thousands upon thousands have unquestionably perished.

The most fascinating member of the Chap-Book series is undoubtedly the *Garland*—not so much a volume by a given author, such as the *Court of Venus* (1558) and Deloney's *Garland of Good Will*, 1596, as a miscellany by sundry hands. The next earliest of these collections known to us at present are the *Muses' Garland*, 1603, and *Love's Garland*, 1624. Those in Pepys's library at Cambridge are of much later date, yet of some no duplicates can be quoted, so vast has been the destruction of these *ephemerides*. Of the Pepysian Garlands a certain proportion are reprints of older editions or repositories of songs and ballads belonging to an anterior date, and here and there we meet with lyrics extracted from contemporary dramatic performances.

Besides Pepys, Narcissus Luttrell the Diarist displayed a taste for fugitive and popular publications, and the copies acquired by him eventually found their way, for the most part, into Heber's hands, whence they have drifted in large measure either into the British Museum or the Miller and Huth collections. Numerous unique examples of the popular literature of his own day, again, are preserved among Robert Burton's books in the Bodleian.

Allied to the chap-book are the broadsides of various classes, including the Ballad, popular and political, the Advertisement and the Proclamation. So far as we know, the second division exhibits the most ancient specimen in our own literature, and is a notification on a single leaf by Caxton respecting Picas of Salisbury use. This precious relic, of which only two copies are recorded, appeared about 1480. It must have been soon after the introduction of printing into London and Westminster that resort was had to the press for making public at all events matters of leading importance; but we do not seem to possess any actual evidence of the issue of such documents save in isolated instances till toward the end of the century, and they are chiefly in the shape of indulgences and other ecclesiastical manifestos, circulated in all probability in the most limited numbers and peculiarly liable to disappearance.

The Ballad proper cannot be said to be anterior to the closing years of Henry VIII., subsequently to the fall of Cromwell, Earl of Essex, when the composition relative to that incident printed in the collections appeared, and was followed by the series preserved in the library of the Society of Antiquaries of London, and reprinted in the writer's *Fugitive Tracts*, 1875. From the time of Elizabeth onward the broadside in its varied aspects grew abundant, and served as a substitute for newspaper notices, so long as the press remained an insufficient medium. The British Museum and Society of

Antiquaries possess large collections of this kind. Lord Crawford has printed a catalogue of his *Proclamations*, and in the writer's *Collections*, 1867-92, occur thousands of these ephemerides arranged under what appeared to be their appropriate heads.

During the sixteenth and seventeenth centuries the sheet *format* lent itself largely and conveniently to teachers, quack doctors, astrologers, announcing their addresses, qualifications, and terms, no less than to the official, municipal, or parochial authorities, and to private persons who desired to give publicity to some current matter by the exhibition of the placard on a wall or a church door. There was yet another purpose which the broadside was made to serve: prospectuses of schemes and reports of companies' or societies' proceedings. The purely temporary interest of such publications accounts for their survival in unique examples and even fragments.

There is a general notion that the *Harleian Miscellany* and the *Somers Tracts* represent between them a very large proportion of the extant pamphlets and broadsheets published during the sixteenth and seventeenth centuries. But, as a matter of fact, they do nothing of the sort. Even in or about 1695 William Laycock of the Inner Temple drew attention to the unsuspected importance of these fugitive publications in his printed proposal for buying them up by a public subscription; but even in the National Library, with all its immense accumulations, and in Hazlitt's *Collections*, many thousands of items are probably deficient; while the two sets of books above mentioned contain a very slender percentage of the whole—in fact, mere representative selections.

There have been men who coupled with a general plan a speciality or two. For instance, Dyce, who laid a collateral stress on *Shakespeariana*; Ireland, who made himself strong in Leigh Hunt and Hazlitt; Crossley, who had a peculiar affection for Defoe; Bliss, who collected books of characters and books printed at Oxford or just before the Great Fire of 1666; Bandinel, who was smitten by the charms of the Civil War literature; Corser, whose bibliographical sweethearts were Nicholas Breton and Richard Brathwaite; and Rimbault, who had two, Old Music and Old Plays. Mr. G. L. Gomme is similarly situated: anthropology and folklore are his foibles. It goes without saying that the Shakespearian and dramatic student, from Sir Thomas Hanmer downward, has usually made a stand on the literary remains and works tending to illustrate their own labours; but of course the relevance may be direct or indirect, and in the latter case the specialist is found to cast his net surprisingly wide.

Specialism, whether on the principle of personal taste or of particular studies, has manifest advantages in an age where the multitude and choice of books are so bewildering, where of every work of any sort of value or interest a man may have, not a single edition—all that in a majority of instances was once available—but a hundred or a thousand in all sorts of sizes and at all sorts of prices. With the discontinuance of the older paucity of literature, the facilities for lodging within a modest bookcase a coterie of literary favourites have sorrowfully decreased, and a collector finds it imperative to draw the line more and more rigidly, if he does not care to fall into one of two perils—excessive outlay or excessive bulk. For we have not, as regards the former, to go very far before we incur a serious expense, if it happens that the run is on the rarer English section or on what constitutes a picked library of the French type.

Of the miscellaneous group there are graduated and varying types. The omnivorous accumulator, especially where he does not insist on condition or binding, is the dealer's idol. In the forefront of this class stand *facile principes* Richard Heber and Sir Thomas Phillipps, for the reason that they bought everything—whole libraries and catalogues at a swoop. Yet both these distinguished men have to be placed on a distinct footing from the normal promiscuous buyer, such as Thomas Jolley, Joseph Tasker, Edward Hailstone, Edward Solly, and a legion of others, to whom anything in the guise of a book was a sure bait, and who spurned Evelyn's motto: "*Meliora retinete.*" Ascending a step or two higher, we come to the men who repudiate specialism as narrowing and troublesome, and who impose on themselves no restraint save perchance in the direction of theology, science, and *arcana*. They stop peremptorily at the *belles lettres*. Singer, Mitford, Bliss, Bandinel, Forster, Cosens, Ireland, Crossley, Sir John Simeon, were more or less of this school. At a still greater altitude we meet with a yet stronger tendency to draw the line at character or condition, and there occur to us the names, under the former head, of Capell, Malone, Douce, Bright, Chalmers, Collier, Ouvry, Bolton Corney, David Laing, E. F. Rimbault, Halliwell-Phillipps, Frederick Locker, W. H. Miller, Henry Cunliffe, R. S. Turner, and Henry Huth. From the same point of view, nearly in the clouds are discovered a small knot of fastidious *dilettanti*, who purchase a volume in the same spirit as they might do a picture or a piece of majolica; and of this minority Sir Andrew Fountaine, Sir David Dundas, and Samuel Addington may perhaps be accepted as types.

The most interesting, and it may with permission be added, intelligent type of book-collector, however, seems to be that where, after a certain measure of preparatory thought and training, one confines acquisitions for permanent ownership to volumes for which the acquirer has a genuine personal relish. In general, the principle of forming a library on this wholesome basis would be found not only more useful, but more economical, since the rarest and costliest articles are by no means, on the whole, the most interesting or the most instructive. In any case, the inconsiderate emulation by one collector of others, who may have different objects and perhaps ampler resources, is a course to be avoided. Even here there is more than a single source or ground of inducement to purchase. Setting aside the mere book of reference, which has to be multiplied to suit various exigencies, there may be said to be three classes of literary property which rationally appeal to our sympathy: (i) the volume which commends itself by its intrinsic value and charm; (ii) that which has grown dear from lengthened companionship and possibly hereditary link; (iii) and that which, unimportant so far as its internal claims and merits are concerned, bears on its face the evidence of having once belonged to a favourite of our own or a world's hero.

One persuasive argument in favour of adopting the miscellaneous or typical course in the choice of a library is the rapid growth of the difficulty of meeting with the rarer items in all important specialities. It is the general plan on the part of every follower of particular lines to commence, very often casually, by bringing home from time to time a few volumes on a certain topic, or in a given class of literature, or by one or two of a school of writers; and such a proceeding succeeds tolerably well, till the owner makes discovery of volumes positively essential to his object, and unattainable save by a heavy outlay—perchance not even to be had at any price. It is nearly always the *lacunæ* for which we yearn; one or two of our richer friends have them, and we have not. What we possess anybody can get in a morning's walk; we find that we have travelled a long distance, and have come to an *impasse*. It is very seldom indeed that a man is satisfied with the cheaper and commoner articles in a series, if he is aware of the existence of those which just constitute the corner-stones of such a collection as his.

On the contrary, by the process of sampling or picking out here and there, now and again, a book or a set of books which chance or circumstances may throw in our path, we may gradually acquire a caseful of most desirable specimens, against which it is out of the question to raise any charge of incompleteness, where incompleteness is the governing aim. Book-buying under these conditions is a humour. We are at liberty to take or leave. Because we conceive a fancy for a work by this or that author, we feel under no obligation to accommodate every scrap which he has printed, or which his friends or followers have penned. The object of our personal selection suffices us; and there perhaps we begin and we end. It is our humour.

The auctioneers' and booksellers' catalogues of the present day supply an instructive demonstration of the gradual withdrawal from the market of many thousands of articles, in Early English literature more particularly, which at one time seemed to be of fairly frequent recurrence. They have been taken up into public collections all over the world; and the very few copies, not to speak of unique examples, which time had spared, are beyond the reach of the private purchaser of to-day. We have only to study with attention the Heber and other leading records of former libraries existing in this and other countries to become convinced that the facilities for acquiring an approximately complete library of the rarer books grow narrower year by year.

There is, I submit, far too prevalent a tendency in collectors to follow suit, to attach themselves to leaders of temporary fashions. I plead for a greater independence of opinion, where the taste is in any reasonable measure cultivated and developed, or, again, where an individual knows what pleases himself. By all means, if it happens that he does not admire Shakespeare and Bacon, Sydney and Jonson, Dryden and Pope, Byron and Shelley, Scott's novels or Lamb's *Elia*, let him leave them alone, and make his own free choice, even if it be to go in for *John Buncle*, the *Adventures of a Guinea*, or Luttrell's *Letters to Julia*. There is always the room for hope that he may quit those pastures after a time and seek more fruitful ones. What is important and desirable, however, is that each person should be his own caterer. Schools are only useful where some writer of real genius has been neglected or overlooked, or been boycotted by the press, and attention to his works is only a fair service to him, or a becoming, if tardy, tribute to his memory.

Apropos of the increasing difficulty of obtaining certain old books noted above, the extensive scale on which reproductions of original editions of Early English literature have of recent years been made is certainly a boon to literary inquirers, since the presence of such reissues in our circulating libraries, if we do not choose to buy them, tends at every step in many branches of work to help us, and to render our undertakings more complete. It frequently occurs that volumes and tracts, which are of very slight literary or intrinsic value, contain valuable allusions and illustrations, which we might miss in the absence of available copies. It is worth while to take in one's hand even some puerile trifle by the author of *Adonais*, if one is not obliged to buy it or asked to become the possessor. One feels a curiosity to glance for a moment at a volume which, we are constantly assured in the catalogue, the writer did his utmost to obliterate; and we sometimes wish that he had fully succeeded.

Any of us, taking in his hands the series of *English Book-Collectors* in course of issue by Mr. Quaritch (Nos. 1-12), will perceive without difficulty, if he go no farther, the two distinct camps, so to speak, into which the collecting fraternity may be, and is, broadly divided and classifiable. You have, on the one hand, the men who followed their personal taste, and amused their leisure in late years after a busy life by purchasing such works or such descriptions of literature as appealed to them and fell within their resources; again, the scholar or investigator who assembled round him what illustrated his studies, not merely with an aim at emulating others; or, once more, the gentleman of fortune, who evolved from his school-day acquisitions a feeling or a passion for higher things, and made it the business of his maturer time—

even made it his career—to carry out on a scale and on lines dictated and governed by circumstances the predilection formed in boyhood. On the contrary, there are for our consideration and instruction the libraries which owed their existence to less interesting motives, to the vague and untrained pursuit of rare and expensive books and MSS., on the judgment of others in rivalry of others, and the enterers into the field of competition with a practical eye and a financial side-look. Of all these great divisions there are varieties naturally arising from personal character; but of the collector pure and simple of the older school, that type, we avow, most warmly and potently attracts us which limited itself to the small and unpretentious book-closet, with just those things which the master loved for their own sakes or for the sakes of the donors—where the commercial element was wanting, and where the library was not viewed in the same light as railway or mining stock. It is a famous principle to invest money prudently and well; but happy is he who is wise enough to keep his library within narrow limits, and rich enough to leave it, such as it may be, out of the category of realisable assets.

Mr. Quaritch's project possesses in our eyes the incidental merit of providing us with personal accounts in a succinct form of many of the past proprietors of English and American libraries, and enables us to see at once how varied and fortuitous were the conditions under which the task was begun and accomplished, with what different measures of success and financial means; and in what a preponderance of instances it was an individual rather than an hereditary trait. Broadly speaking, we recognise two varieties of collector from all time: the one who confers his name on a library, and the other whose library confers a name on him.

Even the family of genuine book-lovers—neither virtuosos nor speculators—presents more than a single type to our notice. We have the student who takes a subject for treatment, and forms a small gathering of the literary material necessary for his purpose, shooting it back perchance into the market, his immediate task accomplished. There is the man like Coleridge, who regarded the volumes which fell in his way as casual and welcome visitors, of whom he asked questions, or who answered his, and whose margins gave themselves up to his untiring habit of registering whatever occurred to him, before the passing—possibly borrowed—volume went on its way again. There is Lamb, who was less addicted to annotating his acquisitions, but who gave them a permanent home, if they had come to him *jure emptionis*, and were of the elect—not presentation—copies, cold and crude, thrust into his hand by some well-meaning acquaintance. There is Edward Fitzgerald, dissimilar from all these, yet so far cognate that he bought only the books which struck him as worth reading, if not turning to some practical account. Nor should we in strict fairness refuse admittance within this highest circle even to such as Selden, Burton, Pepys, and others who might be easily enumerated, who may have been little more than curiosity-hunters, but who had a genuine relish for pieces of old popular literature, the greatest rarities in the language inclusive, when there was barely any competition for them. The man of the old school, who ransacked the shops and the stalls, and even attended the auction, may have been a faddist and a superficial student; but his was an honest sort of zeal and affection; there was no vanity or jealousy; and we meet with cases where one collector would surrender to another an acquisition which the latter happened to have missed, and to want very badly indeed. So Isaac Reed gave up to George Steevens Marlowe's *Dido*, and so George III. enjoined his agent not to bid for him against a student or a scholar.

I have not yet quite done with this aspect of the matter. I have to speak of the personages who have thought fit to impose on themselves a chronological or a financial limit, who drew the line at a given year, or would not go beyond a certain figure. Mr. Henry Pyne laid down 1600 as the latest date which he would admit, and rarely exceeded a sovereign or two for a single article (Dr. Doran gave me to understand that fourpence was *his maximum*). It may appear strange to suggest that the higher the sum paid for a book (assuming it to be worth the money), the slighter the risk grows of the purchase proving pecuniarily unprofitable. Yet at the same time outlay on a library is a relative term, and one individual may account himself as frugal in expending £30,000 in the course of a lifetime, as another may do in expending £300. The late Earl of Ashburnham bought in chief measure during the forties and fifties, when the reaction from the bibliomania still more or less sensibly prevailed, and considering his Lordship's position and resources, he was not much more lavish than the above-mentioned Mr. Pyne, or indeed any other amateur of average calibre, while he was to the full extent as genuine a follower of the pursuit for its mere sake as anybody whom we could name—as the Duke of Roxburghe, Mr. Heber, Mr. Corser, or Mr. Crossley.

In my *Rolls of Collectors* I specify a type under the designation of *Book-Recipients*, and I instance such cases as Dickens and Thackeray; but in fact there are many who would never go in pursuit of anything of the kind beyond a work of reference, and whose utmost exploit is the payment of a friendly subscription. The only title to admittance into my category of such doubtful enthusiasts is the sentimental enhancement of value arising from the transformation of the margins of a common-place volume into a repository for manuscript remarks or graphic embellishments, which may send it back into the market some day a three-figure item in a catalogue.

In attempting to indicate in a sort of tentative manner the publications to which a private collection might be advantageously and comfortably limited, one does not contemplate the shelf or so of mere works of reference, which have to be obtained even by such as are not amateurs in this direction, and, moreover, there is an obvious difficulty in prescribing for persons of infinitely varied ideas and prepossessions. Now, as to volumes for reference, the class and extent of course depend on individual requirements, and the books outside this radius are apt to be subject in their selection to local circumstances, since a man associated with a district or county naturally contracts a sympathy with its special history or its archæological transactions, as well as any miscellaneous monographs relating to particular places or celebrated persons. With such specialities and preferences we cannot presume to interfere; but, as a rule, the aggregate body comprised in them need not be large or very expensive, and in catholic or general literature it becomes almost surprising when we have taken the pains to winnow from literary remains of real and permanent interest the preponderant mass, of which the facilities for occasional examination at a public library ought to suffice, how comparatively slender the residuum is.

CHAPTER VI

The safest course—Consideration of the relative value and interest of books in libraries—The intrinsic and extrinsic aspects—Consolation for the less wealthy buyer—The best books among the cheapest—A few examples—Abundance of printed matter in book-form—Schedule of Books which are Books—Remarks on English translations of foreign literature.

WHEN we inspect a great library, filling three or four apartments lined with cases, the first impression is that the possession of such an assemblage of literary monuments is a privilege reserved for the very wealthy; and to some extent so it is. But certain elements enter into the constitution of all extensive accumulations of property of any kind, whether it be books, prints, medals, or coins, which inevitably swell the bulk and the cost without augmenting in anything approaching an equal ratio the solid value. Not to wander from our immediate field of inquiry and argument, the literary connoisseur, starting perhaps with a fairly modest programme, acquires almost insensibly an inclination to expand and diverge, until he becomes, instead of the owner of a taste, the victim of an insatiable passion. He not merely admits innumerable authors and works of whom or which he originally knew nothing, but there are variant impressions, copies with special readings or an unique *provenance*, bindings curious or splendid; and nothing at last comes amiss, the means of purchase presumed.

Yet, at the same time, he does not substantially possess, perhaps, much more than the master of a *petite bibliothèque*, on which the outlay has not been a hundredth part of his own. A considerable proportion of his shelf-furniture are distant acquaintances, as it were, and those acquisitions with which he is intimate are not unlikely to prove less numerous than the belongings of his humbler and less voracious contemporary.

Even where the object and ruling law are strict practical selections of what pleases the buyer, the range of difference is very wide. One man prefers the modern novelists, prose essayists, or verse writers; a second, collections of caricatures and prints in book-form; a third, topography; a fourth, the occult sciences, and so forth. I offer no objection to these partialities; but I entertain an individual preference for volumes chosen from nearly all branches of the *belles lettres*, each for its own sake. I do not vote of necessity in all cases for a book because it is rare, or because it is old, or because it is the best edition; but I do not think that I should like any scholar my friend to have the opportunity of pointing out to me (as he would, wouldn't he?) that I lacked any real essential, as the child tried to satisfy Longfellow that his shelves were not complete without a copy of the undying romance of Jack the Giant-killer.

It cannot fail to strike any one opening such books as Bacon's *Sylva Sylvarum* or Markham's *Way to Get Wealth*, for how comparatively, indeed absolutely, small a consideration it is possible to obtain two works so brimful of interest and curiosity on all subjects connected with gardening, agriculture, and rural pursuits or amusements. But both these works long remained—the Bacon yet does so—outside the collector's pale and cognisance, and the real cause was that they were alike common; they had been the favourites of successive generations; edition upon edition had been demanded; and the survival of copies was too great to suit the book-hunter, who aims at shyer quarry.

Take again, as a sample, a noble old work like the English Bayle, five substantial folios; it was a question of more than a five-pound note to become the master of a good, well-bound copy; one in morocco or russia by Roger Payne twice that amount could once scarcely have brought down; and now it is *articulo mortis*. The connoisseur finds it too bulky, and he hears that its matter has been superseded. At any rate, it is no longer the *mode*, and the mill begins to acquire familiarity with it. Let the taste return for such big game, and copies will be as Caxtons are. Most part of the editions will ere then have been served up again in the form of cheap book-drapery.

The *ne plus ultra* of interest and respect seems to us to centre in such collections of books as those of Samuel Pepys, Narcissus Luttrell, the Rev. Henry White of Lichfield, and Charles Lamb, where the volumes reflect the personal tastes of their owners, and are, or have been, objects to them of personal regard. What is to be thought or said of the man who simply buys works which happen to be in the fashion for the moment, and for which he competes with others as wise as himself, till the prices become ridiculous? English and American millionaires acquire specimens of early typography, poetry, binding, or what not, because they hear that it is the thing to do. One gentleman will give £100 more for a copy, because he is credibly informed that it is three-eighths of an inch taller than any other known; and a second will take something from the vendor on the assurance that no library of any pretensions is complete without it. This sort of child's-play is not Book-Collecting. The true book-closet and its master have to be kinsfolk, not acquaintances introduced by some bookseller in waiting. Humanly speaking, the poor little catalogue made by Hearne of his own books and MSS. comes nearer home to our affections than those of Grenville and Huth.

In speaking and thinking of real books, it is necessary again to distinguish between articulate productions of two classes—between such a work, for example, as Defoe's *Robinson Crusoe* and such an one as Thoreau's *Walden*, or between Gibbon's *Decline and Fall of the Roman Empire* and Sir Thomas Browne's *Urn-Burial*. The present is an enterprise directed toward the indication to collectors of different views and tastes of the volumes which they should respectively select for study or purchase. There are millions who have passed through life unconsciously without having read a book, although they may have seen, nay, possessed thousands. Those which might have been recommended to them with advantage, and perused with advantage, were too obscure, too dull, too cheap, too unfashionable. It is of no use to read publications with which your acquaintances have no familiarity, and to the merits of which it might be a hard task to convert them. But, as we have said, we want space to enter into these details, and we can only generalise bibliographically, repeating that literature is broadly classifiable into Books and Things in Book-Form—Specimens of Paper, Typography and Binding, or counterfeit illusory distributions of printer's letter into words and sentences and volumes by the passing favourites of each succeeding age— what Thoreau call its "tit-men."

We might readily instance masterpieces of erudition or industry which leave nothing to be desired in the way of information and safe guidance, and which, at the same time, do not distantly realise our conception of Books— real *bonâ fide* Books. They may be the best editions by the best binders, or they may be antiquarian periodicals or sets of Learned Transactions, reducing much of the elder lore cherished and credited by our ancestors to waste-paper; we feel that it is a sort of superstition which influences us in regarding them; but we fail to shake off the prejudice, or whatever it may be, and we hold up, on the contrary, to the gaze of some sceptical acquaintance a humble little volume in plain mellow sheep—say, a first Walton, or Bunyan, or Carew, nay, by possibility a Caxton or Wynkyn de Worde—which a roomful of perfectly gentlemanly books should not buy from us. It may strike the reader as a heresy in taste and judgment to pronounce the four Shakespeare folios of secondary interest from the highest point of view, as being posthumous and edited productions. But so it is; yet Caxton's first impression of Chaucer's *Canterbury Tales*, if we were to happen upon it by accident, is a possession which we should not be easily persuaded to coin into sovereigns, and such a prize as the Evelyn copy of Spenser's *Faëry Queen*, 1590, with the Diarist's cypher down the back and his note of ownership inside the old calf cover, is worth a library of inarticulate printed matter. So, again, Aubrey, in his *Miscellanies, Remains of Gentilism and Judaism, History of Surrey*, and *Natural History of Wiltshire*, presents us with works very imperfect and empirical in their character—even foolish and irritating here and there; but between those undertakings and such as Manning and Bray's or Brayley and Britton's *Surrey* there is the difference that the latter are literary compilations, and the former personal relics inalienably identified with an individual and an epoch.

It is the same with certain others, ancient as well as modern writers. Take Herodotus, Athenæus, and Aulus Gellius on the one hand, and Bishop Kennett's *Parochial Antiquities*, White's *Selborne*, Knox's *Ornithological Rambles in Sussex*, or Lucas's *Studies in Nidderdale* on the other. All these equally tell you, not what some one else saw or thought, but what they saw or thought themselves, and in a manner which will never cease to charm.

There are works, again, which, without professing to entertain for the authors any strong personal regard, we read and re-peruse, as we admire a fine piece of sculpture or porcelain, an antique bronze or cameo, as masterpieces of art or models of style. We are perfectly conscious, as we proceed, that they are not to be trusted as authorities, and perhaps it is so on the very account which renders them irresistibly attractive. Some of the most celebrated literary compositions in our language are more or less strongly imbued with the spirit of partisanship or a leaven of constitutional bias; yet we like to have them by us to steal half-an-hour's delight, just as we resort sometimes to alluring but dangerous stimulants. We have in our mind, not volumes of fiction, not even the historical novel, but serious narratives purporting to describe the annals of our country and the lives of our countrymen and countrywomen. We take them up and we lay them down with pleasure, and it is agreeable to feel that they are not far away; and they will not do us greater harm, if we combine an acquaintance with their deficiencies and faults as well as with their beauties, than the fascinating associates with whom we exchange civilities in the drawing-room or at the club, and with whose haunts and opinions we are alike unconcerned. Of the romances under the soberer names of history, biography, and criticism, which abound in all the literatures of nearly all times, we are at liberty to credit as much or as little as we choose; but in how many instances we should regret to lose, or not to have inherited, these; and the personal partiality which constitutes the blemish here and there equally constitutes the merit.

What makes us return again and again to certain books in all literatures, forgetful of chronology and biographical dictionaries? What draws us irresistibly for the twentieth time to works of such different origin and character as Herodotus, Cæsar, Aulus Gellius, Browne's *Urn-Burial* and *Religio Medici*, Pepys's *Diary*, Defoe's *Robinson Crusoe*, Boswell's *Life of Johnson*, and a handful of authors nearer to our own day? Is it not their breadth, catholicism, and sincerity? Is it not precisely those qualities which no sublunar systems of computing time can affect or delimit? If we take successively in hand the *Odyssey*, the *Arabian Nights*, the *Canterbury Tales*, *Don Quixote*, *Gil Blas de Santillane*, and *Robinson Crusoe*, do we without some reflection realise that between the first and the last in order of production thousands of years intervened? Most of the romances of chivalry and the *Faëry Queen* strike us as more antiquated than Homer, assuredly more so than Chaucer. The secret and the charm seems to lie in the fact that all great books are pictures of human nature, which is and has been always the same; and we are able to account in a similar manner for the stupendous popularity of such works as the *Imitatio Christi* and the *Pilgrim's Progress*. Above all things, they are strictly *bonâ fide*. They are no catch-pennies.

We find ourselves with hundreds, nay, thousands of other books at our elbow or at our command, living in communion with half-a-dozen minds. We read our favourite books, and when we have reached the end of our tether, we recommence as if we were in the Scilly Islands, and there were no more obtainable or permissible. We never wax tired of conning over Bayle St. John's *Montaigne the Essayist*, Thoreau's *Walden*, Howell's *Venetian Life* and *Italian Journeys. Cuique suum*. We have known those who never let the sun set without dipping into Burton's *Anatomy of Melancholy*, or who have some pet volume with which they renew their intimacy every year, as Francis Douce did with *Reynard the Fox*. There must usually be an unconscious sympathy in these cases, a pleasing revelation of extended identity, as if these other productions were what we should have liked to claim as our own, and as if we felt we should have said the same things and thought the same thoughts, if they had been ours.

It is the same with some parts of some writers' labours, to be had separately, as *Hamlet*, *As You Like It*, *A Midsummer Night's Dream*, *The Merry Wives of Windsor*, *Macbeth*, and the *Merchant of Venice*; and with a few detached or select compositions to which one has to thread one's way in a larger volume: a few songs scattered through the early dramatists and lyrists; Gray's *Elegy*; Tennyson's *May Queen* (without the sequel), and *Locksley Hall* and *In Memoriam* (missing the tags).

In the present aspect of our inquiry, *Famous Books* and the *Best* are by no means convertible terms. There are such, it is true, as fall under both categories: the Hebrew Scriptures, Homer, Herodotus, *Arabian Nights*, *Canterbury Tales*, Montaigne's *Essays*, Shakespeare, Gibbon. Famous literary compositions at different levels or in their various classes are Boccaccio's *Decameron*, Ariosto's *Orlando Furioso*, Aretino, Spenser's *Faëry Queen*, Rabelais, *Pilgrim's Progress*, La Fontaine's *Tales*, Rousseau's *Confessions*, *Tristram Shandy*, *Candide*, *Don Juan*; and even among these how fair a proportion depends for its value and fruitfulness on the student? And, again, on his training. For we are aware of readers who prefer Bunyan to Spenser, others who place Sterne, Voltaire, and Byron before both, and not a few who have emerged with profit and without pollution from the perusal of the labours of Rabelais and Aretino. There is a literal deluge of moral and colourless works, on the contrary, from which even the average modern reader comes away only with an uncomfortable sense of waste of time and eyesight.

Of printed matter in book-shape there is no end. The mass grows day by day, almost hour by hour. Yet the successful candidates for admission to our inner circle of publications of all ages and countries, which so far meet on common ground in being provided with a passport to succeeding times requiring and recognising no critical *visè*, increase in numbers slowly, O so slowly! It would be presumptuous and unsafe to attempt to discount the ultimate verdict on many now popular names; but it is to be apprehended that, looking at the much more numerous body of writers, the calls to immortality will hereafter be in a relatively diminishing ratio. The influences and agencies by which certain schools of thought and work are artificially forced to the front are too often temporary, and their life is apt to be, Hamadryad-like, conterminous with that of their foster-parents. It has been my lot to witness the rise, decline, and evanescence of groups of authors and artists, whom it was almost sacrilegious to mention even with qualification. Adverse criticism was out of the question for any one valuing his own repute.

How various all the afore-mentioned standard or permanent books are, and still in one respect how similar! Similar, inasmuch as they or their subject-matter are surrounded by an atmosphere which preserves them as in embalmed cerements. In strict truth, there may be some among the number which are far indeed from being individually important or costly, while others in a critical sense have long been entirely obsolete, or perhaps never possessed any critical rank. It does not signify. Their testimonials are independent of such considerations. Many, most of them, are on ever-living topics; many, again, in their essence and material properties are sanctified and odorous.

I find myself possessed by a theory, possibly a weak and erroneous one, in favour of such a book, for instance, as Johnson's *Lives of the Poets*, as Johnson published it, with all its imperfections, with the full consciousness that improved editions exist. For the original output represents a genuine aspect of the author's mind, prejudices inclusive; and I am not sure that, had he lived to bring out a revised and enlarged impression, I should have looked upon it as so characteristic and spontaneous; and the same criticism applies to a number of other productions, dependent for their appreciation by us not upon their substantial, so much as on their sentimental, value.

What is not unapt to strike an average mind is that, with such a caseful of volumes as my cursory and incomplete inventory represents and enumerates, how much, or perhaps rather how little, remains behind of solid, intrinsic worth, and what a preponderance of the unnamed printed matter resolves itself into *bric-à-brac*, unless it amounts to such publications, past and present, as one is content to procure on loan from the circulating library or inspect in the show-cases of our museums.

Happy the men who lived before literary societies, book-clubs, and cheap editions, which have between them so multiplied the aggregate stock or material from which the collector has to make his choice! There are occasional instances where co-operation is useful, and even necessary; but the movement has perhaps been carried too far, as such movements usually are. Our forefathers could not have divined what an unknown future was to yield to us in the form of printed matter of all sorts and degrees. But they already had their great authors, their favourite books, their rarities, in sufficient abundance. It was a narrower field, but a less perplexing one; and from the seeing-point of the amateur, pure and simple, our gain is not unequivocal.

I shall now proceed to draw up an experimental catalogue of works which appear to possess a solid and permanent claim to respect and attention for their own sakes, apart from any critical, textual, or other secondary elements. Others without number might be added as examples of learning, utility, and curiosity; but they do not fall within this exceedingly select category:—

Æsop's *Fables*.

∴ In a form as near as may be to the original work.

Antoninus, *Itinerary*.

Arabian Nights.

Arthur of Little Britain.

Ashmole's *Theatrum Chemicum*.

Athenæus.

Aulus Gellius.

Bacon's *Sylva Sylvarum*.

Bacon's *Essays*.

Browne's *Religio Medici*.

Browne's *Urn-Burial*.

∴ The latter reminds us of Lamb's style,
allowing for difference of time.

Browne's *Vulgar Errors*.

Bayle's *Dictionary*, in English.

Bidpai or Pilpay [so called], *Fables* of.

∴ A genuine English text.

Boccaccio's *Decameron*.

Boswell's *Life of Johnson* and *Tour in the Hebrides*.

Bradbury's *Nature-printed Ferns and Seaweeds*.

Brand's *Popular Antiquities*.

∴ Latest recension, *not* Ellis's.

Cunningham's *London*, by H. B. Wheatley.

Defoe's *Robinson Crusoe*.

Delany, *Diary and Correspondence*.

Diogenes Laertius.

Browning's *Early Poems*.

∴ A moderate volume would hold all worth perpetuation.

Bunyan's *Pilgrim's Progress*.

Burton's *Anatomy of Melancholy*.

∴ A book of academical cast, abounding
in quaint conceits and curious extracts;
full of false philosophy and morality.

Butler's *Hudibras*.

Byron's *Scotish Bards*.

Byron's *Childe Harold*.

Byron's *Don Juan*.

Cæsaris *Commentarii*.

Carew, Thomas, *Poems*.

Cervantes' *Don Quixote*, by Jervis, 2 vols. 4to.

Chappell's *Popular Music*.

Chaucer's *Canterbury Tales*.

Chronicles (English) Series of.

∴ Including Froissart and Monstrelet, with the original illuminated
illustrations to former.

Cicero, *De Senectute et De Amicitiâ*.

Dodsley's *Old Plays*.

Douce's *Illustrations of Shakespeare*, 2 vols.

Dunlop's *History of Fiction*.

Sir H. Ellis's *Original Letters*, three series.

George Ellis's *Specimens of Early English Romances*.

Elton's *Specimens of the Classic Poets*, 3 vols. 1814.

∴ Elton's versions of portions of Homer appear to be superior to Chapman, and to make it regrettable that he did not complete the work.

Epinal Glossary, by Sweet.

∴ For the earliest English extant.

Evelyn's *Diary*.

Evelyn's *Sylva*.

Fairholt's *Costume*, 1860.

Fielding's *Tom Jones*.

Fox's *Book of Martyrs*.

Fournier's *Vieux-Neuf*, 1877.

∴ In the original Latin.

Cobbett's *Rural Rides.*

Coleridge's *Table-Talk.*

Cotgrave's *French Dictionary.*

Couch's *British Fishes.*

Coventry, Chester, Towneley, and York Mysteries.

Grimm's *Popular Stories.*

Hakluyt's *Voyages.*

Harleian Miscellany.

Hearne's *Diary*, 2nd edition.

Rawlinson's *Herodotus.*

Herrick's *Hesperides.*

Holland's *Heröologia*, 1620.

Homer, by Chapman.

∴ But better in the original.

Hone's Popular Works.

∴ An original copy.

Horace, *Satires and Epistles*, by Keightley.

Horæ Beatæ Mariæ Virginis.

∴ A printed edition for the engravings.

James Howell's *Letters.*

Gayton's *Festivous Notes on Don Quixote.*

Gesta Romanorum, in English.

Gilchrist's *Blake.*

Gilpin's *Forest Scenery.*

Golden Legend, in English.

Goldsmith's *Vicar of Wakefield.*

Goldsmith's *Citizen of the World.*

Keightley's Histories of Greece, Rome, and England (last editions).

Knox's *Ornithological Rambles in Sussex.*

Lamb's *Elia.*

Lamb's *Letters.*

Lamb's *Adventures of Ulysses.*

Lamb's *Rosamund Gray.*

Langland's *Piers Ploughman.*

Latimer's *Sermons.*

Lazarillo de Tormes, in English.

Le Houx, *Vaux de Vire*, in French.

Leland's *Itinerary* and *Collectanea*, 1770.

Le Sage's *Gil Blas*, IN FRENCH.

Lord Lindsay's *Lives of the Lindsays.*

Howells' *Italian Journeys*.

Howells' *Venetian Life*.

Hundred Merry Tales, 1526.

Hunter's *New Illustrations of Shakespeare*.

Hunter's *Historical Tracts*.

Hunter's *Account of New Plymouth*, 2nd edition.

Irving's *Scotish Poetry*.

Johnson's *Lives of the Poets*.

Johnson's *Rasselas*.

∴ For the sake of its story, not of the book.

Junius, Letters of.

Keightley's *Mythology of Greece and Italy*.

∴ Some of the matter anticipated
by Sir T. Browne in his *Vulgar Errors*.

∴ See that passage where the opinion of James, Earl of Balcarres, is quoted in regard to the duty of men to leave behind them some trace or record of their mind. Edit. 1849.

Lockhart's *Life of Scott*.

Lodge's *Portraits*.

∴ An early edition.

Lovelace's *Poems*.

Lucas, *Studies in Nidderdale*.

Lysons, *Magna Britannia*, 6 vols.

Lysons, *Environs of London*, 2nd edition.

Malory's *Morte Arthur*.

Montaigne's *Essays*, IN FRENCH.

Morris's Works on Birds, Birds' Eggs, &c.

Nürnberg Chronicle, 1493.

∴ The Latin text. As a very early picture-book.

Olaus Magnus.

∴ Original Latin, with the woodcuts.

Poets. *Corpus Poetarum Latinorum et Græcorum*.

∴ The same remark applies.

Rabelais.

Randolph's *Plays and Poems*.

Retrospective Review.

Ovid.

∴ Partly as in all appearance
a favourite in some shape with
our
Shakespeare.

Paston Letters.

Pennant's *Tours in Wales and
Scotland,*
and *Journey to London.*

∴ On account of their
personality.
You know that much is
obsolete, and other men have
improved
on them; but there is somehow
the same charm.

Pepys's *Diary*, by Wheatley.

Percy's *Reliques.*

Phillips's *English Dictionary.*

Photii *Bibliotheca.*

Plato's *Dialogues.*

∴ Perhaps the French version
by Cousin is preferable.

Plinii *Epistolæ.*

Plutarch's *Lives.*

Popular (Early) Poetry of England, 4
vols.

*Popular (Early) Poetry of Scotland and
the Border*, 2 vols.

Poets. *Select British Poets*, 1824.

Reynard the Fox, in English.

Richardson's *Clarissa.*

Robin Hood Ballads.

Scot's *Discovery of Witchcraft.*

Selden's *Table-Talk.*

Shakespeare's *Works.*

Shakespeare's *Library*, 6 vols.

Songs of the Dramatists.

Southey's *Commonplace Book.*

Southey's *Select Letters.*

∴ More especially for his
delightful letters to children.

Spence's *Anecdotes.*

Spenser's *Works.*

Sterne's *Tristram Shandy.*

St. John's (J. A.) *Manners and Customs
of Ancient Greece*, 1842.

∴ A lifelong labour, and most
delightful and instructive work.

St. John's (Bayle) *Montaigne the Essayist.*

St. John's English version of Saint
Simon.

Stow's *Annals.*

Stow's *Survey of London*, 1720.

Strutt's *Costume*, by Planché.

∴ Includes ample selections from writers hardly worth possessing
in a separate shape, including many even great and distinguished
names.

Suckling's Works.

Swift's *Gulliver*.

Sydney's *Arcadia*.

Tennyson's *Lyrical Poems*.

∴ A judicious one-volume selection preferable.

Thoreau's *Walden*, 1854.

Thorne's *Environs of London*.

Tottell's *Miscellany*.

Virgil, *Bucolics* and *Georgics*, by Keightley.

Voltaire's *Candide*, in French.

Voltaire's *Philosophical Dictionary*.

Walton's *Angler*.

Warton's *English Poetry*, 1871.

Walpole's *Letters*.

Wise's *New Forest*.

∴ Best edition for engravings.

White's *Selborne*, 1st edition.

Wodroephe's *Spare Hours of a Soldier*, 1623.

Yarrell's *British Birds*.

How passing rich one would be with all these, and no more—rich beyond the greatest bibliomaniacs, and beyond the possessors of the rarest and costliest treasures in book-form! Turn over the pages of the most splendid catalogues, and how few one would find to add! Nor would all the before-recited productions appeal to all book-lovers. There are many who would excuse themselves from admitting Rabelais. Some might not particularly care for the works of foreign origin. Some might be courageous enough to avow an indifference to Milton and Spenser, and even a dislike to Bunyan. Still the rule holds good, we think, that all our chosen authors or books have more or less powerful credentials. There remain to be added Books of Reference, as we have pointed out, curiosities, and this or that person's specialisms.

From a strictly practical point of view, the language and sense of any great writer, ancient or modern, may be as well, nay, better, appreciated in a volume bought for a trifle than in a rare and luxurious edition, where the place and time of origin, the type, the paper, and the binding are adventitious accessories—almost *impedimenta*—and the book itself a work of art like a picture or a coin. But with either of the latter it is different, for there the canvas or the metal is an integral portion of the object. For instance, take the better parts of Tennyson. Is it not sufficient to read them in a modest foolscap octavo? Do we require external aids? The poet is his own best illustrator, and if we purchase a pictorial edition, we are apt to find that the author and the artist are at variance in their interpretations.

Translations are always to be carefully avoided by all who can more or less confidently read the author in the original language. We have yet to meet with a version, whether of an ancient or of a modern classic, which is thoroughly appreciative and satisfactory. The majority are utterly disappointing and deceptive. It is in the transfer of the idiom and costume that the difficulty and consequent failure lie. No one who merely knows at second hand Homer, Herodotus, Plautus, Terence, Horace, Virgil, Montaigne, Le Sage (a metonym for *Gil Blas*), Cervantes, La Fontaine, Dumas, Maupassant, Balzac, can have had an opportunity of forming an adequate and just estimate of those authors. You might nearly as soon expect a Frenchman to relish Butler or Dickens in their Parisian habiliments.

Such a fact—for a fact it undoubtedly is—opens to our consideration a very large and a very grave problem, since the very limited extent to which the English public is conversant with Greek and Latin, and with even the Latin family of modern languages, makes the admission that so many works of the highest importance and interest are only properly and truly readable in their own tongues tantamount to one that they are not properly and truly readable at all.

Of all forms of translation, the paraphrase is perhaps the worst, so far as an interpretation of the original sense goes, but not the most dangerous if we know it to be what it is, and do not look for more than a general idea of the meaning and plan of the author. To be practically serviceable, an English version of any classical or foreign work should be literal, and with the literalness as idiomatic as may be; and if the text to be rendered is in verse, the English equivalent should preferably be in verse without rhyme or in prose. The object to be attained in these cases is a transfer of the conceptions, notions, or theories of writers from languages which we do not understand to one which we do; and therefore the best translator is he who has absolutely no higher aim than this, and does not aspire to make his task a stalking-horse for his own literary ambition.

There is scarcely an end of the various schemes adopted to convey to us intelligibly and successfully the sentiments and conceits of ancient authors as well as of those of other countries, and, all things considered, a *literal* version in prose appears to present the fewest disadvantages, for it disarms the translator of the temptation to poetical flights and metrical ingenuity, and brings us nearer to the man and the age to be immediately and primarily studied.

At best, a translation is an indifferent substitute for the book itself, as it was delivered to the world by some renowned hand, or even by some personage whose individuality is stamped, as in the case of the *Imitatio Christi* or the *Essays* of Montaigne, on every sentence indelibly and untransferably, and seems part of the very Latin or French type. An amusing instance occurred in which a gentleman, having heard of the fine style of A Kempis, bought as a present to a friend a copy of the latest English translation! And it is equally futile to look for the essence and spirit of the great Gascon writer in the pages of Florio or Cotton, both of whom, though in unequal measure, to the exigencies of diction or an imperfect conversance with the dialect in which Montaigne wrote sacrificed precious personal idiosyncrasies.

The majority of the popular and current versions of the classics are unsatisfying and treacherous, because they have been executed either by under-paid scholars, like Bohn's Series, or by persons who have had a tendency to put themselves in the place of their author.

We may not be very willing to part with our old favourites, such as Chapman's *Homer*, Florio's *Montaigne*, North's *Plutarch*, Shelton's *Don Quixote*, Urquhart's *Rabelais*, and Smollett's *Gil Blas*; but it is to be feared that they must be prized as curiosities and rarities rather than as interpreters and guides. If a thoroughly reliable library of classical translations, on as literal a plan as possible, could be formed, it would be a real boon to the public—it would be what Bohn's Series ought to have been. Of course, in the department of translation there are two leading divisions—the ancient and the modern classics; and for much the same reason that a story or a *jeu d'esprit* seldom bears transplanting from one soil to another, both these branches of literature are apt to suffer when they change their garb. Almost every man who writes is influenced by dominant environments, whether he be Greek or Roman, or Oriental, or modern European of whatever nationality; and his mere expressions or sense rendered into a foreign tongue are usually like a painting without a background or an atmosphere. We may range over the whole field from the most ancient times to the most modern, and the same thing manifests itself. Open before me is an illustration which will answer the purpose as well as any other, in the shape of Muirhead's version of the *Vaux de Vire* of Jean le Houx. At page 105 we have the following stanza:—

"Lorsque me presse l'heure,

Je retourne au logis;

Ma femme est la qui pleure,

Ainsi qu'il m'est aduis,

Et me dict en cholere:

'Que fay ie seule au lict?

Est il seant de boire

Ainsi jusqu'à minuict?'"

Mr. Muirhead translates thus—

"When late the hour appears,

  Returning to my home,

  My wife is there in tears,

  As I hear when I come.

  She greets me testily:

  'I lie a-bed alone:

  Do you thus shamelessly

  Carouse till midnight's gone?'"

The same kind of paraphrastic dilution runs through the volume; nor is Mr. Muirhead wholly to blame. The original is idiomatic and terse, and he could not find exact equivalents in numerous cases. *Ab uno disce omnes.* But what a privilege it becomes to be able to dispense with interpreters! My admiration of these festive *chansons* arises from my appreciation of them in their native costume and diction. The Knight of La Mancha was of my opinion herein, for he likened a translation to a piece of Flemish tapestry seen on the wrong side.

A corollary which naturally suggests itself to my mind is that if a familiarity—say, even with Latin and French alone—is expedient on no other account, it is eminently so on this one; and the mastery of the inner sense of a great and famous writer constitutes an ample reward for any expenditure of labour and time in acquiring the language in which he wrote, in making yourself as nearly his countryman as you can. I remember a saying, which may have been a wicked epigram, that the only book in Bohn's Classical Library worthy of purchase or perusal was a version of one of Aristotle's works which a gentleman had executed *con amore* and presented to the publisher.

A voluminous and not very well known body of literary material consists of foreign translations of contemporary English pamphlets of a historical or religious character, from the time of Henry VIII. to the Revolution of 1688, covering the entire Stuart period. They cannot be said to be of primary consequence beyond the proof which they furnish of the interest felt abroad in passing transactions in this country, even in such incidents of minor moment as the trial of Elizabeth Cellier in 1680 for an obscure political libel, and the occasional value which they have acquired through the apparent loss of the English originals. We have, for example, a French account of a London ferryman, who, under pretence of conveying passengers across the river, strangled them (1586); a second, of the misdoings of a minister at Malden in Essex (1588); and a third, of the execution of two priests and two laymen at Oxford in 1590, the last existing also in Italian, but none of them known in English.

CHAPTER VII

Transmission of ancient remains—The unique fragment and unique book—
Importance of the former—The St. Alban's Grammar-School find—A more
recent one or two—Mr. Neal's volume—A tantalising entry in a country
catalogue—*The Hundred Merry Tales*—Large volumes only known from small
fragments—Blind Harry's *Wallace*—Aberdeen and other Breviaries—The
Oxenden Collection of Old English Plays—The idyll of *Adam Bell*, 1536—
John Bagford: his unsuspected services to us—Ought we to destroy the old
theology?—Other causes of the disappearance of books—Unique books
which still preserve their reputation—Rare books which are not rare—
Books which are rare and not valuable—Ratcliff, the waste-paper dealer,
who had a collection of Caxtons—The bystander's manifold experiences—
Narrowness of the circle of first-class buyers—The old collector and the new
one—Speculative investors.

LOOKING at the imperfect and unconsecutive condition in which much of
our most precious early literature has been received by us, we are apt to
reflect to how narrow and close an accident we owe two classes of existing
remains: the unique book and the unique fragment. Of course to term a
volume or production unique is a perilous business; the bookseller and the
auctioneer may do so *ex officio*; an inexperienced amateur may resort to the
term as a pleasant and harmless self-deception; but no responsible writer or
critic dares to pronounce anything whatever unique without an emphatic
caveat. We have personally known cases where a publication by one of the
early printers was first introduced to notice, and created a sort of sensation,
as a mutilated fragment rescued from the binding of another work; this
revelation brought to light, after an interval, a second of a different issue;
anon at some auction occurred a perfect copy; and now the poor damaged
worm-eaten leaves, once so reverently and so tenderly regarded, awake no
further interest; the mystery and romance have vanished; and when we
examine the book as a whole, we do not find its merits so striking as when
we strained our eyes to decipher the old binder's pasteboard.

The FRAGMENT is really an unusually and more than at first credibly
important feature in the elder literature. It may be taken, after all deductions
for occasional discoveries of the entire work, to be the sole existing voucher
for a terribly large section of the more popular books of our forefathers, just
as the Stationers' Register is for another. But it is far more than one degree
trustworthier and more palpable; for it is, like the *torso* of an ancient statue, a
veritable part of the printed *integer* and a certificate of its publication and
former existence. Many years ago there was a great stir in consequence of the

detachment from the binding of another book—Caxton's *Boethius*—in the St. Alban's Grammar-School of a parcel of fragments belonging to books by Caxton; these are now in the British Museum. In the Huth Catalogue are noticed several relics of a similar kind; and indeed scarcely any great library, public or private, is without them. They may be accepted as provisional evidences. A rather curious circumstance seems to be associated with one of the Huth fragments—three leaves of Thomas Howell's *New Sonnets and Pretty Pamphlets*. The relic once belonged to Thomas Martin of Palgrave, and includes two leaves of signature D, which are deficient in the Capell copy of this work at Cambridge. The latter is described as a quarto; but it would be interesting to discover that from the fragment the text could be completed. The inconvenience attending the examination of rare books in provincial libraries is very great and serious.

A copy of Statham's *Abridgement of the Statutes*, printed at Rouen about 1491, and bound in England, had as flyleaves two sheets of Caxton's *Chronicles of England*, possibly some of the waste found in Caxton's warehouse after his death.

There is a weird fascination about a newly found fragment of some lost literary composition. Only a few months since, in a copy of Cicero's *Rhetorica*, printed by Aldus Manutius in 1546, in the possession of Mr. Neal, quite a number of pieces of wastrel were disclosed on the removal of the covers, and among them portions of English metrical effusions of the period (for the volume must have been bound here). We view this *treasure trove* wistfully and indulgently; there it is; no mortal eye had fallen on it in the course of three and a half centuries; and how can we be expected to judge its value or quality by the ordinary standard—on an ordinary critical principle? It has come to us like an unlooked-for testamentary windfall. We are not to look at it in the mouth too curiously or fastidiously, or we deserve to have lost it; and it is the very same thing with scores of remains of the kind, brought to light in various directions and ways from season to season, and (to the utmost extent of my power and opportunity) chronicled by me on my accustomed principle.

When I was younger by some thirty years, I received the catalogue of a provincial bookseller, and was sanguine enough to suppose that I should become the happy master at the marked price (7s. 6d.) of No. 2084, which ran as follows:—

"Pynson and others—Specimens of Early Printing, comprising *Twenty Leaves of the Ballad of Robin Hood, &c. &c.*, taken from the cover of an old Missal."

No time was lost in giving the order; *but the lot was sold, and the proprietors did not even know who had bought it.* I comforted myself as the fox did. Yet such is the frailty of one's nature, that one cannot refrain, after long, long years, from sentimentalising over it. There is something so taking in the notion of a tattered, semi-illegible, unappropriated fractional relic, not a trunk even; it fascinates us like a coin of which the legend is almost beyond identification; there is mystery behind it; we may be on the track of a discovery which will help to make us famous.

We have all heard of the *Hundred Merry Tales*, rescued by Mr. Conybeare in the early years of the century from another book, of which the fragments assisted to form the covers, and how the treasure was prized till a complete copy occurred in a Continental library and dispelled the charm. It was pointed out many years ago by the present writer (*Old English Jest-Books*, 1864, i., Additional Notes) that Scot, in his *Discovery of Witchcraft*, 1584, quotes the story from this miscellany of the miller's eels, and enabled us, before the Göttingen copy was brought under notice, to complete the text, which is almost undecipherable in the Conybeare (now Huth) one.

The fragmentary state by no means restricts itself to literary items of insignificant bulk. For, as we see, a potential factor in the creation of rare books has been a vast temporary popularity, succeeded by a prolonged period of neglect. The result is before us in the almost total evanescence of thousands of books extending to hundreds of pages. Look at Blind Harry's *Wallace*, a large volume, first printed in folio about 1520; a few leaves are all that remain of the *editio princeps*; and others have totally vanished. Many of us are familiar with the tolerably ample dimensions of the service-books of various uses in the English Church; and yet those of Aberdeen, Hereford, and York survive only in fragments or *torsi*; and the modern reprint of the first was formed from a combination of several imperfect originals. A similar fate has all but overtaken such excessively popular works as Coverdale's Bible, 1535, and Fox's *Martyrs*, 1563, an absolutely perfect copy of either of which I have never beheld.

Henry Oxinden, of Barham in Kent, was the earliest recorded collector of old English plays, and bound up his 122 dramatic possessions in six volumes before 1647. He has left a list of them in his manuscript common-place book. Tears almost steal into our eyes as we read the titles: the *Hamlet* of 1603, the *Taming of the Shrew*, 1594, *Ralph Roister Doister*. Of the first we know well enough the history to date: two copies, both imperfect. The second exists in the unique Inglis, Heber, and Devonshire example; it is mentioned in Longman's Catalogue for 1817, from which it was purchased by Rodd, and sold to Mr. Inglis; it is reputed to have once belonged to Pope. The remaining item survives in the titleless copy at present in the library of Eton College, to which Mr. Briggs presented it in 1818, not on account of the association of Udall the author with that seminary of learning, but, curiously enough, by mere accident.

Among Bagford's collections there is a single leaf of an otherwise unknown impression of Clement Robinson's *Handful of Pleasant Delights*, a 1565 book only hitherto extant in a 1584 reprint. This precious little *morçeau* altogether differs, so far as it goes, from the corresponding portion of the volume now preserved in the National Library.

Let me insist a little on the instructive progress of knowledge in one or two cases. A fragment of a small tract in verse by Lydgate, from the prolific press of Wynkyn de Worde, was proclaimed as an extraordinary and unique accession to our literary stores some eighty years since; it was called *The Treatise of a Gallant*, and had been taken from the covers of a volume of statutes in the library at Nash Court. Some time after, a complete copy of another impression turned up, and ultimately a third, quite distinct from either of the previous two, was discovered in a volume of marvellously rare pieces sold by a Bristol bookseller to the late Mr. Maskell for £300, and by him to the British Museum. Take another case connected with the same press. A piece entitled *The Remorse of Conscience*, by William Lichfield, parson of All Hallows, Thames Street, who died in 1447, leaving a larger number of MSS. behind him than Lamb once humorously made Coleridge do, long enjoyed the reputation of being a solitary survivor; but at present the world holds four, two recovered from bindings, and a third titleless, and all, in fact, more or less dilapidated by unappreciative or over-appreciative handlers. Last, not least, the delightful idyll of *Adam Bell*, of which we were so glad on a time to follow the Garrick exemplar, is now proved to have been in type in the reign of Henry VIII.; and a piece of a pre-Reformation issue luckily preserves enough to show how, even in a production probably sold at a penny, it was thought worth while to alter a passage where the Pope was originally alluded to.

There are instances where we are deprived of the gratification of beholding so much as a morsel of a book sufficient to establish its former existence in hundreds, if not thousands, of copies. Of the *Four Sons of Aymon*, from the press of Wynkyn de Worde, 1504, not a vestige has so far accrued; yet it once existed, as it is expressly cited in a later issue. So it is, again, with Skelton's *Nigramansir*, printed by De Worde in 1504, which was actually seen by Weston the historian in the hands of Collins the poet, and with *Peter Fabyl's Ghost* (the Merry Devil of Edmonton) from the same press.

We are accustomed to associate with the black-letter fragment the name of JOHN BAGFORD, who, in the closing years of the seventeenth and beginning of the next century, distinguished himself by the zeal with which he collected typographical specimens and memorials. In Bagford's day, the relative value of old books was scarcely at all understood; there was no adequate discrimination between the productions of Caxton and his immediate successors and those of living or recent printers; and, again, which was more excusable, volumes by early divines or by writers of established repute were more generally sought than those by schools of poetry and fiction, which at present command chief attention and respect. If we turn over the pages of an auctioneer's catalogue belonging to that era, we perceive, side by side, items estimated at about the same figure, of which many have become worth perhaps even less, while a few have left their former companions immeasurably behind, and one or two rank among the *livres introuvables*. Those were the days when the classics were preserved with the most jealous care, and acquired at extravagant prices, and when our vernacular literature, from the introduction of typography down to the Restoration, was an object of attention to an extremely limited constituency, and could be obtained for a song.

The Bagford collection of title-pages and fragments formerly constituted part of the Harleian manuscripts in the British Museum, but has been chiefly transferred to the printed book department of recent years. It resembles a Typographical Cemetery, a charnel-house of books crowded together without respect to their subject-matter or their literary rank: the leaf of a Caxton, another of a valueless legal treatise, the title-page of *Romeus and Julietta*, on which Shakespeare founded, as the phrase goes, his own play, and a broadsheet preserved entire, there being no more of it. But Bagford, who helped Dr. Moore, Bishop of Ely, and perchance Lord Oxford, to some of their rarities, does not stand alone. He had many followers; but the scale of operations diminished as the orthodox collector multiplied and prices rose. Sir John Fenn, editor of the *Paston Letters*, whom we have named above, was a disciple, however, and Martin of Palgrave was another. Many years since, for a proposed new *Biographia Britannica* by Murray of Albemarle Street, the present writer collected all the known particulars of Bagford himself, who spent his last days in the Charterhouse. His episcopal client or patron died in 1714.

Before we condemn these biblioclasts, let us recollect one thing. It is not so much that they have rendered books imperfect by the abstraction of leaves or title-pages, as that they have actually preserved the sole testimony for the existence of hundreds of books, tracts, and broadsheets of which we should have otherwise known nothing, amid the wholesale destruction of early literature, which was not arrested till the close of the last century, and still proceeds in a modified form and degree. Not many years since the *Troy-Book* printed by Caxton was discovered hanging up in a water-closet at Harrogate; a portion had disappeared, but the remainder was secured, and was sold to a dealer in Manchester for thirty guineas. It must be, and is, Bagford's apology that he sacrificed to his typographical scheme material which was almost universally neglected, and for which there might seem, two hundred years ago, scarcely any prospect of a future call. Yet, oddly enough, this very person was one of the pioneers, by his labours and example, in bringing back a taste for the older English school; he appeared at a juncture when sufficient time had elapsed for the destruction by various agencies of a vast proportion of the products of the press; but until the fashion, which he and others set, had begun to spread, it remained unknown how much was reduced from its original volume, and how much had perished. We have the less pretence for censuring the biblioclasts of the past, who could only use the eyes and experience of their own epoch, when instances are reported from time to time of the same ruthless practices even by those who might have been expected to know better; and there is more than one way of viewing the present notorious tendency to exterminate the old theology on the plea that it is worthless, since a generation may arise which will upbraid us for having converted to pulp this part of our inheritance, till it comes at last to survive in a stray leaf here or a mangled fragment there. An altogether different quarter from which a result conducive to the shrinkage or disappearance of copies of early works has arisen is the print-collecting movement, involving the devastation of the innumerable volumes which contain portraits, frontispieces, and other engravings, and the more than incidental risk of the consignment of the unvalued residue to the waste-basket; and it may be mentioned that within our personal knowledge hundreds upon hundreds of scarce old books have been destroyed by editors, lexicographers, and other literary workers, to save the trouble of transcribing extracts. It might be impossible to exhaust the variety of ways in which an extraordinarily large body of publications of former days has been reduced or raised to the position of rarities of graduated rank.

After all these ages, all the indefatigable researches which have been undertaken for profit or for pleasure, all the libraries which have been formed and dispersed, true it is that the Unique volume, which of course enjoys its designation only till a second copy is producible, still survives in such abundance, that one, if it were otherwise feasible, might form a library composed of nothing else. Does it not become curious to consider to what lottery, as it were, we owe them—owe their arrest just at the dividing line between living and lost literature? Whatever may be the cause, we have hitherto failed to trace duplicates of the metrical *Ship of Fools*, 1509, *Queen Elizabeth's Prayer-Book*, 1569, Watson's *Teares of Fancie*, 1593, *Venus and Adonis*, 1593, 1599, and 1617, and of *Lucrece*, 1598. Copies of these later productions must have found their way to Shakespeare's country at the time. Malone met with the *Venus and Adonis* of 1593 at Manchester in 1805, and another collector with that of 1594 in the same shire; and the Florio's *Montaigne* of 1603, the only volume with the poet's autograph yet seen, was long preserved at Smethwick, near Birmingham. It was at Manchester, too, that the copy of the *Tragedy of Richard III.*, 1594, came to light as recently as 1881. Several of the works of Nicholas Breton and Samuel Rowlands survive in isolated copies. Upwards of a century has elapsed since a medical man picked up in Ayrshire in 1788 an assemblage of quarto tracts belonging to the ancient vernacular literature of Scotland and to the parent press of Edinburgh; and not a whisper has been raised to suggest the existence of a second copy of any of them, which is to be regretted so far, as some are imperfect. During years on years, the authorities at the Advocates' Library, Edinburgh, kept this inestimable relic in a cupboard under the stairs. In the find at Lamport Hall, Northamptonshire, thirty or forty years since, there were items upon items utterly unknown. It was the same at the Wolfreston sale in 1856. It goes without saying that among the Heber stores the uniques were barely numerable; and many yet preserve their reputation as such. Mr. Caldecott, Mr. Jolley, and Mr. Corser were lucky in falling in with scores of tracts of the first order of rarity. No one has beheld the double of the *Jests of the Widow Edith*, purchased by Lord Fitzwilliam for £3 10s. at West's sale in 1773, and formerly Lord Oxford's; and the citation of the last name prompts the remark that many a book in the Harleian Library still awaits recovery, assuming the description in the catalogue to be correct. On the contrary, there are serious warnings to enthusiasts not to rely too implicitly on the reputation of a volume for uniqueness or high rarity in view of such phenomena as the occurrence within a short period of each other at the same mart in 1896 of two copies of the first edition of Chaucer's *Canterbury Tales*, printed by Caxton. Here was a case where the publicity afforded to these matters brought out a second example, which the owner found to be worth a small estate.

The writer's publication, *Fugitive Tracts*, 1493-1700, 2 vols., 1875, very aptly and powerfully illustrates the present bearings of our subject. Of the sixty pieces there reproduced, two-thirds appear to be unique, and only four are traceable in the Heber Catalogue. Yet many of the items are of historical or biographical importance, and were, in fact, selected from a much larger number with that view; which seems to be tantamount to a recognition of the truth, that, enormous as is the total surviving body of early English and Scotish Literature, it represents in some sections or classes only a salvage of what was once in type, or, to speak more by the card, of what we have so far been able to recover.

There are rare books which, paradoxical as it may seem, are not rare. Take, for example, Burton's *Anatomy of Melancholy*, 1621; the first folio Shakespeare, 1623; Milton's *Lycidas, Poems, Paradise Lost, Paradise Regained*, in the *editiones principes*; the works of the minor poets, Suckling, Carew, Shirley, Davenant; Walton's *Angler*, 1653; Bunyan's *Pilgrim's Progress*, 1678; the Kilmarnock Burns, 1786; and many first editions of Wordsworth, Lamb, Shelley, Keats, Tennyson. Every season swells the roll of existing copies. On the contrary, Spenser's *Faëry Queen*, Books i.-iii., 1590, and Milton's *Comus*, 1634, are authentically scarce, the former especially so in fine state; and the same may be predicated of Lovelace's *Lucasta* (the two parts complete). But the real meaning of the rarity of the other books above specified—and the list might be readily enlarged—is that, although the copies are numerous enough, the taste for capital productions has increased within a few years out of proportion to the recovery of new or unknown examples.

We are finding frequent occasion to cite works of foreign origin, which are more or less habitually taken up into our own collections by miscellaneous or general buyers; and there is among these one which forms a signal illustration of the fallacy of uniqueness. It is the Gutenberg or Mazarin Bible. Scarcely a library of the first rank occurs here or elsewhere without offering a copy; and we are persuaded that at least forty must exist, either on paper or on vellum, throughout the world. The book occupies the same bibliographical position as the first folio Shakespeare, the first edition of Walton's *Angler*, and the first Burns; it tends to grow commoner, yet, so far, not cheaper.

There are other books which, as it may be more readily understood, are rare without being valuable, and of which such of the commercial world as has it not in its power to expend large amounts on individual purchases, naturally seeks to make the most. It was almost amusing, some time since, to note the entries in some of the booksellers' lists under "Black Letter," "Gothic Letter," "Rare Law," "Curious Early English," and so forth; and the names of Caxton, Wynkyn de Worde, and other ancient printers were freely introduced to help off a rather lame foreigner, who was alleged to have been professionally associated with one or the other of them. If the bookseller knows the book-buyer, it is highly requisite that the latter should study what he is going to buy.

Illustrations are not wanting of the loss of untold treasure through a medium more fatal than any other—through exhaustive popular demand. Entire and large impressions of books, pamphlets, and broadsides have succumbed, not to the sacrilegious hand of the spoiler, but to the too affectionate, and not too cleanly, fingering of the multitude of men and women who read and then cast the sources of entertainment away. If we remember that certain of the Bibles ordered to be kept in churches for general use chiefly survive in crumbling fragments, or at best woefully dilapidated copies, we cease to be surprised at the easy prey which more fugitive compositions have formed to a succession of careless and indifferent owners. The illiterate inscriptions on many books, which have thus become valuable, point to the hands through which they have passed, and tell a story of prolonged neglect, too often culminating in appropriation to domestic requirements.

It is, anyhow, perfectly undeniable that of the miscellaneous early literature of all countries, the proportion which exists is in very numerous instances no more than a simple voucher for the work having passed the press. A single copy has formerly occurred or occurs fortuitously, and no duplicate can be cited. This is the position of thousands of volumes, and of many it is the chief merit.

Infinitely numerous are the strange tales, sometimes drawing up the moisture into the mouth, sometimes sufficient to make one's hair rigid, of books of price hung up for use at country railway stations, or employed by a tobacconist to wrap up his pennyworths of snuff, or converted by a lady of quality into curl-papers. What has become of the Caxtons sent over to the Netherlands in the last century by a confiding English gentleman their owner, for the inspection of a nameless Mynheer his friend, who, when he was invited to restore them, lamented their disappearance in a fire?

There was beyond a question an epoch, and a prolonged one, when the mill shared with household demands an immense quota of the cast-off literature of these islands. One of our early collectors of Caxtons, Ratcliff, whose books were sold in 1776, acquired his taste (one in a thousand) through his vocation as a chandler or storekeeper in the Borough. We may surmise how his Caxtons came to him, and at what rates!

These episodes appertain to the romantic and speculative aspect of book-collecting; but they really have another side. Here, at a time when the first-fruits of the English press were unregarded, we find a man of Ratcliff's status acquiring thirty Caxtons. He lived just to see a rise in their value, yet a very slight and fluctuating one; for at last he went into the open market and purchased a few lots at West's auction in 1773, and the Caxtons thus obtained re-sold after Ratcliff's death in one or two cases at a lower rate. He had inflated the market; the competitors were not more than two or three. But the time was soon to come when such persons could no longer afford to hold this kind of property—when it became fashionable for dukes and earls and men of large property to make our early typography an object of research; and so it continued down to the present time, till the agricultural depression arrived to create another organic change, and to direct these, as well as other costly luxuries, into new channels. Not the chandler, or the Government official, or the private gentleman of modest means, but the great manufacturer or the merchant-prince entered on the scene, and wrested from the landowner his long-cherished possessions. The West and Ratcliff sales (1773-76) were the two golden opportunities, however, of which the advisers of George III. wisely availed themselves to purchase volumes at what we have been taught to consider nominal prices; and there they are in the British Museum to-day, a recollection of one of the better traits in the character of that prince. When we say that the market for Caxtons in 1776 was beginning to expand, we mean that the day for getting such things for a few pence or a shilling or two had gone by. Here, for example, are some of the quotations from the Ratcliff auction:—

	£	s.	d.
Chronicles of Englande, fine copy, 1480	5	5	0
Doctrinal of Sapyence, 1489	8	8	0
The Boke called Cathon, 1483	5	5	0
Tullius de Senectute, in Englyshe, 1481	14	0	0
The Game and Playe of Chesse	16	0	0
The Boke of Jason	5	10	0
Legenda Aurea; or, the Golden Legend, 1483	9	15	0

These figures make even some of those in the West auction, 1773, appear by comparison rather extravagant. For his Majesty's agent at the latter gave as much as £14 for the romance of *Paris and Vienne*, from the Caxton press, 1485. True, it seems to be unique, and might to-day require its purchaser, if it were for sale, to have £500 in his pocket or at his bank to secure it. Yet strange events still continue to happen from time to time. Not Caxtons nor Shakespeares, but excellent books which command prices in the open market, are yet occasionally given away.

A case occurred in Lincolnshire about a year ago, when a library of some 2500 volumes was sold by an intelligent provincial auctioneer *al fresco* in the dogdays, and put up in bundles, nearly all of which were knocked down at the first bid—*threepence*. Say, 150 lots at 3d. per lot = £1 17s. 6d. for the whole. There must have been an *entente cordiale* among those in attendance, the gentleman in the rostrum inclusive.

These instances of misdirection, which have been in times past more numerous than now, although two of the most recent and most signal have occurred in the same county (Lincolnshire), inevitably tend to the destruction of copies, and so far illustrate our remarks on the causes of the gradual disappearance of books during former periods.

There are, however, circumstances under which prices are depressed by collusion, as where a first folio Shakespeare was knocked done for £20 in an auction-room not five hundred miles from Fleet Street; or by an accident, as when the original *Somers Tracts*, in thirty folio volumes, comprising unique *Americana*, fetched *bonâ fide* under the hammer only £61. A single item was re-sold for sixty guineas, and would now bring thrice that amount. What a game of chance this book traffic is!

Imperfect Books, as distinguished from Fragments, constitute a rather complex and troublesome portion and aspect of collecting. They are susceptible of classification into books—(1) Of which no perfect copy is known; (2) Of which none is known outside one or two great libraries; (3) Of which even imperfect examples, as of a specimen of early typography or of engraving, are valuable and interesting; (4) Of which copies are more or less easily procurable. It is only the last division at which an amateur of any pretensions and resources draws the line. With the other contingencies our keenest and richest book-hunters and our most important public collections have been and are obliged to be satisfied. When it is a question of a unique, or almost unique, Caxton, Wynkyn de Worde, or Pynson, or quite as much of a volume from the London, St. Albans, Tavistock, York, or Edinburgh presses, what is to be done? The object, no doubt, *laisse à desirer*; but where is another? This sentiment and spirit operated twice, as we have elsewhere noted, within three months in 1896 in the case of two incomplete copies of the first edition by Caxton of Chaucer's *Canterbury Tales*. But for the defective copy of a common book some find an apology and a home: they cannot afford a better, or they require it for a special purpose. The upshot is, that for every old volume there is a customer, who is pleased with his acquisition according to his light; and we have met with such as seemed disposed to view the missing of damaged leaves as negative evidence of antiquity and genuineness.

The bystander who has had the benefit of as long an innings as the present writer, witnesses perpetual changes and vicissitudes of sentiment; and from one point of view, at all events, the minute details, into which the too generally despised bibliographer enters, are valuable, because they present to us, in lists of editions of authors and books published from age to age, the astonishing evidence of mutable popularity or acceptability. There is a feature, which is almost amusing, in the ideas and estimates expressed of many works by our earlier antiquaries, when we look to-day at their position and rank. If we turn over the pages of Hearne's *Diary*, for instance, we constantly meet with accounts of literary curiosities and rarities, which we regard with different eyes by virtue of our enlarged information, while thousands of really valuable items—valuable on some score or other—go there unnoted, although copies of them must have passed through the sales, even more frequently than at present. The close of the nineteenth century has brought these matters to a truer level. We are better able to gauge the survival of books and editions.

Even in the sometimes tedious enumeration of editions of early books bibliography confers a sort of benefit, for it demonstrates the longevity in public estimation and demand of a host of books now neglected, yet objects of interest and utility to many successive ages.

We have seen so many cranks and fancies successively take possession of the public. Early typography; early poetry and romances; books of hours; books of emblems; Roman Catholic literature; liturgies; Bewick; Bartolozzi; the first edition (which was sometimes equally the last); books on vellum, on India-paper, or on yellow or some other bizarre colour or material, debarring perusal of the publication; copies with remarkable blunders or with some of the text inadvertently omitted—all these and a legion of others have had their day; and to some of them it happens that they drop out of view for a season, and then reappear for a second or third brief term of life and favour; and therefore, it being so, who can have the heart to blame the parties that in the exercise of their vocation make hay while the sun shines? There is one personage, and one alone, who makes it whether or no, summer and winter, to wit, the auctioneer; his commission is assured; on what or from whom he gets it he cares not. He cheerfully leaves the adjustment of accounts to gentlemen outside.

The circumstances under which a new departure takes place, often without much previous warning, in the book-market, and disturbs the calculations of holders of certain classes of stock, are infinitely varied. The bibliographical barometer is surprisingly sensitive, and the slightest change of fashion in the older literature, and even in those sections of the more recent which embrace acknowledged rarities, is instantaneously felt. In some branches of collecting, and where the prices of commodities are such as to exclude all but a knot of wealthy amateurs, the entrance of a new-comer on the ground makes a vital difference, especially if the market is in need of support from existing wants having been supplied; and if one goes about a little, one hears men whispering in corners and questioning who the stranger is, and for what he is likely to prove good. Should he be a strong man, that is, in purse, you will soon perceive, if you keep your eye on the auction-room, another strong man buying at all costs against all comers just the articles which commend themselves to the first *dramatis persona*. He buys nearly everything; they are for him alone, unless there are two in the field concurrently, and then one may be conveniently played off against the other. A small field it is!

And this interesting commercial strategy is always going on, while the objects of pursuit continually vary. The dealer looks after, not his own desiderata— for he has none—but those of his immediate clients. In a large business a man is likely to have many; but the class which repays study, which turns sovereigns into bank-notes for him, is not a numerous one. Half-a-dozen first-rate customers keep a shop open even in the most fashionable and expensive thoroughfare. The late Joseph Lilly leant during his last years mainly on one. A collector of the stamp of Mr. Hartley was almost sufficient to support such an establishment as Newman's in Holborn or Toovey's in Piccadilly. You might pass the latter, or both, day after day and week after week, and not see a soul enter or leave the premises; all was done by correspondence and flukes and a few real good buyers in the background. Mr. Quaritch in London or M. Fontaine in Paris will clear more in an afternoon by the change of hands of two or three heavy items than a small dealer, even if he is unusually lucky, will do in a twelvemonth out of thousands of petty and troublesome transactions. It is not particularly unusual for a big firm to sell at one sitting four or five thousand pounds worth of property. There are others which have not sold as much during the entire term of their career, and never will.

The works which enjoy their turn of public favour are generally recognisable in the catalogues by the type in which they are set forth; and any one who has stood by and witnessed all the changes of the last thirty or forty years observes periodical phenomena in the transfer of typographical honours from one school of authors, or one group of subjects, to another. The most recent auctioneers' catalogues reflect the sentiment of the day in lavishing capitals on trifles from the pens of more or less ephemeral modern writers, and registering with corresponding brevity much of the old English literature, which a few years since was in the ascendant. A rare volume of Elizabethan verse or prose halts after an insignificant brochure by Lamb, Dickens, or Thackeray, which the respective authors would have judged scarcely worth preserving, to which their indifference, in point of fact, constitutes the cause of scarcity and consequent appreciation.

So it was once upon a time, to be sure, with the Caxton, the quarto Shakespeare, the ballad, the penny black-letter garland, and many another article which we now hold so precious. The man who could secure Caxtons and Shakespeares for pence, was he happier? Why, no; for he simply followed the market and nobody was envious. He lifted his acquisition off the counter or stall for the best of all reasons—because he fancied it—nay, because he intended to read it when he reached home.

A plea from the absolute collector's point of view—I fear, a weak and false one—is occasionally advanced for books which were formerly in fashion and favour; for example, Sylvester's *Du Bartas*, the Platonic romances, Townley's French *Hudibras*, and a hundred—a thousand—ten thousand more. It is thought to be worth while to have a few of these deposed idols to show to your friends when they visit you, that they may join in a homily on changes of taste. Perhaps it would suffice to compare notes through the medium of some *Censura Literaria*, or Beloe, or Collier. With most people space is a consideration, with a few, money; and an incidental and passing reflection need not be so costly in either way. For that reason such works as I have indicated, and a few others similar to them, are apt to prove serviceable and economical.

The periodical reinforcement of the ranks of the book-collecting world, in the higher latitudes at least, is obviously imperative, as individuals do not usually commence investments of such a kind till they are well on in life and have put by a fortune, or at all events retired from business. Some purely accidental matter directs attention to a line of bibliography which appears attractive and important; the money is there, and the expert will undertake the rest. It is not the interest of those engaged in the business to be critical; they are merely executive agents. But the demand for the costlier rarities and curiosities is so narrow, that the fresh aspirant is soon the central object of attention to the few who can provide him with what he imagines he wants. As a rule, where a man has no personal knowledge, and finds that he is gradually becoming a milch-cow for the trade, the hobby is not of long duration; it is only where the buyer can control and check the vendor that satisfactory relations are likely to continue, perhaps for years, perhaps for a lifetime. There is ever a tendency, on the part of the bookish commissariat, to strike the iron too hard.

It does happen here and there that collectors are enabled to make their own prices for their acquisitions either by extraordinary reputation for judgment and by virtue of a well-known name, or by the fact of being carried by our common lot beyond earshot of their good fortune, or, once more, by the force of peculiar circumstances. As an almost inexorable rule, the stocks of dealers are coldly regarded, and even those of William Pickering and Joseph Lilly were allowed to drop, so that, in the latter instance more particularly, some real bargains were obtained. Yet, on the contrary, the books thrown on the market after the retirement of F. S. Ellis and the death of James Toovey went capitally, partly because they were supported by Mr. Quaritch (rather glad perhaps to get rid of his two confrères). Then, more recently, the collection formed by Mr. Warton brought quite unexpected figures, and we feel justified in adding, figures sometimes scarcely warranted by the property. These instances, and this other aspect of the subject, strengthen our contention that the whole affair from beginning to end is a sort of lottery, a type of gambling. If those who enter into the fray do so with their eyes open, and do not object, who should?

But assuredly the most egregious case in modern times of the absolute despotism of name and ownership over all other considerations was that of the portion of William Morris's library submitted to public sale in December 1898. The books themselves were, as a rule, below mediocrity in state, and could not have well possessed for the new acquirers even that special interest and value which Morris recognised in them as aids to his artistic and literary labours. Yet the prices realised were beyond anything on record, and were simply absurd. There seemed to be a violent struggle on the part of three or four competitors to secure these treasures at any cost, and they did so. Let the very same copies recur, and in the hands of a person of inferior celebrity, and the shrinkage will probably be serious. The direct association was dissolved when the lots were adjudged to the highest bidders, and here the highest bidders were high indeed.

To the speculative investor in literary property what can we have to say? He works with his eyes opened to their widest possibility of expansion, and carries his fortune or success in his hands. No doubt there are occasional flukes for him; but, generally speaking, the greatest have been for collections formed and dispersed without any view to profit, where the state of the market has accidentally favoured the owner, or there was some nimbus round the name.

Before you set about forming a library, you should consider in what sort of atmosphere, of your own or your friends' creation, it is likely to be sold hereafter. You ought almost to be able to calculate how celebrated you will die.

CHAPTER VIII

Early English literature—Absorption of the rarer items by public libraries or by America—Future of collecting—Poetical writers of the sixteenth and seventeenth centuries—Fruits of a long neglect—Want of discrimination among private buyers—Necessity for a better training or sounder advice—Remarks on our early literature—Small proportion of high-class authors—Safe and unsafe investments—Condition of copies—Writers whose works are of mysterious rarity—Nicholas Breton—"Three-halfpenny ware"—Paucity of great names in the post-Restoration period down to our own—Foreign works belonging to the English series: their chief places of origin—English presses—Typographical vicissitudes of London—The Scotish Series—Scotish presses—The Irish Series—Irish presses—The Irish Stock—The List of Claims, 1701—Anglo-American literature and early American editions of English Classics—The American Colonial group of books—The *Bay Psalm-Book*, 1640—The volumes of Statutes printed at Boston, Philadelphia, and New York—Sources of information on Anglo-American bibliography—Caution against impatience and enthusiasm.

THE entire range of the earlier English and Scotish romantic, poetical, and even historical literature embraces so many items, which are either unattainable from their rarity or their cost, if they happen once in a lifetime to occur, that it may be said to be ground almost closed against the ordinary private buyer. Articles which are to be seen by the hundred in the priced catalogues of libraries dispersed twenty or thirty years since with fairly moderate figures attached to them, have, owing to severer competition from America as well as at home, either for public or private purchasers, trebled or quadrupled in value. With the more modern literature, of which the positive scarcity does not warrant this great inflation, we may reasonably look for a fall; but in the case of volumes which are really rare, it is hard to see how the chances of collectors can be improved in the future. The upshot will be, that they must be satisfied with smaller fish or modify their lines; for of old and elderly books of intrinsic value and interest there is a plentiful choice. With regard to a considerable body of Early English volumes, which formerly appeared in the catalogues of Thorpe, Rodd, the elder Pickering, and others, it is to be said that the fewness of survivors was not appreciated, and half-a-dozen public or closed libraries have absorbed them all.

It exemplifies the remarkable revolution in feeling and taste when we turn over the pages of one of William Pickering's catalogues—that for 1827—and observe a perfect set of the four folio Shakespeares, 1623-85, marked £105, while a large-paper series of Hearne's books, or of some standard edition of the classics in morocco, cost more; whereas at present the Hearnes and the classics are barely saleable at any price, and the dramatic volumes might be worth twenty times more than they brought seventy years since.

The poetical writers of the Tudor, Elizabethan, and Stuart eras have had, in a commercial sense, two or three reverses of fortune. From the period of publication down to the last quarter of the eighteenth century they were to be bought at prices little beyond waste paper, so soon as the original interest in them had subsided. The editors of Shakespeare—Pope, Hanmer, Theobald, Warburton, Capell, Steevens, Malone, Farmer, and Reed—awakened a sort of new interest in the subject, just in time to save the slender salvage of a century and a half's neglect or indifference from the mill and the kitchen-fire; and their example led to others coming upon the ground, such as West, Major Pearson, the Duke of Roxburghe, Lord Blandford, Lord Spencer, Bindley, and Heber, whose motives were primarily acquisitive. In or about 1833 a strong reaction set in, and prices fell till 1842-45, when the Bright and Chalmers sales, and the more sensible competition of the British Museum, again restored confidence and strength to the market. Since that time, our old poets have not, on the whole, suffered any marked decline, and the most recent revival is in their favour.

The Americans, it seems, call for first editions, and they have not to call twice, though they may be required to pay smartly. This new ticket owes its origin to the usual agency. One or two Transatlantic book-lovers gain the information from some source that this is the real article, that if you want fine poetry you must go to these fellows—not exactly Shakespeare and Spenser, for they had heard of them before—but to Gascoigne, Sydney, Herrick, Carew, Suckling, Lovelace, and the rest of the company; and above all, if you desire to enjoy their beauties and appreciate their genius fully and absolutely, you are referred to the *editio princeps*—not that which the author corrected and preferred, but the one in morocco extra, which your bookseller recommends to you.

It is by no means that we seek to ridicule or discourage the pursuit, but we want and wish to see a more healthy and discriminating spirit among buyers. Let intending collectors devote a reasonable time to a preparatory study of the subject and survey of the field and then they will perhaps accomplish better results at a lower cost. Let them, once more, not be in too violent a hurry. The abundance of transmitted writings in a metrical shape only proves more conclusively the familiar fact that it is as easy to compose verses as it is difficult to compose poetry. The long succession of authors who fall within the category of poets has received an extent of editorial care and illustration in the course of the century, however, which argues the prevalence of a more favourable opinion of their merits. The names which are at present commanding chief notice are those which have always been esteemed:

Shakespeare, Fletcher, Beaumont, Jonson, Daniel, Drayton, Wither, Sir John Davis, Herrick, Carew, Lovelace, and Suckling; and among the Scotish bards Drummond takes the lead. The most singular feature about the matter is that, in the presence of all kinds of critical editions, the demand is not for them, but for the originals. The mission of the modern recensor comes to an end when, by a stupendous amount of research and erudition, he has emphasised the characteristics and gifts of a writer. Then the amateur steps forward, and expresses his readiness to give any price for the good old book, undisfigured by notes and emendations!

It is perhaps fruitless to attempt to turn the tide of common sentiment, and gentlemen must be permitted to choose their own money's worth. They may think and say that they want the volume as it left the author's hands, not diluted and overlaid by commentators. Granted, it is a product of the time, even though the author did not see the proofs, and the printer could not always decipher the MS. But then comes the larger and more general question: How much of the better class of early verse-writers are worth reading? The present deponent, without being conscious that he is very hyper-critical, states the deliberate result of actual examination and perusal when he affirms that of the minor poets of the sixteenth and seventeenth centuries, save perhaps Randolph, the productions of enduring value and interest could be brought within the compass of a moderate volume.

It would be eminently unwise for any one who treats his library as an investment to yield to the existing tendency to exorbitant prices for the later poets and playwrights, as the rise is due to ephemeral causes, and the demand, for the most part, is not likely to exhaust the supply.

If the truth may be told, the literature of past ages in all countries, and nowhere more so than in England, is, in proportion to its immense extent, excessively barren of high-class writers or written matter. Each generation of collectors discovers this fact at last; but it discovers it for itself. We disdain to profit by the experience of our precursors, just as the little girl insisted on learning at her own cost how foolish it was to do a certain thing. Because there are a few highly interesting catholic publications, your amateur must be absolutely complete in the series. If it seems expedient to possess an example or two of ancient typography, he ends by doing his best to accumulate every example in the market. There is more than a probability that the service-books of the Romish Church have their archæological and literary value: *ergo*, he orders every one which he sees advertised, albeit the differences are substantially far from momentous. He understands that some very curious volumes illustrative of ritualism and the various holy orders were printed here or abroad, and he proceeds to drain the booksellers' shelves throughout the universe of every bit of sorry stuff answering to this description. There are a dozen or so of Collections of Emblems, English or foreign, which are supposed to throw light on passages in Shakespeare and other authors; this is sufficient leverage for the concentration under the unfortunate gentleman's roof of a closely packed cartload.

Seriously and bibliographically speaking, there is a fairly wide difference and disparity among the old editions of the poets and romancists; and there are, and always will be, a distinguished minority, of which the selling prices may be expected to remain firm. Such men as Shakespeare, Jonson, Beaumont, Fletcher, Chapman, Massinger, and among the lyric group Barnfield, Watson, Constable, Wither (earlier works and *Hallelujah*), Carew, Herrick, Suckling, and Lovelace, are to be viewed as standard and stable.

Then in the Scotish series there is permanence in Lyndsay, Drummond, and Burns. But, on the contrary, the minor, more obscure, or commoner productions must be carefully distinguished and circumspectly handled by those who do not desire or cannot afford to throw away their money. The names above cited are themselves very unequal; some, like Breton, Churchyard, Whetstone, Barnfield, Watson, and Constable, are sought, and will ever be sought, by reason of their peculiar rarity; and, save in a sentimental way, no one would probably dream of placing Beaumont, Chapman, Wither, and some of the rest on a par with Shakespeare, Fletcher, and Massinger. There has been, however, a tendency to force on the notice of book-buyers, *faute de mieux*, many writers whose productions are neither rare nor of the first class—Heywood, Dekker, Webster, Ford, and Shirley— and to bracket them commercially with authentic *desiderata* either on the score of merit or of scarcity. Of the three former, the most difficult pieces to procure are the Civic Pageants. Nearly all Ford's and Shirley's works, except the *Echo* of the latter, 1618, are classable among common books even in the first editions.

Again, condition is a postulate which begins to assert itself in the book-market. Poor and bad copies are eschewed by many or most of those who are willing to pay handsomely for fine specimens; and the worst type of indifferent exemplars is the sophisticated volume, which can be manipulated by experts to such an extent that even a person of considerable experience will now and then be at fault. The American collector grows more fastidious every day, and discovers blemishes which we on this side of the water try to tolerate, if the article is rare or we badly want it. Our Transatlantic friends, however, are more inexorable, and go so far as to return purchases not answering the description in the auctioneer's catalogue to their English commission-agents.

We have instanced above two or three writers whose works command excessive prices mainly by virtue of the paucity of surviving copies, seconded by a faint and indirect literary interest; but we see that the list is open to extension. During the last half-century and upward the publications of Nicholas Breton have fetched sums, when they have occurred, totally incompatible with any intrinsic value; with some few exceptions they belong to the category of "three-halfpenny ware," as Chamberlain the letter-writer styles such things in his correspondence with Sir Dudley Carleton; half-a-dozen or so out of forty and more are undoubtedly curious and illustrative; but Mr. Corser and one or two other collectors made a speciality of the author. It is only the other day that Sir John Fenn's copy of Breton's *Works of a Young Wit*, 1577, recorded by Herbert in his *Typographical Antiquities*, and the only perfect one known, occurred at an auction and fetched £81! A fine book it was, too, with the blank leaf at end. Doubtless, the reason for the evanescence of Breton's literary labours is to be sought in their estimation by many, besides the letter-writer above quoted, as barely more than waste paper. Verily, their substantial worth is barely tangible.

Speaking from a connoisseur's rather than from a reader's point of view, when we leave behind us the pre-Restoration writers of Great Britain and Ireland, we do not encounter much difficulty in a commercial sense, if we consider the length of time and the almost innumerable names, excepting Bunyan's *Pilgrim's Progress*, Swift's *Gulliver*, Defoe's *Robinson Crusoe*, Goldsmith's *Vicar of Wakefield*, and a few early Byrons and Shelleys, unless the buyer schedules among his *desiderata* the earlier Anglo-American literature. For as we draw nearer to our own day, items which were thought to be superlatively uncommon, including sundry pieces by Tennyson and Browning, have failed to maintain their reputation for scarcity, as any one might have foreseen that they would do. The preposterous prices paid for some copies have brought out others, and the ultimate supply will probably exceed the demand.

Even where an English collection may not enter the Continental lines, but preserves its national character, there are numerous classes of books of foreign origin and from foreign presses, which are fairly entitled to consideration and admittance. These publications embrace not merely religious and controversial literature, but a large and important body of material for English and Scotish biography and history, and for the elucidation of Irish affairs. Every season brings to light some new features in this immense series, which is, of course, susceptible of a classifying process, and may be ranged under such sections as we have above indicated, besides a considerable residue which falls under the head of poetry and typography, the latter constituting a branch of the History of English Printing, and the former being worthy of notice as embracing some of the rarest metrical productions of the sixteenth and seventeenth centuries, which owed their issue from presses in Germany and the Low Countries to various agencies, but chiefly to the exigencies of foreign military service by English and Scotish officers during the English operations in the Netherlands under Elizabeth and during the Thirty Years' War.

The foreign sources of English books, or books written by or about English, Scotish, and Irish folk, have been—

Aire	Leyden
Amsterdam	Lyons
Antwerp	Malines
Arras	Middelburg
Augsburg	Milan
Basle	Munich
Bologna	Munster
Boulogne	Paris
Breda	Parma
Bruges	Pisa
Brussels	Rome
Constantinople	Rotterdam
Dort	Strasburg-in-Elsass
Florence	The Hague
Flushing	Tournai
Geneva	Utrecht
Ghent	Venice
Gouda	Vevey
Haarlem	Wesel

Leipsic   Zürich

It is always to be borne in mind that these adjuncts at the foot of title-pages in troubled periods are not unfrequently fictitious; and we have elsewhere equally shown that Greenwich and Waterford are names appended to early controversial works of which the writers desired to conceal the real parentage.

Of English presses it might seem almost superfluous to speak; but in fact the typographical fortunes of London have experienced their flux and reflux. At first we find the City itself in sole possession of the industry and privilege; then Westminster came; thirdly, Southwark. Of the provincial places of origin, Oxford appears to have been the foremost, and was followed at intervals by York, Cambridge, Canterbury, Ipswich, Worcester, and other centres, of which some preserved their reputation down to comparatively recent times, while Oxford and Cambridge of course remain important and busy seats of printing. Beverley, Nottingham, Derby, Northampton, Bristol, Birmingham, Gateshead, and Newcastle-on-Tyne have never been more than occasional sources of literary production, and certain towns, such as Lincoln and Gainsborough, are only known from local or small popular efforts; there is an edition of *Robin Hood's Garland* with the Gainsborough imprint. One or two publications purporting to have been executed at Sherborne in Dorsetshire belong to the firm of William Bowyer of London.

There was a distinct centralising tendency at a later period, by which the English metropolis absorbed the principal share of work, and it was followed, owing to economical causes, by a reaction which we know to be at present in full force, and which has restored to the provinces, but to new localities, Bungay, Guildford, Bristol, no less than Edinburgh and Aberdeen, an appreciable proportion of the custom of the London publishing houses; nor is it unusual to send MSS. abroad for the sake of the advantage accruing from cheaper labour. We not long since secured this boon in Scotland; but Scotland has grown as dear as London.

The SCOTISH SERIES is a difficult and costly one to handle. The early vernacular literature of that country has suffered from two classes of destructive agency, neglect and fanaticism, to a greater extent than England, and the disappearance of the more popular books and tracts has been wholesale. The attempt on the part of a collector, however rich and persevering he might be, to form a complete series of original editions of the poetical and romantic writers of North Britain, could only be made in ignorance of the utter impossibility of success. The late David Laing abundantly illustrated this fact in his numerous publications, and further evidence of it may be found throughout the bibliographical works of the present writer.

The old Scotish presses were Edinburgh, Leith, St. Andrew's, Glasgow, Stirling, and Aberdeen; but a large proportion of the literary productions of Scotish authors, including much of the historical group relative to Mary Queen of Scots, proceeded from foreign places of origin, where the writers had settled or were temporarily resident.

The principal channels through which we have in modern times augmented our information of their products are the catalogues of Fraser of Lovat, Boswell of Auchinleck, the Duke of Roxburghe, Pitcairn, Constable, Chalmers, Maidment, Gibson-Craig, David Laing, and the Rev. William Makellar, the last a cousin of Sir William Stirling Maxwell of Keir, and a collector from 1838 to 1898.

A purely IRISH LIBRARY would inherently differ both from one limited to English or to Scotish books. There is no early typography or poetry, no works printed on vellum, no masterpieces of binding. The collectors in that part of the empire have always been few in number, and in fact Irish books have been chiefly collected by persons who were not Irishmen, nor even residents in that country. It used to be the case that, where a book was remarkably successful in England, the Dublin booksellers reprinted it, and, as these reproductions are generally scarcer than the originals, doubtless in limited numbers.

The series consists of a handful of books and tracts of the Elizabethan and Jacobean periods (1570-1625); of publications relative to the Civil War (1644-48); of others relative to the Commonwealth and Jacobite troubles (1650-90); of literary illustrations of the state of Ireland under the Houses of Orange, Stuart, and Brunswick or Hanover, and of modern days. The bibliographical writings of Sir James Ware are usually quoted and consulted for the literature within his time, but they have become almost obsolete. The two other works of reference for amateurs and students are those by Charles Vallancey (*Collectanea de Rebus Hibernicis*, 1786-1807, 7 vols.) and Charles O'Conor (*Rerum Hibernicarum Scriptores Veteres*, 1814-26, 4 vols.).

But we have to go to more recent authorities to discover that the typographical productions of Ireland in the first decade of the sixteenth and seventeenth centuries comprise a few books of the greatest rarity and one or two of which no copies are at present known. On the other hand, certain Elizabethan volumes, purporting to have proceeded from Irish presses, are generally believed to have an English origin, while others with German imprints of a later date (second half of the seventeenth century) are absolutely proved to have been clandestinely executed at home.

A very fair and comprehensive idea of the salient features in the present series may be gained from the Grenville and Huth catalogues and from Hazlitt's *Collections* (General Index). Considerable stress is laid by collectors on a large-paper copy with the *Decisions* filled in in MS., the Memorandum, &c., of the *List of Claims*, 1701, in connection with the Irish forfeitures. But in fact a copy of this work is always available, when any one wants it, which is seldom enough.

There was no *regular* printing here till the beginning of the seventeenth century, although one or two Marian tracts falsely purport to have come from the Waterford press. Dublin had a printer, John Frankton, who worked from 1601 to 1620 or thereabout, and produced many books, tracts, and broadsheets, some not yet recovered; the city also boasted a Society of Stationers in 1608, and many volumes appeared at London "Printed for the Partners of the Irish Stock," referring to the Plantation of Ulster. The places in Ireland itself, where the art of typography was pursued, were Dublin, Cork, Waterford, Drogheda, Kilkenny, and Belfast (as in the section just dismissed). But the rarest articles in the earlier series emanated from London or from Continental presses, the writings of Nicholas French and Cranford's *Tears of Ireland*, 1642, taking a prominent rank in the latter category.

The leading collectors on Irish lines have been Sir Robert Peel, Mr. Grenville, Mr. Huth, Mr. Bradshaw, Canon Tierney, Mr. Shirley, and Bishop Daly.

In the English series I have supposed the admission of a certain number or proportion of foreign books, which are of catholic interest, and have acquired a standing among many classes of collectors whose bias is principally national. But there are two other series of very unequal extent, importance, and costliness, which more directly appeal to the buyers of these islands, namely, the earlier Anglo-American literature belonging to the Colonial period, and the American reproductions of the favourite books of Lamb, Leigh Hunt, Hazlitt, Thackeray, and others in the present century. The latter category enters into the department of curiosities, and has yet to acquire bibliographical importance. In one or two cases, works issued at home in numbers have been published in the States in book-form prior to their appearance here. This happened with the *Yellow-Plush Correspondence*, reprinted direct from *Fraser's Magazine* at Philadelphia in 1838, and curious as the writer's earliest separate publication. These papers were not collected in England till 1841.

The products of the Colonial period include all the books emanating from American presses between 1640, the date of the *Bay Psalm-Book* at Cambridge, N.E., from the press of Stephen Day, and the Declaration of Independence. There has been a disposition to treat the whole of this output of printed matter with a special tenderness and reverence on political grounds; but it obviously is of a very mixed and unequal character, and, as time goes on, there must be a continuous winnowing process, and a consignment to oblivion of a vast assortment of the dullest theology and of political *ephemerides*. There will always remain a rich heirloom to our American kinsfolk and ourselves of historical nuggets in the shape of narratives of the fortunes and careers of the Pilgrim Fathers, their experiments in statecraft, their religious trials, their early superstitions and strange intolerance of personal liberty in a land chosen by its settlers for liberty's sake; and of course there is a section of literary products appertaining to the New World, namely, ritualistic ordinances, liturgical manuals, and collections of statutes, which derive what one is bound to term an artificial interest from the local circumstances, or, in other words, from the place of origin. A theological treatise, a Bible, a volume of prayers, or a law-book, published in England in the second half of the seventeenth century, may be worth from sixpence to a sovereign; if it bears the imprint of Boston, Cambridge (N.E.), New York, Philadelphia, or New London, its value may be computed in bank-notes. The *Laws of Massachusetts*, 1660, was lately sold for £109, and the *Papers Relating to Massachusetts Bay*, 1769, for £8, the latter in boards. The reason (so far as there is any) for this inflation is twofold: the patriotic sentiment which leads American amateurs to desire the oldest and most precious typographical and historical monuments of their country, and, secondly, the perhaps less justifiable enthusiasm of some Englishmen for books which, as they may plead, are the offspring of the States while they were still English settlements. A copious and fairly contemporary view of the extensive family of works belonging to the earlier Anglo-American library may be found in the bibliographies of Stevens, Sabin, and Harrisse, and in the Grenville, Huth, Lenox, and Tower catalogues. There is not only no line of collecting which is more difficult and more costly than the present, but none which, within the last twenty years, has, so far as first-rate rarities are concerned, more seriously advanced, even inferior copies of certain books fetching at times five times as much as good ones did in the seventies. Just lately the call appears to come from the other side of the Atlantic. There are two or three new bidders. That is sufficient.

CHAPTER IX

The Modern Side—Words of advice—The place and functions of Free Libraries—Coleridge and Byron period—Unhealthy state of the market—The Dickens and Thackeray movement—Fashions in books—A valuable suggestion—Slight actual demand for costly modern productions—Two often make a market—Effect of time in settling value—Forecast of the durability of a few names—A large-paper copy of Byron's poems, 1807—Cheap literature not a modern invention—The published price noted on the face of early volumes—An episode—Practical buyers not to be considered collectors—The first edition considered from editorial and other points of view.

IN the acquisition of modern books, far greater caution is requisite than in that of the older literature, since the output is so enormous, and the changes in taste and depreciation in value so rapid and so capricious. The Free and other Circulating or Reference Libraries throughout the country must prove of immense service in superseding the necessity of purchasing volumes of temporary interest or of expensive character; and the average collector will, and does, find that a certain number of dictionaries of various kinds, and of works which happen to be favourites, suffice to exhaust his space and resources. The Free Library is an undoubted boon in two ways: in enabling us to read or consult books which we do not care to buy; and again, in affording us an opportunity at leisure of judging whether such and such a volume merits more than a passing notice and perusal. The sole method of arriving at this information is to take the publication home. Even where shelf-room and funds are forthcoming, there is slight danger of any large percentage of recent literature being added to the stores of a judicious householder. To read, perhaps only to skim, and return, will be the general rule.

It is inexpedient to lend oneself too exclusively to a period or a school; for even where one has to study for a purpose a particular class of authors, or a particular subject or group of subjects, the local institution is at hand to help one; and the cheap reproductions of the writings of the earlier centuries, erring, as they do, on the side of indulgence, place it in the power of individuals of modest means to have at their elbows a representative assemblage, not necessarily a cumbrous one, of the literature from Chaucer to the present day, so that they may form a comparative estimate of the intellectual activity and wealth of successive ages, while, at the same time, the Greek and Latin authors are procurable in a collective shape, if they desire to compare notes and satisfy themselves on the obligations of the moderns to the ancients.

It amounts to this, that the Free Library is an agency which should save us to a very material extent from actually acquiring books which are not worth holding; it is not only a medium for reference, but for testing and winnowing. But for the select private bookcase it is not, or ought not to be, a substitute.

The Free Library is in its infancy and on its trial. In course of time the spread of education and the force of experience will confer on it better governing bodies, and better governing bodies will guarantee better curators. The actual generation of librarians, or so-called librarians, is the product of inefficient committees of control and selection; and the worst part is that some of these gentlemen receive salaries which would almost enable their employers to secure the services of qualified officers.

I am not personally of the opinion that those institutions are an unmixed blessing. For already there was a marked tendency to a decline in the taste for collecting among the middle classes in the United Kingdom, available resources being devoted to other outlets more generally acceptable to families; and the facilities afforded by the Free Library virtually amount to each individual parishioner being enabled, without appreciable cost, to possess books on a far larger scale than if he had a collection actually his own. The unfavourable operation of this state of affairs is twofold: it injures the literary market, and it promotes superficiality of study in the case of books which should be owned, not borrowed, to be thoroughly mastered and understood.

The range of choice, which embraces the writers of the modern school in prose and verse, is both wide and difficult. During many years past the number of authors within these lines has been continually on the increase, yet, while merit and value may be questions of opinion, there can be no serious or legitimate doubt that the output of literary work of high character is not greater than it was, if indeed as great. In the course of a quarter of a century many popular names have either fallen or faded out of remembrance, alike of authors who belonged to antecedent generations, and of those who have enjoyed a transient and artificial celebrity, and have come and gone, as it were, under the eyes of their immediate contemporaries. With the advantages offered by lending libraries, it appears to be imprudent on the part of any one who cannot conveniently form an extensive collection of modern books to buy on the recommendation of the press or the trade new favourites; for literary acquisitions are unfortunately apt to occupy space, and, save in very exceptional cases, to deteriorate in value. Even the original editions of the later works of Tennyson are not in great demand, and the high figures realised by one or two of his early productions are explainable in the same way as those given for Byrons and Shelleys.

The Modern Side of collecting is classifiable into numerous branches, according to the point of departure, as some differ in their view of what is modern from others. If we have to lay down a dividing line, however, we should make it comprehend the last decade of the eighteenth century, when many of the writers who were the contemporaries of our immediate foregoers began their literary careers.

Then, again, there are two branches of the later literature: the more recent writers themselves, and the reproductions, as I have noted, of the writers of former periods; and the extent to which the edited collections have been carried places it within the power of many who so desire to specialise on a certain line, and to deal representatively with the rest.

The specialist who proposes to himself as a field for his activity the Coleridge and Byron period, or who, again, confines his efforts to the writings of one or two of that set, has his work before him. Generally speaking, the first editions, which are those usually desired, are not uncommon; but there is almost always a *crux*, an *introuvable*, for which the not altogether blameable dealer puts on the screw, and charges more than for all the remaining items. Bohn's *Lowndes* yields a fair account of this family of literature; and Alexander Ireland, Richard Herne Shepherd, and others have bestowed vast pains on drawing up monographs on Coleridge, Hazlitt, Hunt, Shelley, Lamb, Keats, Browning, Tennyson, and the rest. It is difficult to foresee what the final upshot may be; probably, when fabulous prices have drawn forth from their hiding-places additional copies of many of these latter-day objects of keen pursuit, the market will fall and the craze will subside. It is a purely artificial and spurious one.

A second group, to whose books a collector may reasonably and conveniently confine his attention, consists of the poets and prose-writers who are still, or who were till lately, among us; and a fairly numerous body of matter falls within this class, as we may judge from a glance at the names which present themselves in the publishers' and booksellers' lists. In selecting the contemporary school, there is the undoubted advantage that you can institute a comparison between the book and its author, and that you may fall in with him at dinner, in a drawing-room or in a shop, and congratulate him or solicit an explanation of some fine but obscure passage; and should you also be literary, he has the opportunity of exchanging compliments with you. The old dead writers receive praise and offer no equivalent.

During a series of years there was a notorious run, which, as usual, became indiscriminate, on first editions of the writings of Dickens, Thackeray, and other foremost men of the period, eclipsing, as it seemed, even the demand for the earlier English classics, till the auctioneers and booksellers in their catalogues underlined at a venture every *editio princeps*, though it might be the last as well as the first, and, whether or no, a book of no mark. But the enthusiasm has at last contracted itself within narrower and more intelligent limits, and is restricted to productions which rank as masterpieces or are special favourites, and then all postulates have to be satisfied, all bibliographical minutiæ have to be studied. It is impossible to foresee how far this latest compromise may last; but whatever it is, there must always be some novelty to keep the market going, and bring grist to the mill. The world of fashion comprehends books as well as bonnets and dresses; but the literary section is a humble one by comparison, and is in few hands. Every fresh *mode* has somewhere its starter, and it usually prevails long enough to suit the purposes of the trade, when it makes way for its successor.

If one had the ordering of these strategical devices, one would imagine that the true policy was to buy up a given class of books, procure the insertion of a clever article or two in the press, extolling their merits and lamenting the public ignorance and neglect, and then launch a Jesuitically constructed catalogue devoted to such undeservedly disregarded treasures. But we may have been forestalled. Who knows?

The less current and every-day literary ware appeals to a more or less narrow constituency. There is a proverb, "The wool-seller knows the wool-buyer;" and it has to be so in books. There are volumes which, if they do not from their character or price suit one of a circle of half-a-dozen collectors, with whose means and wants the whole trade is generally familiar, are exceedingly likely to suit nobody outside the public libraries at public library prices. So much is this the case, that many booksellers do not think it worth their while to publish catalogues, and content themselves with reporting to the most probable purchaser fresh acquisitions. With certain very special and costly rarities *two* often make a market.

Time will perform its habitual office or function for us and our successors of separating from the multitudinous accumulation of modern published or printed matter such portion as, on deliberate inquiry and scrutiny, appears to be of permanent value. There is no doubt that much will be thrown aside; but the *residuum* which will bear the test of dispassionate judgment must prove considerable in itself, and also when taken into account as an appendix to the record left by preceding generations of writers. There may be certain authors and authoresses whom our descendants will like to have by them, even though they may no longer exert a sensible influence on literature and thought, just as we prize many of the older schools and types for characteristics and allusions which strike us as curious or entertaining; and soon, as decade follows decade, and the twentieth century has well opened, men and women, who were our grandsires' contemporaries, will seem through the lengthening vista almost as remote as they were from the Stuart epoch with its Elizabethan and Shakespearian traditions.

It is useless and invidious to particularise, and, besides, when one has drawn up a list of names, which are more or less obviously ephemeral, one cannot be certain as to the rest. Some must live; some may.

The astonishing demand for the first editions of our modern poets and novelists has, as was generally anticipated, subsided, and in some cases almost ceased; and it is extremely doubtful whether the taste will ever assume again the same unhealthy proportions. For one result of the matter has been to make it perfectly clear that copies of Byron, Shelley, Keats, Coleridge, Lamb, Dickens, Thackeray, Tennyson, and so forth, exist in much greater plenty than was at first supposed, though very little reflection should have sufficed to establish the fact as an eminent probability; and all that was needed to draw them from their resting-places was the series of paragraphs in the press conveying to holders how valuable their property had unexpectedly become. Shall we not have more copies of Shelley's poor little brochure of 1810 offered for sale ere long, as well as of Thackeray's *Exquisites* and *King Glumpus*?

At the same time, while we insist that the survival of means of supply is too large, and the market too limited, to sustain the extravagant quotations of recent years, there will ever remain persons prepared to give generous prices for absolutely first-class examples of the best modern authors. There must be no qualification, nothing secondary, nothing dubious; and with these provisos, we do not venture to predict that the competition might not become keener than ever. The same experience will result here and there, whenever a book forming a desideratum in more than one cabinet occurs for sale, and is perhaps the first copy which has been offered. At Sotheby's in June 1896, Shelley's *Œdipus Tyrannus*, 1820, it is said, was carried under these circumstances to £130. It was, we believe, one of two copies, picked up by a well-known amateur for fourpence each. On another account—its perfectly immaculate state in boards—a large-paper copy of Byron's poems, 1807, was thought by Mr. Edward Huth not too dear at £105. It had been acquired by a London bookseller in exchange for one in morocco from a correspondent in Yorkshire, the latter receiving the bound book (which cost the vendor £27) and £18 difference, so that there was a profit on the transaction of £60. Seriously speaking, the purchase was extravagantly dear, for the book on large paper is at all events not scarcer than on small. One of the most signal incidents, however, in modern auctioneering annals was the sale of MSS. copies of the *Endymion* and *Lamia* of Keats in the poet's handwriting for £1000, and the subsequent offer to the purchasers at that figure of a large advance for their bargain. These two items are printed, and the written copies were those employed by the printer, as upon the first leaf of each MS. were the directions as to size. They were in the familiar round schoolboy hand, and presented occasional corrections. We heard a suggestion that there might have once, at all events, been a duplicate copy in existence. If the lots were worth the money, what would the manuscript of *Venus and Adonis* or *Hamlet* fetch?

The mischief which proceeds from the advertisements through the press of sensational sale prices is not one for which either the buyers or the sellers are responsible. It is due to the notorious circumstance that very few persons are able to discriminate accurately between an important item in an auction or elsewhere, and another submitted to their approval, ostensibly and professedly identical, but actually very different. A certain familiar type of bookseller will tell you that a copy of such or such a work fetched £50 under the hammer last week, but that he can let you have his—same edition, same date, same nearly everything—for fifty shillings. Of course it is no such matter; yet the bait is often swallowed, and the poor (or possibly rich) fish caught.

The relatively cheap literature of the present day has been thought to be a revival rather than an invention. We meet with tracts published in the reign of Elizabeth with the express notation of the price of issue, namely, one penny. The *Book of Common Prayer*, 1549, was to be sold at 2s. 2d. unbound, and 4s. in paste or boards. The ordinary amount charged for a tract extending to thirty or forty pages, and for a quarto play, was 4d. or a groat. The first folio Shakespeare, 1623, cost the original purchaser 20s.; Percival's *Spanish Dictionary*, 1599, appears to have come out at 12s. There are lists of advertisements attached to publications of the later Stuart era showing that a large variety of popular productions brought the printer or stationer twopence or a penny. A curious little edition of *Coffee-House Jests*, 1760, bears the imprint:—

"Drogheda. Printed for the sake of a Penny:

Sold in Waterford, Cork, and Kilkenny."

But throughout these statistics, which are capable, of course, of infinite augmentation, we have to keep before us the difference in the value of money, and the purchasing power of the same amount in other and more practical directions; and it follows that the printed matter offered to-day for threepence or sixpence had no real parallel in former times, and that the absolutely cheap book is a product of modern facilities for manufacture.

The published price not unfrequently presents itself at the foot of the title on books of the late seventeenth and earlier eighteenth centuries. The simplicity of some individuals who are ranked among occasional or casual buyers was illustrated many years since by a man going into a shop in Fleet Street and putting down eighteenpence in payment of Hubert's *Edward II.*, 1721, in the window. The bookseller explained to him that his price was 5s. "But," insisted the customer, "look at the title-page; it was published at 1s. 6d." "Then you had better go to the publisher," observed the other, replacing the volume.

Book-collecting seems scarcely to concern very closely those who regard the pursuit from a severely practical point of view, or in the aspect of absolute intrinsic importance. It is true enough that one may form, not only a library, but a remarkably extensive one, of books of reference and study; but this does not quite answer to the idea of a bibliophile—in fact, it is little more than the digestion into book-form of a mass of learning and useful information. Again, if, without embracing such classes of volumes, we limit ourselves to those which, as we express the matter above, are positively important, we of course find on our shelves all the capital authors, ancient and modern; yet how many we should have to reject which are accounted indispensable to a choice cabinet! And such is apt to be more peculiarly the case in a selection formed on Anglo-French lines, as anybody may readily judge by examining a catalogue of this kind, where pages and pages are occupied by irritating trifles of no solid pretensions whatever, not even those evident in personal or heraldic accessories.

The general rule may be applied to our modern books, that, whatever they may be for purposes of instruction or entertainment, they seldom represent the outlay, and still more rarely a profit upon it when the day arrives for realising. During some time past we have witnessed the rise and fall, or at least disappearance from the front rank, of individuals and schools of individuals whose writings no amount of friendly support in the press was capable of propping up beyond three or four seasons. It is not that some of them may not hereafter, like our older authors, return to notice and currency; but they will suffer that intermediate period of neglect which has been experienced by well-nigh all our greatest names in letters. There is for literature, in common with its buyers, an earth, a purgatory, and a heaven— or something else. The public cannot keep pace with the vast and unbroken succession of literary produce, and the favourites of the day pass over to neutral ground, with very few exceptions, when their honeymoon has expired, to await the deliberate verdict of posterity on their merit and their station. To the investor for a more or less immediate return, however, they are precarious possessions, unless the market be carefully watched. The wealthy and absolutely uncommercial amateur disregards these risks and these counsels; and he is in a sense to be envied.

The question of the First Edition is not limited to any era of literary history and production, and the call for this class of book, at first (as usual) rather unreasoning, begins to be more critical and narrow. The author to be thus honoured by his posterity must have a certain bouquet and vogue. He must be a Shakespeare, a Jonson, a Herrick, a Burton, a Defoe, a Bunyan, a Burns, or (if we cross the sea) a Molière, a Montaigne, or a Cervantes.

With the first edition in some bibliographical schemes is associated the Best One. The possessor of both may pride himself on being able to show the earliest and latest state of the writer's mind, what he originally conceived, and what he decided to leave behind him as his *ultimum vale*. For the most part, however, first thoughts are treated as better than second, and it may actually be the case that, alike in ancient and modern books, the too fastidious and wavering ancient poet, or playwright, or essayist has done himself in maturer years an injustice by blotting the fresh impulses of his noviciate. It is a case, perhaps, where the public is entitled to intervene, and taking the two readings, deliver its award—always supposing that the text is that of a man worth the pains, and, again, that both versions are the language of the author, not that of the editor. It is obvious that, as a matter of literary and scientific or technical completeness, the last edition of a work is the most desirable; but it is particularly the case with volumes endeared by personal associations, such as Gilbert White's *Selborne*, that one prefers the text as the author left it, even if one has to be at the pains to consult a second publication for up-to-date knowledge. The present point is one to which I have adverted in an earlier place.

Apart from the collector, the first and the best impressions of writers of importance, whose texts underwent at their own hands more or less material changes, are necessarily an object of research to the editor or specialist who has dedicated his attention to such or such a study; and he is apt to pursue the matter still further than the amateur, who does not, as a rule, esteem the intermediate issues. It is this feeling and need which have led, since critical and comparative editions came into fashion, to the accumulation by their superintendents of an exhaustive array of titles and dates, with hints of the most remarkable various readings; and the cause of bibliography has gained, whether, in drawing together the series, the book-hunter or the literary worker be the pioneer. From the editorial and bibliographical points of view a complete sequence of the writings of our more distinguished and durable authors is generally practicable; but of excessively popular or favourite books, even of the Elizabethan era, it is imperfect. We refer to such cases as the so far unseen second impression of Shakespeare's *Passionate Pilgrim* and the ostensible disappearance of the original quarto of *Love's Labor's Lost*.

Two questions connected with the present part of the subject before us, now better understood and managed, were under the old system, so far as we can ascertain or judge, permitted to remain in a very loose and vague state. We allude to the law of copyright and the revision for the press. Prior to the institution of the Stationers' Company and the existence of a Register, the sole protection for authors and publishers was by the grant of a privilege or a monopoly for a term of years; yet even when registration had become compulsory, and was supposed to be effectual, spurious editions constantly found their way into the market, while books of which the writers might desire, on various grounds, to keep the MSS. in their own hands, found their way into print through some irregular channel. Such was the case with Shakespeare's *Hamlet*, 1603, and (in a somewhat different way) with the third edition of his *Passionate Pilgrim*, 1612; and we perceive that of Bacon's *Essays* during some years two parallel impressions were current without ostensible interference or warrant. There are frequent instances in which authors state that their motive in hastening into type was the rumour that a surreptitious and inaccurate text was threatened, as if there was no legal power to prevent such a class of piracy.

The correction of proofs by early writers, if we except books of reference, and those not without qualification, was evidently very lax and precarious. The entire body of popular literature, the drama included, offers the appearance, when we investigate examples, of having been left to the mercy of the typographers, and the faulty readings of old plays are more readily susceptible of explanation from the fact that we owe their survival in a printed form as often as not to the clandestine sale of the prompters' copies to the stationer. The editors of our dramatists have consequently found it an extremely laborious task to restore the sense of corrupt passages, and have sometimes abandoned the attempt in despair. Not a few of the pieces in the last edition of Dodsley come within this category; and we may signalise the unique tragedy of *Appius and Virginia*, 1575, as a prodigy of negligent and ignorant execution on the part of the original compositor. But to the same cause is due our still remaining uncertainty as to the true reading of numerous places in Shakespeare himself.

Our collectors, however, are not particularly solicitous to study the present aspect of the matter, and the hunter for First Editions is by no means likely to care an iota about the purity of the text, but may be more apt to congratulate himself on the ownership of the genuine old copy with all the errors of the press as vouchers for its character. Who would exchange a second *Hamlet* of 1604 for a first one of 1603, simply because the former happens to contain as much more, and the latter is little better than a *torso?*

The long uncertainty and insecurity of authors' rights, whatever may be thought of the present position of the matter, led at a very early date to the adoption of such safeguards against plagiarism as it was in the power of specialists, at all events, to impose. Some time after its original publication in 1530, we find John Palsgrave, compiler of the *Eclaircissement de la Langue Françoise*, prohibiting the printer from giving or selling copies to any one without his leave, lest his profits as a teacher of the language should be prejudicially affected; and so it was that preceptors often reserved the right of sale, and dealt direct with buyers, and in one case (only a sample) a treatise on Shorthand by Richard Weston (1770) is delivered to purchasers at eighteenpence on the express condition that they shall not allow the book to leave their own hands or premises.

CHAPTER X

Our failure to realise the requirements of Illustrated Books—The French School—La Fontaine's *Contes et Nouvelles*, 1762—Imperfect conception of what constitutes a thoroughly complete copy—The Crawford copy—Comparative selling values of copies—The *Fables* of the same author—Dorat—La Borde—Beaumarchais—Contrast between the English and French Schools—Process-printing—The *Edition de Luxe*—Its proper destination and limit—The Illustrated Copy—Increasing difficulty in forming it—Unsatisfactory character of the majority of specimens—Analogy between the French taste in books and in *vertu*—Temper of the foreign markets—The Anglo-American collector—The Parisian *goût*—The famous mud-stained volume of tracts in the British Museum—Foreign translations of early English tracts.

OF the *Illustrated Book*, the *Illustrated Copy*, and the *Edition de Luxe* we have spoken a few words elsewhere.[2] These are three forms of competition, which represent as many sources of danger and disappointment to the inexperienced. When we refer to illustrated books we of course signify books with woodcuts and other graphic embellishments from the earliest period, such as the Block Books, the *Game and Play of the Chess*, the Caxton *Æsop*, the *Nürnberg Chronicle*, 1493, the *Poliphilo*, 1499, the *Ship of Fools*, 1497, and the *Dance of Death*; collections of Portraits and Views; down to the productions of the modern school, and comprising the popular abridgments of Crouch or Burton, of which an idea may be gained from the list printed at the end of Bliss's *Reliquiæ Hearnianæ*, 1857, and the cheap editions of romances and story-books brought out by sundry stationers at prices ranging from threepence to a penny in the closing years of the seventeenth century. In the English series, independently of the woodcuts which incidentally occur in the books printed by Caxton and his immediate successors and the *Emblem* series, there are Roeslin's *Birth of Mankind*, by Raynald, 1540, Braun's *Civitates Orbis Terrarum*, Gemini's *Anatomy*, 1545, Godet's *Genealogy of all the Kings of England*, 1563, Saxton's *Maps*, Holinshed's *Chronicles*, 1577, Harington's *Ariosto*, 1591, Holland's *Baziologia*, 1618, and *Heröologia*, 1620, the various works illustrated by Pass, Elstracke, Hollar, Barlow, and others, Vicars's *England's Worthies*, 1645, Ricraft's *Survey of England's Champions*, 1647, and other publications by Ricraft with engravings, till we come down to the pictorial histories of England by Bishop White, Kennett, and Rapin and Tindal, Pine's *Horace*, and Buck's *Views*. No doubt among these there are interesting specimens for the respective periods. It is noticeable that in the Holinshed of 1577 the illustrations are frequently repeated without regard to the context. The engravings by Hollar and Barlow are the most pleasing. But the *Basiliologia*, 1618, is the rarest book in the whole range of this class of literature. Pine's *Horace*, even in the first edition, 1733, with the *Post Est* reading, is common enough; and it has been found uncut. So far as we are concerned, we should prefer it in the original morocco. As a text it is of no account.

Coming lower down, we may specify or emphasise a few *chefs d'œuvre*, such as Hogarth's Prints in the first or best states, Turner's *Liber Studiorum*, Sir Joshua Reynolds' Graphic Works, and Lodge's *Portraits*. But we are neither so wealthy nor so advanced as our French and German neighbours in this direction, and the former may be affirmed to stand alone in the possession of a class of books with engravings germane to the national genius and to the feeling and spirit of the time which produced such masterpieces in their way. Of works illustrated by copper-plates, that by Roeslin on Midwifery, 1540, above-named, seems to be the first in chronological order; but both this and the Gemini of 1545 probably owed their embellishments to foreign sources.

Our own country is probably weakest in this department; many of the engravings in our early literature are direct copies from the German, Dutch, or French masters; the names of some of our leading artists are those of foreigners; and we have comparatively little to show of strictly original work till the last quarter of the eighteenth century, when we may place our national efforts side by side with uninterrupted Continental series from the middle of the fifteenth. We are also poorly provided with books of reference enabling amateurs to form an idea of the extent of the field and of the relative practicability and costliness of given classes or lines, whereas the foreign collector enjoys the advantage of many excellent and fairly trustworthy manuals. We want a General Guide to English Illustrated Literature, which should exhibit its sources and inspiration, and the epochs and schools into which it is divisible.

Of course, it stands with the present description of literary monuments as it does with the normal book. An enterprise which should aim at being exhaustive would prove excessively serious in point of outlay, and would hardly be so satisfactory as one either on a miscellaneous or a special principle.

Meanwhile, it is desirable that statements offered in catalogues of various kinds should aim at accuracy as far as possible. It is singular what a vitality resides in errors when they have been pointed out by experts, and ought to be recognised. The auctioneers seem to keep the type of certain notes standing, as they are repeated in catalogue after catalogue without any other gain than that of misleading such as know no better. One familiar acquaintance of this class is the *dictum* that the copper-plates in Hugh Broughton's *Concent of Scripture*, 1596, are the earliest of the kind executed in

England, although they had not only been preceded by the prints in Harington's *Ariosto*, 1591, but by those accompanying the *Birth of Mankind* by Roeslin, 1540, and the *Anatomie Delineatio* of Thomas Gemini, 1545.

The average collector, who possesses tolerable judgment, and has the authorities at his elbow, cannot go far astray if he buys what pleases him among the ordinary books of medium price, and may acquire examples of every period and place of origin, as opportunities arise. Or he may limit himself to early German, Dutch, Italian, or French books with woodcuts, to the French illustrated literature of the eighteenth century, to volumes with engravings by Bewick, Stothard, or Bartolozzi, or to modern works with proof-plates, etchings, and other choice varieties. It is literally impossible to fix any *maximum* or *minimum* of cost in this case; so much depends in graphic publications on niceties of difference; and a law prevails here analogous to that which governs the Print, that is to say, that a more or less slight point of detail vitally affects values. Let us take such a familiar instance as Lodge's *Portraits of Illustrious Personages*. One may have a copy in Bohn's Libraries for a dozen shillings; and one may give seventy or eighty sovereigns for a large-paper copy with india proofs of the four-volume folio edition of 1821. On the whole, the twelve-volume quarto book is almost preferable, as in the folio there is the disadvantage of three volumes having copper-plates and one (the fourth) steel engravings, and the quarto is obtainable for £20 or £25 in morocco.

Very few of the English portraits in the engraved series antecedent to Lodge are trustworthy, as this branch of specialism was not properly studied and understood down to the present century, and even the heads executed by Houbraken are not unfrequently apocryphal. Such a criticism applies less to royal personages than to private individuals, of whom the painted likenesses were apt, after the lapse of years, to be not so easily identifiable.

We have excellent monographs on Bewick and Bartolozzi by Mr. Hugo and Mr. Tuer respectively; and there is the delightful biography of Stothard by Mrs. Bray, 1851, with profuse illustrations of his various artistic productions and progressive style. Many of the scarcer examples of Bartolozzi have been imitated. To the collector who limits his interest to artists in book-shape, the first editions on large or largest paper of the *Birds*, *Quadrupeds*, and *Select Fables* of Bewick are most familiar and most desirable. Stothard is seen to advantage in the engravings to Ritson's *English Songs*, 1783. Much of his work lies outside the mere library. For a general view of that branch of the subject, Jackson and Chatto's *Treatise on Wood Engraving*, 1839, may be recommended, so far as the printed book is concerned.

We do not dwell on the modern illustrated literature, which demands less study, and offers few features of interest, especially that produced at home.

Too large a proportion of it, however, whatever may be the origin, is indifferent in quality and permanent worth. Publications are at present, like other commodities, prepared with a main eye to sale; the sense of pride and honour on the part of the producer is dulled; he manufactures in gross. There are the showy volumes of Yriate on Venice, Florence, and other subjects, with letterpress written apparently to accompany blocks and plates in the publisher's warehouse.

Perhaps, if we seek something more elevated and creditable, it will be in certain periodicals conducted on higher lines than those to which the ordinary publisher has from financial exigencies to be bound; and of these there are several both in France and England—nay, in Italy, in Australia.

The Illustrated Book, as we are familiar with it here, affords innumerable examples of varied treatment, as the school of design and the public taste differ or fluctuate from century to century, from age to age, and even from season to season. We do not speak of the cheaper literature in this class, accompanied by engravings so intolerably poor as to disarm criticism, but to the higher efforts of the artist to respond to the author, and to appeal more directly to the eye. In this country, however, we have not so far been so fortunate, or otherwise, as to attain the Continental ideal of what the graphic portion of a literary performance should be; and the question is intimately associated, particularly in France and among foreign buyers of the French school, who are numerous in all parts of the world, with that of binding, inasmuch as a volume possessing pictorial embellishments of whatever kind must fulfil all requirements in that respect no less than in the outward vesture, and what may be termed the complemental book-plate.

One of the eighteenth-century French productions which answers most thoroughly to the just foregoing description, is the "Fermiers Généraux" edition of the *Contes et Nouvelles* of La Fontaine, 2 vols. 8vo, 1762. The ordinary copies of this work, of which the whole charm lies in the meretricious plates by Eisen (for the text is inoffensive enough), are distinguished by the presence or otherwise of two or three plates in a particular state, those left as originally printed being preferred, because they offer certain unconventional details subsequently modified. But, in fact, to make a perfect exemplar of the work, to satisfy the demand of a rigid connoisseur, you have to combine features in the shape of proofs before letters and vignettes taken off separately, besides extra engravings by other artists not strictly belonging to the edition, until you have a complete album of *bijoux indiscrets*, and in the old French morocco by Derome or Bozerian a £200 lot. The Earl of Crawford's copy, which was to have been sold at Sotheby's in July 1896 (No. 493 of catalogue), was a masterpiece of this description; but it was withdrawn. It has since been sold to another noble lord—the Earl of Carnarvon.

A copy of the normal *decouvert* type of the *Contes et Nouvelles*, 1762, may be had, according to condition and binding, for between £10 and £50. It has been said of the extra plates to the *Contes et Nouvelles* of La Fontaine that their rejection as part of the published work ought to be a matter neither of surprise nor of regret, for they are not only flagrantly indecent, but are poor and unsatisfying from an artistic point of view. Another favourite edition of the *Tales* is that with the plates by Romeyn de Hooge, 1685, 2 vols. 8vo; but you must have it on fine paper in old morocco.

Looking at the illustrated editions of the *Tales* generally, the plates, except the charming head and tail pieces, do great injustice to the text, which the author can hardly have foreseen the possibility of being deformed and discredited by such forced and exaggerated constructions of his meaning.

The edition of La Fontaine's *Fables* by Oudry, 4 vols. folio, 1755-59, is almost equally sought by connoisseurs, though on somewhat different grounds. Some copies in one of the plates, where there is a tavern sign, have on the board a lion rampant. In the Bibliothèque at Paris is a copy on largest paper bound for Marie Antoinette with original decorations by Oudry himself on the covers; it is only a single book out of thousands which they have there, yet it might make a day's sale, and a remunerative one, in Wellington Street in the Strand! Boccaccio, 5 vols. 8vo, 1757, with plates by Eisen, Gravelot, and others, enters into this series; it is not an uncommon book, and is found with a French and an Italian text, of which the former is generally preferred. It is necessary to secure a copy in all respects faultless. But far more important and relatively costly are the *Baisers* of Dorat, 1770, printed on *grand papier de Hollande*, with the title in red and black, and, above all, Laborde's *Choix de Chansons*, 1773, always a dear publication when the state is right, and excessively difficult to obtain with proof plates; the Magniac copy was bought by Mr. Quaritch at Phillips's a few years since for upwards of £200, and sold by him, we believe, to Lord Carnarvon. Another copy, with the plates in unlettered proof state, is marked £250 in Pearson & Co.'s Catalogue, 1897-98. *La Folle Journée*, by Beaumarchais, with engravings of the same period and character, is also a charming production, and commands a good price.

The minutiæ into which the enthusiasts for the graphic French literature produced in the closing years of the ancient régime permit themselves to enter is rather bewildering to a novice or an outsider, and certainly asks as much study as it can well be worth. The cultivation of the pursuit has naturally brought into existence a small library of monographs, of which that by Cohen is one of the best known and the most frequently quoted. There is an equal degree of difference between the pictorial features of books produced in England and on the Continent during the past and the present centuries. In France there still reigns the spirit of enterprise conducive to the execution of high-class work; but among ourselves it is painful to contemplate the decline, not of power, but of encouragement, and the unhealthy tendency to a style of illustration which will not probably be very creditable to the country in retrospect. A collection of modern illustrated works of mixed origin may well dispense, except by way of sample and contrast, with much of the fantastic and preposterous creations of some of the latter-day masters.

The *Edition de Luxe*, the *Large*, *Larger*, and *Largest Paper*, the copy on yellow paper, blue paper, writing paper, on *papier de Hollande*, *de Chine*, or *d'Inde*, or on Japanese vellum, the very limited impression, are among the fancies and demands of the omnivorous past. A short study of the supplement to Bonn's *Lowndes* and of Martin's *Privately Printed Books* will suffice to show that not only a library, but a tolerably extended one, might be formed of these classes of literature exclusively; and indeed the thing has been more than once actually done. Utterson, Halliwell, Laing, Maidment, Eyton, Turnbull, and others have contributed to leave to us a voluminous inheritance of now rather neglected and undervalued curiosities of this kind. But even here the discriminating collector may still advantageously pick out items worth buying and holding, for in the case of every artificial *furore* the good, bad, and indifferent are apt to rise and to fall together, while it is reserved only for the first to experience a revival—the Revival of the Fittest.

The Illustrated Copy is an indefinite quantity as to character and importance or estimation, since no two correspond. Nearly all those which have been formed are more or less unequal, even where there has been no regard to cost, and every care has been exercised in the selection of objects; for there is a chronic tendency to become complete. But so far as the normal undertaking of this class is concerned, we usually perceive a few desirable and appropriate prints or drawings as a sort of *pièce de resistance*, and the remainder is made up anyhow. Even such a book as the Pennant's *London* in the Huth Collection strikes us as unsatisfactory on the ground stated; there is a share of merit in the choice of embellishments; there is also too considerable a residuum of comparative rubbish; and if it is so here, the reader may judge how the matter stands with illustrated books of the ordinary stamp made up for sale. There is one remark to be offered. The really fine prints and other similar productions are too valuable to treat in this way, as they would necessarily render the work, when it was ready for the client, too expensive. A Pennant, for example, exclusively composed of first-rate material, and tolerably representative in regard to names and localities, would be worth thousands of pounds. The time for securing prizes for this purpose at a moderate figure has gone by. The catalogues advertise copies "extensively and tastefully" illustrated with hundreds or thousands of portraits and views; and the bidding or demand, as the case may be, is carried to £20, £50, or £100. Our advice is, Not to touch. It is preferable to have a few chosen examples in a portfolio.

It is not always that the Illustrated Copy is restricted to engravings and other works of art. Autograph letters enter into the plan, and facsimiles of title-pages or other cognate and more or less relevant objects. One of the most recent enterprises of this nature—a Boswell's *Johnson*—cost the actual possessor about £10,000; it was extended to forty-two volumes, and aimed at having a token of some kind of every one mentioned in the text. So we advance. It was deemed a piece of extravagance when, forty or fifty years ago, the late Sir William Stirling-Maxwell expended about £1000 in forming an illustrated copy of his own *Cloister Life of Charles V.*

The Nature-printing, Autotype, Photogravure, Collotype, and other processes strike us as hardly falling within the category here contemplated, although that they are material accessions to our resources is undoubted. They are the fruit of a combination between nature and mechanical science; their fidelity for portraiture and technical purposes may be granted; but they do not realise the notion of artistic embellishment or interpretation, nor are they capable of rendering with anything approaching truth the more delicate and subtle touches of the miniaturist.

The *Edition de Luxe* is dilettantism *in extremis*. It is a movement which seems to rest on a false theory and basis. It should have limited itself to *nugæ literariæ*, to *bagatelles*, which no mortal sought to read, and which might be harmlessly printed on any material, of any latitude and longitude, in any type, or else to graphic works where the luxury would more comfortably and more suitably make itself manifest in illustrations varied and duplicated to whatever extent it pleased the issuer, or was calculated to gratify his clients. But to apply the principle to books so essentially appealing to practical readers as Dickens, Thackeray, Scott, and others, was an unfortunate step and precedent, which has thrown on the market a large amount of stock not easily moved even at a heavy discount on the published price.

Merely looking at the *bibliophile* pure and simple, and shutting our eyes to those phases of book-collecting, where the principle or sole aim is educational or religious, we incline to the conclusion that foreigners, and above all the French, are less practical than ourselves, and lay far greater stress on sentiment.

The French, and we may perhaps add the Anglo-French school of book-collecting, works on lines which to a normal lover of books must at first appear rather mysterious and strange, if not absolutely irrational. The closest analogy which it is in our power to suggest is the almost parallel sentiment and policy in regard to other branches of inquiry—china, furniture, numismatics. The Frenchman and his English disciple have no respect whatever as *collectionneurs* for substantial value, and agree in ignoring everything, good, bad, indifferent, outside a prescribed limit.

The temper of the foreign markets, especially the French one, is so essentially different from that of England, that it demands an almost life-long study of the subject to comprehend the true principles by which they are guided and influenced. In what we are just now urging, we must of course be understood to allude to the *amateur* pure and simple,—in fact, if it may be said without offence, to the virtuoso. There are foreign book-collectors, as there are English, who seek copies of works within their lines, whatever those lines may be, for the sake of information and reference. The collector has no such aim. He aspires to make himself master of so many items answering to certain inexorable postulates laid down by the experts in such matters. His taste has happened to take a bibliographical direction and shape; it is hardly a literary one; and the objects of his pursuit, instead of being pictures, prints, antiquities, gems, or coins, are things in book-form.

Monsieur and his British satellite cultivate exclusively what is French, just as in the numismatic department Monsieur will only buy French coins or Franco-Italian ones, or the money of Monsieur's direct ancestors, the Greeks and Romans. It is the same principle throughout; and the undoubted fact is before us that, if the article to be sold is right in all respects, the price is marvellous. One can understand a high appreciation of some superb or unique example of ancient typography, of a book which has belonged to a famous person, or of a manuscript like the *Bedford Missal* or the *Hours* of Anne of Brittany. One can understand, again, the enthusiasm for an unrecorded old poem, romance, or play, for a production by an eminent author supposed to have perished, or for a precious relic such as the Manesse MS., presented by the German Emperor Frederic to the library at Heidelberg, from which it had been taken by the French during the wars of the Revolution. But the Parisian *goût* is less intent on such matters than on flimsy and effeminate specialities. A copy of a book, it does not signify how valuable intrinsically it may be, is worth nothing in the eyes of *Monsieur* and *Monsieur d'Angleterre son ami*, unless it is in a particular vesture, with a particular *ex libris*, and of a particular measurement in *millesimes*. MM. *les amateurs* reject not merely calf, but that vellum wrapper and that stitched paper envelope so dear to us English—so dear that when one of us has given hundreds of pounds for a book thus clothed, rather than commit it to a binder, we employ him to make us a case for the gem. The volume of tracts which Charles I. borrowed of Thomason the stationer, and let fall in the mud, what could Monsieur do with it? Absolutely nothing. But the British Museum cherishes the relic, and would not on any account, we solemnly believe, suffer the stains to be removed. They are the credentials, the link between the king and ourselves.

On the subject of French books in regard to their bindings we shall have more to say below.

FOOTNOTES

[2] *Four Generations of a Literary Family*, 1897, ii. 371.

CHAPTER XI

The extrinsic features in books—Autographs—Inscriptions—Various classes of them and of interest in their subject-matter—The Henry VIII. *Prayer-Book* of 1544—Some account of it—Gabriel Harvey—Spenser—Evelyn—Milton—Hypothetical *grands prix*—Classification of inscriptions—Examples—Dramatists—Poets—Jonson, Massinger, Drayton, Wycherley, Killigrew—Mere signatures—Shakespeare's copy of Florio's *Montaigne*, 1603—The Earl of Essex's copy of Drayton's *Eclogues*, 1593—Humphrey Chetham—Strays from his library—Beau Nash as a collector—Sir Joshua Reynolds—William Beckford and his *Vathek*—Foreign autographs and memoranda—A whimsical note in a copy of Shakespeare's *Passionate Pilgrim*, 1599—Interesting MS. matter in a copy of Stow's *Survey*, 1633—Pepys's binder—Dr. Burney and his verses in *Sandford and Merton*—Napoleon and Josephine—The Lutheran Testament given by the latter to General Buonaparte—A charming presentation copy from Josephine of Voltaire's *Henriade*—What makes the interest in autographs—Ineptitudes—The reviewer's copy—Latter-day vandalism—Arms on books—Prefaces and Dedications—*Imprimaturs*.

WHAT may be treated as the casual accessories of books of nearly all periods and countries—the autograph inscription testifying to the ownership or signalising a gift from one possessor to another—have manifold and diversified elements of interest and attraction. These features offer a graduated scale of importance, just as it happens. The question depends on the donor, or the recipient, or the article given and received; and where all these combine to augment the charm and to complete the spell, the issue is electrifying. No more impressive corroboration of this truth could well be desired or produced than the Henry VIII. *Prayer-Book* of 1544 on vellum, from the Fountaine Collection, with the MSS. notes and autographs of the King, the Princess Mary, Prince Edward, and Queen Catherine Parr. It fetched about 600 guineas at Christie's in 1894.

In the *Bibliographer*, *Bookworm*, and his own *Collections*, the writer has formerly assembled together notices of all the most remarkable examples of English books, both printed and in MS., with inscriptions, *marginalia*, and other records of prior and successive possession, brought within his reach during more than thirty years past. There are not unreasonably people who may not see in an ordinary copy of a volume much tangible interest, yet who are prepared to recognise the value, and even importance, of one with the autograph and memoranda of some illustrious personage, of some great warrior or statesman, or of a famous man of letters, artist, or sculptor. The accidental and secondary feature in the work takes precedence of the rest; he pays for the sentiment and association. The direct human interest resident in such a relic is apt, in the opinion of many, to surpass that of the finest binding; for one has here the very characters traced long ago by the holder; one can imagine him (or her) seated at the table engaged in the task of leaving to the times to come this memento. The book is the casual receptacle; perchance in itself it is of inconsiderable worth; but the manuscript accessions are as an embalmment and a sanctification. The copy is not as others; it has descended to us as a part of a precious inheritance, of which the mere paper and print are the least significant; we are to approach and touch it reverently, as if the individual to whom it appertained were standing by, to reprove an ungentle hand and take back the legacy.

It would be barely possible, were it of essential use, to schedule all the existing presentation or annotated copies of books in our own and other literatures, but we shall here make an effort to offer a general view of what is intended, and what may in some instances become attainable by watching opportunities:—

- Monastic or collegiate literature.

- Editions of the Bible.

- Editions of the New Testament.

- Editions of the Prayer-Book.

- Royal Books:—

    o (i) With autograph notes by the owner.

    o (ii) With inscription by the giver.

    o (iii) With both.

    o (iv) In binding identifiable with a royal personage.

- Books which possess the signatures of noble or illustrious individuals, politicians, statesmen, soldiers.

- The same categories apply.

- Books with literary inscriptions:—

    o (i) Presentation copies with author's inscription.

    o (ii) With his inscription and additional matter by him.

    o (iii) With inscription by recipient.

    o (iv) With autographs and MSS. notes by both.

- Foreign books:—

    o   Monastic and mediæval.

    o   With MS. matter of historical or genealogical interest.

    o   Books from royal or noble libraries.

    o   Books of literary interest.

Monastic inscriptions are generally limited in their interest to casual light shed by them on personages connected with the institution or on some local circumstance.

Of royal books, genuine and otherwise, the number has had a tendency to increase through the successive dispersion of old libraries everywhere, combined with the additional facilities for gaining access to those which still remain intact. The Henry VIII. *Prayer-Book* on vellum is the only copy known in any state of the edition of 1544, and may not have been publicly issued with this date.

Some of the royal memoranda are of signal interest and curiosity. On the back of the title, under the royal arms, the king himself says: "Remember thys wrighter wen you doo pray for he ys yours noon can saye naye. Henry R." At the passage: "I have not done penance for my malice," the same hand inserts in the margin: "trewe repentance is the best penance;" and farther on he makes a second marginal note on the sentence: "thou hast promysed forgyveness," . . . "repentance beste penance." This was a sort of family common-place book. Inside the cover Prince Edward (afterward Edward VI.) writes: "I will yf you will." The volume, which contains other matter of great historical value, appears to have been given by Henry VIII. shortly before his death to his daughter Mary; for on a small piece of vellum inside the cover he has written: "Myne owne good daughter I pray you remember me most hartely when you in your prayere do shew for grace to be attayned assurydly to yr lovyng fader Henry R." The Princess subsequently gave it to her stepmother, Catherine Parr, and it has a motto and signature of that lady's second husband, Lord Seymour of Sudeley, the Admiral.

The old king, we observe, grew rather nervous about the future just at the last, and he at all events admitted that there was room for contrition.

A companion volume and monument was the copy of the Sarum *Horæ* of 1520, printed on vellum, in the second portion of the Ashburnham sale. This precious book belonged to the Parr family, including the mother of Queen Katherine Parr, and at any rate contained an inscription in the hand of the Queen's brother, and of those of members of the Carew, Vaux, Tailboys, Nevill, and other families, besides being in beautiful condition; and the same library yielded a second copy of *Hours*, 1512, which had passed through the hands of Henry VIII. himself, as attested in one place by his autograph memorandum: "Pray yow pray for me your loving cousin Henry Rex." Such relics appear to bring back before us the dead players on the human stage, divested of all but their more redeeming characteristics.

In the British Museum we have the *Great Bible* of 1540 on vellum, which enters into the present category by reason of its association with the same prince, though in a different way. On the reverse of the fly-leaf occurs: "This Booke is presented vnto your most excellent highnesse by youre loving, faithfull, and obedient subiect and daylye Oratour, Anthonye Marler, of London, Haberdassher." Truly a gift worthy of a king; and there it remains, a precious link with the past and a splendid memorial of the citizen of London who laid it at his sovereign's feet.

Propriety and sympathy of costume go very far indeed to establish and augment the estimation of printed volumes with manuscript tokens of former proprietorship. The collector who chooses this field of activity has to weigh the correlation and harmony between the volume itself and the individual or individuals to whom it once appertained. We have usually to content ourselves with the interest resident in an autograph, with or without further particulars; it is a book, perhaps, which formed part of the library of a distinguished Elizabethan or Jacobean writer or public character; but, if it were not, its worth might be nominal. Again, the book is possibly one of great value, and exhibits an early autograph and MSS. notes; it would be better without them. Find the copy of *Venus and Adonis*, 1593, given by Shakespeare to Lord Southampton, the poet's copy of the *Faëry Queen*, 1590-96, Sir Fulke Greville's copy of Sydney's *Arcadia*, 1590, or a book of Voyages belonging to Drake or Raleigh, and it is worth a library, and a good one too. The nearest approach we have yet made to this kind of combination is the first folio Montaigne and the original edition of Lord Brooke's works, 1633, with the signature of Jonson, and the Spenser of 1679 with the notes of Dryden, unless the *Paradise Lost*, 1667, with Milton's presentation to a bookbinder at Worcester be authentic.

We must not omit in the present connection the copy of the prose story-book of *Howleglas*, given in 1578 with others by Edmund Spenser to Gabriel Harvey. But an almost equally covetable possession was the copy just referred to of Milton's *Paradise Lost*, 1667, which occurred only the other day at a sale, where it was, as too often happens, mis-described, and brought £70. It bore on a small slip inlaid in a fly-leaf: "For my loving ffreind, Mr. Francis Rea, Booke binder in Worcester these," and on another piece of paper: "Presented me by the Author to whom I gave two doubl sovereigns" = £4, nearly as much as the poet had for the copyright. The story of the book is unknown to us; it seems eminently likely that the first memorandum was written by Milton; but whether it belonged to a wrapper forwarding the gift, or to a letter accompanying it, is problematical.

Rea of Worcester must be the same individual who is described as having re-bound in June 1660 the Jolley and Ashburnham copy of Higden's *Polychronicon*, printed by Caxton, 1482; but there an earlier owner, Richard Furney, calls him "one Rede of Worcester."

At Trinity, Cambridge, there is the edition of Spenser, 1679, with a memorandum on the fly-leaf by Jacob Tonson, testifying to the MSS. notes in the book being by Dryden, and at Wootton formerly was the *Faëry Queen*, 1596, John Evelyn's cypher in gold down the back of the cover and seventeen lines in his autograph on the fly-leaf.

Among our dramatists, Ben Jonson is conspicuous by the number of copies of his own performances which he presented to royal and noble personages or to private friends. Of three gift-copies of his *Volpone*, 1607, one has an inscription to John Florio, the other to Henry Lambton of Lambton. The almost unique large-paper one of *Sejanus*, 1605, in the Huth Collection, was given to the poet's "perfect friend," Francis Crane. In the Museum are the *Masque of Queens* and the *Masque of Blackness and Beauty* offered to the queen of James I. But of Shakespeare, Beaumont and Fletcher, and many others, we have not a single memorial of this kind. Of Massinger there is one: the copy of his *Duke of Milan*, 1623, received from him by Sir F. Foljambe. In the case of Taylor the water-poet, the nearest approach to anything of the sort is the MS. note of the recipient of a copy of his Works, 1630.

Of two equally prominent poets of the same epoch, Daniel and Drayton, the latter seems to have had a partiality for inscribing his autograph in presentation copies of his books, while of Daniel in this way we do not recollect to have met with a single example.

Very engaging, on account of its manly and cordial tone, is the autograph epistle by Sir Richard Fanshawe accompanying an extant copy of his translation of Guarini's *Faithful Shepherd*, 1648. The whole production may be seen in the Huth Catalogue (p. 633), where we inserted it as a favourable sample of this kind of poetry or verse. The lines are headed: "To my deare friend Mr. Tho. Brooke with Pastor Fido before an entended voyage," and commence:—

"This to the man I most affect I send,

  The faithfull Shepherd to as true a friend.

  There on each page thou'lt tenderest passion see,

  But none more tender than my own for thee."

The volume belongs to the series of memorials, which we possess in not too ample abundance, of the regard entertained by men of letters of former days for each other, or for their intimates, and ranks with the priceless copies of his own books presented by Jonson to some of his distinguished contemporaries. If he, or any one else, made gifts of such things to the greatest of them all, every trace of such an incident has apparently disappeared.

Rarity of occurrence is not by any means an imperative feature in influencing or determining the value of inscriptions. No examples are probably more abundant than the books of Izaak Walton, either with an ordinary note of presentation, or with MSS. notes in the writer's hand, if not with both; yet they invariably command a liberal price from the admission of Walton by common acknowledgment into the select circle of literary men, whose works we love for the sake of the author.

The following inscription in contemporary MS. occurs on the reverse of the Old Testament title to a Cranmer's Bible of 1540: "Thys byble ys John Crogdens, Cytyzen and merchant taylor of London, dwellynge in Wattlynge Street at ye syne of Y^e Whyte Horse, 1550."

Occasionally more or less curious personal traits or family clues are yielded by the memoranda on fly-leaves. A Latin Testament of 1563 bears: "e libris Thomæ Northcote e dono Joh. Rolle Armig. de Stephenstone in agro Devoniensi;" a copy of Jewell's Sermons, 1583, has "John Willoughby, 1591," and "Amor vincit omnia." In the Savile copy of Sir Thomas More's Works, 1557, we read: "de dono H. Savile anno 1600; found by Mary Savile, Dec. 12, 1635, amongst other books at Metheby: for my daughter Mary Savile."

If the reader will cross over with us into Scotland for a moment or so, we will introduce him to a very interesting relic in the shape of a Latin Aristotle of 1526, in which a Cistercian monk of Kinloss Abbey, Andrew Langland, has enshrined two metrical compositions from his own pen; an epitaph on the Regent Murray, and an epistle to Joannes Ferrerius, Professor at Kinloss, 1542, and continuator of Hector Boece. The epitaph is dialogue-wise between the Bishop of Orkney, who was absent from the funeral, and Ferrerius, who attended it.

At the sale of the library of the Duke of Leeds, a large-paper copy of Wycherley's *Miscellany Poems*, 1704, apparently given by the poet to Lord Treasurer Danby, produced the outrageous price of £46. A far more interesting example was that which he presented to Mistress Mary Twysden, as noticed in the *Bibliographer*. A more important souvenir was the Latin Testament given by Pope to Bolingbroke in 1728 (Christie's, April 3, 1895, No. 339); and a yet stronger sympathy must be felt with the Juvenal and Persius, 8vo, Amsterdam, 1684, which once belonged to T. Killigrew, and subsequently to Pope, whose English version occupies the interleaves, if the description given by Wake of Derby be correct, as the book itself we have not seen.

We approach a different class of consideration when we leave behind us the more or less factitious and artificial attractions of early bindings and autograph memoranda, and pass to books which owe their extrinsic interest to a mere signature, as in the case of the copy of Florio's *Montaigne*, 1603, which belonged to Shakespeare, and possesses his autograph on the fly-leaf, and of which the *provenance*, as stated by Madden in his pamphlet, 1838, favours the authenticity; and again, in that of Mr. Collier's copy of Drayton's *Shepheard's Garland*, 1593, which bears on the title-page the signature of Robert, Earl of Essex.

There quite casually fell into our own hands a copy of one of Archbishop Usher's books, a stray from Manchester, with "Humfrey Chetham's Booke, 1644," on fly-leaf, and with it came a MS. on vellum, also formerly Chetham's, of the *Stimulus Conscientiæ* in English verse. They long lay in a garret at Pennington Hall, Leigh, Lancashire, the seat of the Hiltons, with whom Chetham was intimate, if not connected.

We meet with a surprise now and then, as when such a work as the English *Reynard the Fox* of 1681-84 carries on its face a proof of the prior ownership of Beau Nash: "Rich. Nash Arm. Bathoniæ, 1761," but it is quite natural to find the autograph of Sir Joshua Reynolds accompanying a series of French plates illustrative of the *Odyssey*, 1639.

In old books, and in new ones too, there are inscriptions and inscriptions. We are all familiar with the scrawl of the clown, who has handed down to us his unconsecrated name on the title-page or fly-leaf of some volume of ours otherwise irreproachable. Just a step above him is your fellow who writes some objurgatory *caveat* against the malappropriator, and brings the Almighty without scruple into the witness-box, in case any varlet should make free with his property:—

"Hic liber est meus,

  Testis est Deus;

  Si quis me quærit,

  Hic nomen erit."

      "Will. Morsse, 1678."

Of the whimsical entries in old English books the diversity is endless. On the fly-leaf of a copy of Roger Edgworth's *Sermons*, 4to, 1557, occurs: "Bryen O'rourke his hand and writting by fore God and man." A singular application of the Holy Scriptures presents itself in a couple of *IOU*'s written by James Haig of Prettisides in Longwood, co. Wilts, on the back of the title to a New Testament of 1584. There is a curious, almost pathetic form of this habit of writing in books, practised from very early days down to our own, when we may easily remember how Lamb and Coleridge used to fill the blank leaves of a work of common interest, as it kept passing to and fro like a messenger, till the worth of the manuscript matter left that of the printed far behind indeed. In a mild kind of way this sort of thing was already going on in the sixteenth century. A copy of the English version of the *Paraphrase* of Erasmus on the New Testament, 1548, passes similarly between two Tudor-period intimates, and there is this: "Mr. Dunes, I woulde wish you to peruse V. chapter of Marke, and there you shall finde great comforte to your soules health. Thus fare you well in the Lorde. Wyllyam Byrde."

In the copy of Shakespeare's *Passionate Pilgrim*, 1599, bound up with an early edition of *Venus and Adonis*, a former owner represents with perfect justice, that although he gave three-halfpence for the two volumes in one, a corner of a leaf was defective; and there has been furthermore a profound arithmetical computation that if this gentleman and his heirs or assigns had invested the amount in good securities, the capital at this moment would have reached the vicinity of £1000. In a copy of Stow's *Survey*, 1633, which once belonged to Sir Thomas Davies, Lord Mayor of London in 1676, we encounter a memorandum on the fly-leaf: "I pray, put in the loose leaues Carefully. John Meriton. For Mr. Richardson, bookbinder in Scalding Alley." Richardson bound for Pepys. In an odd volume of *Sandford and Merton*, which fell in Dr. Burney's way, and which he gave to his daughter—Johnson's "little Burney"—he wrote:—

"See, see, my dear Fan,

  Here comes, spick and span,

  Little Sandford and Merton,

  Without stain or dirt on;

  'Tis volume the second,

  Than the first better reckoned;

  Pray read it with glee,

  And remember C. B.

      "April 18, 1786."

Beauty has been said to depend on Variety, and so we ought not to object to examples selected from widely different sources.

BOOK SALE AT SOTHEBY'S AUCTION ROOMS

From the original Water-colour Drawing by Thomas Rowlandson, in possession of Messrs Sotheby, Wilkinson & Hodge, London

Horace's *multa renascentur* comes into our mind when we stumble on a remark by Wodhull the collector in an *Acta Apostolorum* printed at Oxford in 1715: "In May, 1810, Mr. Leigh, auctioneer, told me that a copy of this edition had lately sold for £20, observing, 'these are the times to sell books, not to buy them.'" A more notable man, William Beckford, appears in a copy of the original French *Vathek*, 1787, as the second person of the drama by reason of the written matter referring to him, and being in the hand of M. Chavannes of Lausanne. The note occupies the whole of the available space on the title, and is as follows:—"A la demande de M. Beckford je me suis chargé de corriger son Manuscrit et de le faire imprimer à Lausanne. M. Beckford en quittant Lausanne se hata de le faire imprimer à Paris au Prejudice de l'Imprimeur de Lausanne, et je dus menacer M. Beckford de mettre dans les papiers son infidelité . . . et M. B. se hata de dedomager l'Imprimeur pour éviter la publicité."

So far as books with the autographs and MSS. notes of men of the modern school, such as Byron, Coleridge, Lamb, and Shelley, are concerned, the opportunities for securing specimens have certainly grown more numerous.

We have already in the places specified above furnished many illustrations of this section, and they might be readily extended.

In the foreign department there is a perfectly inexhaustible store of material under a variety of heads: evidences of ownership and descent, biographical suggestions, historical links and side-lights, dated armorial *ex libris*. In 1869 the author met with a thick 4to volume, including the Cologne edition of the *Legenda Sancti Albani Martyris*, printed about 1475, on the fly-leaf or cover of which was a list of contents made in 1475; and in the Hopetoun copy of the *Ethica* of Aristotle the original owner had established the place of printing, otherwise unspecified, by a MS. note, dated 1469, in which he stated that the book was presented to him by its typographer, "Johannes Mentelin Argentin."

In a copy of the works of Petrarch in Latin, folio, 1501, occurs on the title: "Liber Antonij kressen juris vtriusq. doctoris emptus venecijs ligatus nurenberge Mccccv;" and the noble old volume (now in the British Museum) is accompanied by a memoir of Kressen, printed about 1600, of uniform size, with a splendid portrait of the interesting Nüremberger.

A copy of the Vulgate of 1484 commands attention from the presence of a coeval MS. note pasted on the first leaf: "Hec Biblia est Petri Dominici Boninsegnis qui a fratre Cosmo empta fuit Anno MCCCCLXXXU. xviii. die Februarii." A Latin *Horæ* of the fifteenth century contains on a fly-leaf the ensuing little family story: "Ces Heures apartiennent a Damoyselle Michelle Du Derè Femme de M. Loys Dorleans Advocat en la Court du Parlement et lesquelles luy sont echeués par la succession de feu son père M. Jehan Duderè Conseiller du Roy & Auditeur en sa chambre des comptes 1577. Amour & Humilité sont les deux liens de nostre mariage." A St. Jerome's *Epistolæ*, printed at Mainz about 1470, is accompanied by the dated book-plate, 1595, of Christophorus Baro à Wolckhenstain.

In the French series the number of interesting items from a personal or historical point of view, if not both, is of course great, although, as a rule, French collectors have been rather sparing as annotators of their literary possessions. In a copy of De Bure's Sale Catalogue, 1786, now in the Huth Library, occurs a peculiarly striking exception, however, in the shape of a MS. note in the handwriting of Louis XVI., only three years prior to the fall of the Bastille, "Marquer les livres que je desire pour moi."

In the Duke of Sussex's Library was a New Testament in French presented by Josephine before her second marriage to Napoleon. She had inscribed on the spare leaf preceding title: "Au General Bonaparte ce Testament Lutherain est presenté de part la veuve Beauharnois," and below occurs in the illustrious recipient's hand, *Buonaparte*. An association fully as historically and personally significant appertains to the Voltaire's *Henriade*, 1770, in one of the volumes of which the to-be Empress writes: "Donné part Madame la Viscontesse de Beauharnois: pensez à elle, aimez-la, n'oubliez jamais qu'elle est vôtre amie la plus attachée." Was this an oblation at the same shrine? But this is a slight digression, warranted by the twofold circumstance that all these examples have belonged to English collectors, and are of a class quite as interesting to us as to those with whom they are more immediately associated by origin. The same may perhaps be said of the MS. sold in London in 1899, formerly belonging to two persons so widely different as Marie Antoinette and Robespierre, of the latter of whom it possessed the autograph. The interest seemed to centre in the signature of the Revolutionary leader.

The interest and respect with which the presence of handwriting in books is regarded are indefinitely varied. But the preponderance of worshippers is no doubt on the side of those who have shone in the *belles lettres* and in society. Sovereigns, unless it be Frederic the Great or Napoleon, Mary of Scotland or Marie Antoinette, generals, politicians, professional men, do not go for much. The competition is for the poet, the novelist, the newsmonger, or some *enfant terrible*, whose autograph is rare to excess. To be on thoroughly good posthumous terms with collectors, one has no need to have been respectable, sober, benevolent, or pious; these are rather in the nature of draw-backs; but one must have possessed a strong personality. That is the secret. Personality. Schedule the illustrious of the past on this guiding principle, and you cannot err. Men and women without infirmities, without vices, why, ask any dealer of repute and experience, and he will tell you that there is no call for their signatures or for their correspondence. They have too much character in one sense and too little in another. An autograph of Dick Turpin or Claud Du Val would be worth a dozen of Archdeacon Paley or even of Archbishop Tillotson.

The autograph collector certainly forms a separate *genus*. He does not buy books. He does not affect MSS. where they exceed the limits of a fly-leaf or title-page entry. We are accustomed to criticise Master John Bagford unkindly because he stripped the volumes of their titles and then cast them away. But he lived a long while ago, when the value and rarity of many of these things were not so generally understood, and there were not customers all over the Old and New Worlds as many as one can tell on one's fingers to take an early book, if it was offered to them. Even now it not seldom happens that an exceedingly interesting signature or note accompanies an item worth only so much per lb., and your connoisseur in the autograph surrenders all but his portion to its destiny. Who can gainsay him? He shrugs his shoulders; he is no bookworm; he wants autographs alone.

Exceptions to the governing principle arise, however, and sometimes they are recognised, sometimes not. The most beautiful examples for internal condition, binding, even intrinsic interest, are occasionally sacrificed to this

Procrustes—this case-hardened Bagford of our own day. Not so long since we remarked as a treasure beyond our purse a copy of Donne's *Sermons*, with a brilliant portrait of the author, and a long inscription by Izaak Walton presenting the volume to his aunt. It was in the pristine English calf binding, as clean as when it left Walton's hands *en route* for his kinswoman, and such a delightful signature. What has become of it? It is sad even to commit to paper the story—one among many. An American gentleman acquired it, tore the portrait and leaf of inscription out, and threw the rest away! Why, forsooth, should he keep a folio volume against his inclination? He left that to whomsoever it might chance to fall—a mangled corpse!

It is not peremptorily necessary, however, that there should be witness in black on white to the prior holder of a literary *bijou*; for the external evidence may prove abundantly adequate to the satisfaction of the most sceptical. A binding is quite capable of serving as a voucher and guarantee for the *provenance* of a printed book or manuscript, provided that all the links in the chain are sound. The Prayer-Book of Queen Henrietta Maria, the *Fables* of La Fontaine with the arms of Marie Antoinette as Dauphine, an unquestioned Grolier or Maioli, and still more such a bibliographical phœnix as that volume bound in gold of Lady Elizabeth Tyrrwhit's *Prayers*, formerly belonging to Queen Elizabeth, which the late Sir Wollaston Franks purchased at an incredible price and presented to the British Museum— these, and many more, speak for themselves. Yet where a royal or noble personage is not in the case, when it is only some Shakespeare or some Milton who is concerned, let us preferably have the written internal passport. We would barter all the books which we have indicated for the Florio's *Montaigne* with the poet's signature on the fly-leaf, albeit it is in no better a covering than its Shakespearian jacket of shabby old calf.

More than one volume in the earlier range depends very disproportionately for its interest on the preliminary matter in the form of a Preface or Dedication. In *Prefaces, Dedications, Epistles*, 1874, the writer drew attention to this point, and furnished a considerable series of such *prolegomena* in illustration of the fact. But there are cases, of course, where the inscription is of a piece with the book, as in Davenant's *Madagascar*, 1638, where the poet wrote and printed on the leaf following the title: "If these Poems live, may their Memories, by whom they were cherish'd, *End. Porter, H. Jarmyn*, live with them."

The Imprimatur, or License to the Printer, occasionally supplies a curious literary or biographical side-light. That to Davenant's play of the *Witts*, 1636, runs: "This Play, called the WITTS, as it was Acted without offence, may be Printed, not otherwise, 19 Ianuary, 1635. Henry Herbert;" and before Blount's *Jocular Tenures*, 1679, we find: "I well knowing the Learning and industry of the Author, do allow the Printing of this Book. Fra. North." Once more there is Sir Isaac Newton's *Principia*, 1687, with "Imprimatur. S. Pepys."

CHAPTER XII

Materials on which books are printed—Early popular works printed on vellum—The *edition de luxe* again—Binding of books—Earliest method and style—Printers who were also binders—Superiority of morocco to russia and calf—Influence of climate and atmosphere on bindings—Character of old English bindings—Charm of a Caxton or other precious volume in the original covers—A first folio Shakespeare in old calf—Our latter-day literature compared with the old—Splendour of the liveries of books in the libraries of France under the ancient régime—Disappointment at the interiors of well-bound volumes explained—The author plays a subordinate part—The Parisian book-binding Code—The difference between the French and ourselves—The original publisher's boards—The Frenchman's *maroquin rouge*—A suggestion to collectors—Bibliographical *simulacra*—Do not touch!—Sentiment finds a place in England in regard to the treatment of old books—Thoughts which a book may awaken.

IT may be necessary to introduce a few words about the material on which the Printed Book has at various times been brought before its readers, or at least its purchasers. The oldest European fabrics employed for books of this class (not MSS.) were paper and parchment, the latter very often prepared with very slight care, but the former of remarkable strength and durability. The cost must have been at first very onerous; but impressions of ancient volumes were usually limited. By degrees, fine vellum, alike conspicuous for its delicacy of quality and beauty of tone, was introduced, and became fashionable among the patrons of literature in Italy and elsewhere during the Renaissance. No such luxurious mode of presenting the type and giving full effect to the work of the illuminator, which so constantly formed a feature and a charm in the productions of the presses of the Continent of Europe in the fifteenth and sixteenth centuries has ever since been found possible. It is rather singular that not merely classical authors and other *editiones principes* received this sumptuous treatment, but even such books as grammars and theological treatises. A copy of the *Grammatica* of Alexander Gallus (or *De Villâ Dei*) was lately offered for sale by auction, and realised £23; it was printed on vellum of excellent character and colour about 1480.

A visit to the galleries where the show-cases are ranged at the British Museum in intelligible order, is by no means the worst method of arriving at an introductory or general acquaintance with this aspect of the matter. For there examples of printing on parchment or vellum in all countries from the earliest period are conveniently grouped together. The National Library is fairly rich in treasures of the present class, partly owing to the two facts, that it has inherited a good deal from the old royal collections and the Grenville one, and that it was already in the field when prices were more consistent with the financial resources of the institution. Among the productions on vellum here to be found are the Gutenberg, and Fust and Schoeffer, Bibles (1455-62); the Psalters of 1457 and 1459; the Cicero of 1465; the Livy of 1469; the *Book of St. Albans*, 1486; one of the two known Caxtons on vellum (the *Speculum Vitæ Christi*, bought of Mr. Maskell in 1864); the Sarum Missals of 1492 and 1497; the Great Bible of 1540; and the Works of Aquinas, in seventeen folio volumes, formerly belonging to Pope Pius V. and Philip III. of Spain. A curious episode is connected with the last item. In the time of Panizzi the copy was offered for sale, and the Museum commission (£300, we believe) was topped; but the book occurred again, and was acquired by Coventry Patmore, who presented it to the establishment, where he had for many years been an officer.

On the whole, there is no doubt that the English, and much more the Scotish, printers employed this costly and durable substance far more sparingly than those of the Continent. Of many no specimens whatever have descended to us; and the circumstances render it improbable that we shall hereafter add sensibly to our stores in this direction. In the case even of the Romish service-books, printed on paper, it is a matter of common knowledge among book-lovers that the *Canon Missæ*, which was subject to exceptional wear and tear, is usually on vellum.

In our own language, works which we are accustomed to view as essentially popular were occasionally struck off (in a few copies, no doubt) on parchment. There is the edition of *Helyas, Knight of the Swan*, printed by Wynkyn de Worde, 1512, of which only one copy remains, and the metrical version of the *Ship of Fools*, from the same press, 1509, of which an unique copy is in the National French library. Let us recollect, too, the Scotish Boece of 1536, the Great Bible of 1539, and the Tudor Prayer-Book of 1544.

Except paper, parchment (called in some old documents *parthemen*), and vellum, there are no substances which can be said to boast any degree of antiquity, so far as European literature is concerned. We have, as is sufficiently well known, many others of comparatively modern introduction, which tend to impart to the editions or specimens for which they are employed a special value and curiosity. Such are: (1) Whatman's hand-made paper; (2) Dutch paper (*papier de Hollande*), of which there are cheap and worthless imitations; (3) China paper; (4) India paper; (5) Japanese (so-called) vellum; (6) tinted paper; (7) writing paper; (8) motley paper or paper of different colours; (9) silk; (10) satin.

The *edition de luxe* has consumed in its time an enormous total of some of these descriptions of receptacle for literary products. The lovers of the Select in Books, who more commonly regard their possessions as *vertu* rather than as vehicles of instruction or amusement, not unnaturally prefer something which the ordinary purchaser cannot procure, or at any rate does not seek. The fancy appears to be, for the most part, worse than futile, unless it is that books with engravings sometimes gain by being taken off on one or another of these materials; although in practice illustrations are found to be just as apt to come out well on ordinary paper of good quality as on spurious vellum. It was not unusual in the last century, in Mexico and in South America, to print on silk even ordinary works; it may have been possibly found cheaper than paper. Satin is purely ceremonial.

Certain books occur of various dates, such as the *Livre de Quatre Couleurs*, printed on paper of various shades or colours, either for some passing reason or as a mere matter of fancy. A modern jest-book appeared not long since, harmoniously executed on motley paper in a motley binding—a humorous conceit!

It is sufficiently remarkable that neither the Printing nor the Book-binding industries ever erected themselves into societies or guilds, as did the representatives of so many trades far less important in the nature as well as the influence of their products. All the early typographers, at all events from the sixteenth century, were members of the Stationers' Company, and the investiture of books in liveries of different kinds became the function of an unprivileged and unchartered body, of which our knowledge is on that account even more limited and imperfect than it would otherwise have been. It is only through occasional and casual notices in correspondence or diaries that we hear of those who bound volumes for the older collectors, and we have to wait till we come down to the Harleian era, before we find artificers of this class in possession of a recognised calling and competent staff. Three employments, which have long been independent and distinct, those of the printer, stationer, and binder, were therefore at first and during a prolonged period in the same hands and under the same roof.

Anterior to the introduction of printed books, the literary product or record was either rolled up (*volutus*) or stitched, with or without a wrapper; and hence, when there were no volumes in the more modern acceptation in existence, there were rolls. We do not agree with the editor of Aubrey's *Letters*, &c., 1813, where, in a note to a letter from Thomas Baker to Hearne, he (the editor) remarks that the term *explicitus* was applied to the completion of the process of unfolding a roll: it always signified the termination of the labour of the scribe, and even in early printed books occurs in the form *explicit* to convey the same idea on the part of the printer.

The most ancient binders were the monks, who stitched together their own compositions or transcripts, or, when the volume was more substantial, encased it in oaken boards, which a subsequent hand often improved and preserved by a coat of leather. But laymen were occasionally their own binders, as we perceive in the note to Warton's Poetry,[3] where a "Life of Concubranus" in MS. is said to have been bound by William Edis, afterward a monk at Burton-on-Trent, while he was a student at Oxford in 1517.

At Durham and Winchester there were notable schools of art of the present class in the Middle Ages, and specimens occasionally occur, though rarely in good state. A very fine Winchester piece of work was sold in 1898 among William Morris's books (No. 580), and all over the country and abroad, even down to the present time, the inmates of religious institutions occupy themselves with the same industry on a less ambitious scale, and with infinitely less artistic and picturesque results.

When Barclay wrote his English paraphrase of Brandt's *Stulltifera Navis* about 1508, it almost seems as if the type of connoisseur, who understood the outside better than the interior of a book, was already in evidence, for the writer says:—

"Still am I busy bookes assembling,

  For to have plentie it is a pleasaunt thing

  In my concept, and to haue them ay in hand:

  But what they meane do I not vnderstand. . . .

  Lo in likewise of bookes I haue store,

  But fewe I reade, and fewer vnderstande,

  I folowe not their doctrine nor their lore,

  It is ynough to beare a booke in hande."

In Barclay's English *Ship of Fools*, 1509, it is stated that at that time damask, satin, and velvet were employed as luxurious materials for the covering of books, and it seems to have been usual to draw a curtain before the case in which they were preserved. Showy or gay bindings were approved, especially where the owner was not a reader, but, to quote the Latin text, was "Viridi contentus tegmine libri."

The formation of Book-binding into a distinct employment and organisation must have preceded any explicit evidence of the fact. The gradual increase in the output of literature of all kinds from the days of Elizabeth necessitated the surrender to an independent craft of the envelopment of volumes in various liveries, more especially when the French and Italians had set the fashion of elaborate ornamental patterns and rich gilding. Already in the time of Edward VI. the tariff chargeable for certain quasi-official publications, such as the Bible and Book of Common Prayer, was fixed by Government, and at a later date scales of prices for binding in different styles or materials were periodically printed. That of 1646 is reprinted entire in the *Antiquary* for 1886.

The most usual styles were plain brown sheep or calf without any lettering, a publisher's label inside the volume sometimes supplying the latter deficiency, and communicating to a shelf of books an aspect far from picturesque; but vellum or parchment of varying consistence was also a favourite and inexpensive mode of covering the contents of a library. Morocco and russia were later innovations, and the former is not unusually found altogether free from decoration or gilding and with a lettering, probably abbreviated and obscure, on the back. Very sumptuous examples alike of calf and turkey leather binding frequently present themselves, either executed for ordinary persons, or without any note of the original owner; many are more or less successful copies of Continental models, such as the Lyonnese calf, the Grolier and Maioli pattern; but in general our ancestors seem to have been satisfied with the paned sides and floriate back, unless heraldic accessories intervened to usurp the space occupied by the lateral ornament or (as in some of John Evelyn's or his sovereign's books) a gilt ornamental cypher formed the dorsal embellishment.

A visit to some old church or parish, or even cathedral, library nowadays may afford a notion of the external aspect of the early book-closet of the English student or amateur. The glass case is conspicuously absent; the shelf on which the volumes are ranged has to our eyes a ragged, slatternly look; and nothing can well be more opposite to modern taste. Yet the feeling for the printed matter between the two covers or behind the paper label was more genuine, may be, and more practical when a handful of volumes, reflecting the personal predilections or requirements of the owner, gradually accumulated, and the acquisition did not amount to a pursuit, much less to a passion and a competitive race.

The professional binding of books in our country, whether they had been actually produced here or had been purchased abroad, was at the outset almost exclusively executed by printers, who must have had a special department to carry out this branch of work. We hear of the site of Dean Colet's original school having been a bookbinder's, and of the teaching establishment occupying the upper part of the building. The usual style of binding appears to have been the covering of stamped leather, of which such a rich store of examples still survives, and which was copied from the German and Low-Country models. For weightier books oaken boards frequently served as a foundation, on which the leather was laid. Our sovereigns and nobility employed Pynson, Berthelet, Raynes, and other typographers to clothe the volumes which formed their libraries, before the more luxurious and splendid fashion was introduced of investing them in richly gilt calf bindings, with or without armorial cognisances, and these were again superseded by the adoption of the Continental taste for Levant morocco (*maroquin de Constantinople*).

Down to the time of the earlier Stuarts the binding department more than probably remained part of the printer's functions, and calf or sheep was the usual material employed. Thomas Vautrollier, however, the Elizabethan typographer, who carried on business in the Black Friars, and who adopted the *Anchora Spei* as a device on his title-pages, seems to have occasionally bound copies of his own publications in morocco with the same symbol on the covers in gold—perhaps to order; and Lyonnese calf was another style in favour at the same date. Some highly preserved specimens of the latter have descended to us.

Another of the earlier essays in England in the direction of morocco bindings appears to have had in view as a model the Grolieresque style of decoration. A copy of a Latin Bible printed at Venice in 1537, and presented in 1563 by the Earl of Arundel to Sir William Petre, bears the crest of the Fitzalans, a white horse, on sides enclosed in a painted design, the compartments filled in with a dotted pattern. But examples of the same or a similar class are by no means uncommon. A copy of a very common volume, Knolles's *History of the Turks*, 1638, was sold among the Morris books in 1898 at a high price on account of the very charming red morocco binding, richly gilt, with the unusual feature of side-panels filled in with dotted scrolls.

Early Continental collectors more usually than our own registered not only the place and date of purchase on the fly-leaf or title-page, but the circumstances attendant on the binding, as we find in the volume of tracts elsewhere mentioned, put into their existing covers in 1469, in the nearly coeval assemblage of tracts formed and bound by Udalric Ellenbog in 1476, and in the Latin *Petrarch* of 1501, bound for Antonius Kressen of Nürnberg in 1505, now in the British Museum.

The middle-period schools of collectors and binders, who displayed a preference for morocco over russia and calf, were assuredly wise in their generation. Much of the russia has perished, or is perishing fast, under a variety of deleterious agencies; and the more modern calf, at least, does not bear its years well. But morocco, at first more expensive, withstands infinitely better and longer the incidence of social life. What noble sets of books, as well as single volumes, have almost crumbled away in damp country-houses, sometimes relegated to the garret or the stable by the intelligent and highly-educated proprietors, while others have fallen a prey to gas and dust in town. These sources of injury and natural ruin no material can of course long resist; and, the foreigner often enjoying the advantage of a less impure atmosphere, and not usually aiming at a larger collection than may be necessary as chamber-furniture, his acquisitions are apt to come down to us in a more contemporary state, although we grant that, where certain postulates have been fulfilled, we have shown our capability of presenting to a distant age an assemblage of the ancient literature of our own and other countries as immaculate as when it changed hands over the counter in Tudor or in Stuart times.

Binding and Bibliography, no less than literature, are in opposite lobbies as regards the character of the objects which one sees submitted to periodical competition. The taste in books has undergone revolutionary changes; the volumes on which early owners lavished extravagant sums have too often become *per se* waste paper; and it consequently happens that a catalogue devoted to an account of such relics of the past has to register titles and names which play a subordinate part in the matter, and are, as it were, merely useful as a means of identification.

While a large number of splendid examples of binding in russia and morocco have been produced in Great Britain, there has scarcely been at any time a school of binding analogous to those which France, and even Italy, have known, each with its distinctive and recognisable characteristics; nor have we attained in the liveries of our books to the same splendour and beauty of decoration, or to an equal degree of historical or personal interest.

A large number of fine examples present themselves in our sale-rooms here, formerly ornaments of some of the noble collections formed in different parts of Germany; too often they show traces of neglect, yet occasionally they have preserved their pristine beauty and freshness almost unimpaired. They are, for the most part, of the very favourite class, where the oaken boards constitute a receptacle or foundation for an encasement of leather (frequently pigskin) stamped with some beautiful historiette on either side, and carrying the date and other particulars of origin and ownership. We meet with numerous specimens from time to time of the libraries of the Electors of Saxony and Bavaria in this picturesque and becoming raiment.

There should be by right, and with advantage, as distinct an intellectual spirit or element of thought in the binding as in the writing and printing of a book. A man who traces on the covers and back of a volume lines, curves, circles, crescents, scrolls, and other figures without harmony and without significance—in other words, without *mind* or *esprit*—is no true artist, but either an unskilful copyist or a rude beginner. Different schools naturally adopted new ideas of the beautiful or the elegant; some of our most ancient patterns were scriptural or mathematical; the age ruled the prevailing taste and fashion, and everything in and out of Nature has had its turn and its day. Then, again, nationality goes for something: the Frenchman is fond of his *lis* and the Scot of his thistle.

Artistic and historical book-covers have more than a special and technical importance, inasmuch as they contribute to enrich a pursuit which might otherwise become more limited in its interest than it is. For gay or splendid bindings assist in bringing the Book, manuscript or printed, within the category of antiquities or curiosities, where it awakens sentiments in the breasts of persons, neither literary nor bibliographical in their tastes, akin to those which they entertain for a specimen of old furniture or old porcelain; and so indeed we see entire libraries, which are little more than assemblages of triumphs of the binder's art and agreeable memorials of prior ownership. A once rather famous emporium in Piccadilly was known as the Temple of Leather and Literature, because the extrinsic was supposed to govern; and the same point is illustrated by the enormous difference in pecuniary value between copies of many old works in morocco and in more humble garb. Here Dress makes the book no less than in the song it is said to make the man. So it was with the three independent libraries of *Mesdames de France*, daughters of Louis XV. Each of these ladies had her favourite hue in morocco, with the royal arms on the sides; for Madame Adelaide it was red, for Madame Sophie, citron, and for Madame Victoire, green or olive. The ornamental details of early bindings, especially those of Continental origin, embrace nearly every section of natural history: beasts, birds, fishes, insects, flowers, and fruit, and endless varieties of geometrical lines and curves. A Spanish New Testament, printed at Venice in 1556, even presented on its sides what were described in the Ashburnham Catalogue as "richly gilt raindrops." Among flowers we most frequently meet with the rose, the daisy, the lily, and the tulip.

Many varieties of form in connection with the gift of books to friends or patrons formerly subsisted, apart from the autograph note inside the volume. We have adverted to the Grolier group of bindings and certain other allied types perhaps borrowed from Grolier, and the practice was followed, though on a very limited scale, in England, where the token in all cases was mainly confined to the title or fly-leaf, and consequently enters into a distinct category. A very unusual example of presentation occurs in a copy printed on vellum of Voerthusius' *Consecrationis Augustæ Liber Unus*, printed at Antwerp in 1563, where the centres of either side of the volume are occupied by an inscription in gold letters to the Archbishop-Elector of Cologne.

Of the Grolier examples which have descended to us—and possibly the greater part has done so—we possess two or three types as regards the mode of registering the proprietorship; the books occur with and without the autograph: "Jo. Grolierij Lugdunensis: et Amicorum," which generally occurs at the end, and with variant mottoes: "Portio mea Domine sit in Terra Viventium," "Spes mea Dominus et verbo ejus fidem habeo," and "Æque difficilior." He was a noble patron of learning, and on the title of a volume on Music, printed in 1518, dedicated to him, appear his arms and the motto, "Joannes Grolierius Musarum Cultor."

To the same school belongs the equally well-known Maioli, with the similar method of establishing his claim: "Tho. Maioli et Amicorum;" Cristoforo Beneo of Milan ("Questo libro e de Christophore Beneo de Milano e soi Amize"); Antonio Maldonado, of whom a volume of Petrarch has on the upper cover the name of the poet, and on the reverse, "D. Antonio Maldonado," with a shield enclosing five fleurs-de-lis; and Penelope Coleona, with flowering vases heightened in silver, and her initials at the foot of the book.

This is, of course, a most fascinating and covetable class of possession, and the difficulty of procuring genuine specimens of the Henry Deux and Diane de Poitiers bindings, and of all the other sumptuous and artistic productions of a like character belonging to the fifteenth and sixteenth centuries, has naturally suggested to certain ingenious persons the desirability of counterfeiting them. The Maioli bindings have long been subject to this treatment and abuse; but at present almost every other book which offers itself in a fine state of preservation is suspicious from a wholesale system of forgery, which has more or less recently been introduced with considerable success, and culminated in an entire sale at a leading auction-room of a library almost exclusively composed of such fabrications.

Of the genuine old English bindings, the usual materials are vellum or parchment and sheep or calf. All these may be, and in general are, ostentatiously plain; but they are, on the contrary, susceptible of being rendered in the highest degree ornamental. Nothing is more agreeable to the eye, and even the touch, than an old book in contemporary gilt calf, with arms on the sides, or in the original vellum wrapper, or, again, in the plebeian *mutton*.

The two former modes of treatment may, as we have said, be developed to any extent in the direction of tooling and gilding; the sheep has to be left unadorned—*simplex munditiis*.

What can we desire more characteristic and harmonious than a Caxton, uncut and in oaken boards, or even in a secondary vesture of vellum, like the Holford copy of the *Life of Godfrey of Bouillon?* Or than a volume of Elizabethan poetry or a first Walton's *Angler*, in the primitive sheep, as clean as a new penny, like the Huth examples of Turbervile, 1570, and Walton? The purest copy of the first folio Shakespeare we ever saw was Miss Napier's, in the original calf, but wanting the verses. It sold at the sale for £151, and subsequently for over £400. There exist such things as Laneham's *Letter from Kenilworth*, 1575, Spenser's *Faëry Queen*, 1590, Allot's *England's Parnassus*, 1600, and Davison's *Poetical Rhapsody*, 1611, in the pristine vellum wrappers; and one of the Bodleian copies of Brathwaite's most rare *Good Wife*, 1618, is just as it was received 280 years since from the stationer who issued it. Would any one wish to see these remains tricked out in the sprucest, or even the richest, modern habiliments?

Among ourselves in these islands we commonly prize and preserve (even in a leathern case) a highly preserved specimen of Tudor or Stuart binding; and there are instances where to exchange the old coat for a new one, however magnificent or (so to speak) appropriate, is not merely sacrilege, but absolute surrender of value. A copy of the first folio Shakespeare, of a Caxton, of Spenser's *Faëry Queen*, in unblemished primitive clothing, could not be re-attired without making the party convicted of the act liable to capital punishment without benefit of clergy.

Besides the methods and kinds of binding above mentioned, there are others of a metallic and a textile character. We find volumes clothed in bronze, silver, silver-gilt, gold, and embroidered silks, the last variety usually associated with the Nunnery of Little Gidding, without absolute certainty of correctness so far as the claim set up on behalf of that institution to be an exclusive source of such products goes. Mr. Brassington has furnished in his well-known work examples of all these more or less exceptional and luxurious liveries. In the most precious metal the most celebrated specimen is the *Book of Prayers* of Lady Elizabeth Tirrwhyt, 1574, formerly belonging to Queen Elizabeth, and ascribed to the Edinburgh goldsmith, George Heriot. Next in point of rarity to gold comes bronze; silver and silver-gilt are comparatively frequent; and the embroidered style is only uncommon where the execution and condition are unimpeachable, as in the case of a few in our public libraries. The most ordinary books found within embroidered covers are small editions of the Common Prayer and Psalms; and they are almost invariably in a dilapidated state. Gilding books was usually considered at a later epoch, at all events in France, part of the business of a binder, and so perhaps it may have been in the case of Dubuisson, who flourished about the middle of the last century at Paris; yet we observe on his ticket attached to an exquisitely gilt copy of an almanac for 1747, in red morocco of the period, simply "Doré par Dubuisson," as if that portion or branch of the work only had been his.

Some curious episodes have ere now occurred in connection with sets of books, or even works in two or three volumes, in historical bindings, or with a remarkable and interesting *provenance* of another kind. It was only at the sale of the last portion of the Ashburnham Library (1898), No. 3574, that the third and fourth parts of Tasso, *Rime e Prose*, 1589, bound together by Clovis Eve for Marie-Marguerite de Valois Saint-Remy, was acquired by a French firm through Mr. Quaritch, the purchaser having already secured at the Hamilton Palace sale the first and second portions, also in one volume, in the same binding, and the set still wants Parts v.-vi., so that it will demand a small fortune to effect a perfect reunion.

It is hazardous to discount the durability and permanence of our best modern bindings of English origin, and to answer our own question, whether hereafter they will be appreciated in the same way as those of the old masters here and abroad. Yet we think that we can offer a valid and persuasive reason why we shall fall short of former ages in this handicraft. The feudal conditions and atmosphere, which go far to win our regard or arrest our attention in the case of the older binders and their work, have vanished, and can never revive. It is with the book from this point of view as it is from that of the autograph inscription or signature; both are extensions of the owner's personality; and what a personality it was! Those who follow us at a distance may find reason to think and speak differently; but we can at the present moment scarcely realise the possibility of our latter-day literature acquiring a pedigree and an incrusted fragrance such as belong to works, however dull and worthless in themselves, from the libraries of Grolier, Maioli, De Thou, Peiresc, or Pompadour. There is a sort of sensation of awe in taking up these volumes, as if they had passed through some holy ordeal, as if they had been canonised. It is not the piece of dressed leather with its decorative adjuncts which casts its spell over us: it is the reputation of the courtly patron of learning and art; of the statesman and soldier who sought a diversion in the formation of a library from severer employments; of the prince who loved to gather round him such evidences of his taste, or to lay them at the feet of *a chère amie*; of the licentious but superb Lady Marquise, who vied with her king in the magnificence of her books, as she did with his consort in that of her toilette—it is this which exercises upon our imagination its ridiculous yet unalterable sway.

It is impossible to avoid the discovery, if we take for the first time a survey of a library chiefly conspicuous for the splendour of its bindings, how almost invariably we are disappointed by the contrast between the exterior and the contents. It would probably be far from easy to fill a small case with examples where a really valuable book was enshrined in a covering of corresponding character. It is our ordinary experience to meet with some obsolete nondescript classic, or some defunct theological treatise of alike infinitesimal worth, in a sumptuous morocco garb, bestowed on it by the author as a compliment to his sovereign, or by the sovereign as an oblation to his mistress. In those princely establishments for which such things were destined and reserved, it was necessary that all the constituent features should correspond in external grandeur, the costumes of the great folks themselves, the furniture, the decorations, the equipages, the dependents, the book-bindings.

The remarkable changes of taste in books cannot be more powerfully and decisively exemplified than by the thousands of volumes which have descended to us in all languages and many branches of literature in liveries once only a subsidiary feature in the eyes of the possessors or acquirers, and at present often the sole title to regard and the sole object of competition. The work has become mere printed paper; but it is perhaps not less covetable as a triumph of bibliopegistic art, than as a memorial of the distinguished or interesting personages through whose hands it has passed to our own. The book, alas! has degenerated into a vehicle for external accessories. We are asked to admire, not the quality of the text or the style of the writer, but the beauty of the type, the splendour of the ink, and the elegance of the initial letters, on the one hand; on the other, the excellence of the leather, the brilliance of the gilding, the ingenuity and skill of the design, and the curiosity of the *ex libris*. But this has to be kept well in mind. It is the binding which constitutes the supreme feature of importance and attraction. A second copy in shabby attire may plead in vain its merits of production; but it fares as ill as a person of the highest respectability who labours under the misfortune of being badly dressed.

There is no point of distinction on the part of our own countrymen more marked and enduring than the very qualified allegiance which they give to the Parisian book-binding code. It is true enough that in England we admire not merely the old French School, but the modern one; but our loyalty and liking are by no means unreserved. A Frenchman, in nine cases out of ten, will not, in the first place, buy any book that was born out of France, any more than he will buy an article of furniture or china, or a coin, emanating from a less favoured soil; nor will he willingly acquire even a volume of native origin in any state but the orthodox morocco; but his first impulse and act, if he does so under protest, is to strip and re-clothe the disreputable article, and have it put into habiliments worthy of the *cabinet choisi* of Monsieur.

Now, we have had, and no doubt have still, on this side of the Channel certain heathens in the likeness of collectors who, no matter how perfect and how fresh, and how suitable, the original jacket, commit the heinous offence of following the Continental mode, and in such a way thousands of lovely examples, transmitted to us as heirlooms from our ancient families, have been sacrificed. But let us congratulate ourselves that we have among us many who know better, who will not even let the binder desecrate a faultless copy of Tennyson, Byron, Shelley, or Keats in the publisher's boards.

This is, however, not exactly an analogy. The analogy arises and grows possible when we compare such writers as Montaigne, Molière, Corneille, or again, certain of the Elzevir series, with our corresponding foremost names. If we meet with the latter in vellum or in sheep, we only too gladly preserve them as we find them, provided that the outward garb is irreproachable. Of how many gems do we not know, in all the peerless glory of their pristine life, tenderly ensconced in morocco envelopes. Let them never be acquainted with another existence! Let no binder's unholy hand come near them! Let them be exhibited as historical monuments.

On the other hand, if we could oblige Monsieur to comply with this law, he would be _désolé_; for it is not the matter which makes the book; it is the _maroquin rouge_.

Even in England, where we are more robust in our taste, the true collector is not a reader. He may buy a cheap book now and then; but he hands it to the cook when he has perused it. Such things are outside his category; they are for those interesting creatures the toiling million. His possessions or _desiderata_ are not vehicles of instruction; they are far too valuable; they are objects of ocular and sensuous indulgence equally with china, paintings, sculpture, and coins. They are classable with bric-à-brac. You have an opportunity of appreciating the quality of the paper or vellum, the type, and the binding. The merits of the author are reserved.

It is better, if a gentleman leans a little to the practical side, and chooses to admit literature for actual reading, to have two cases, one for Books, the other for Bibliographical _Simulacra_. For it is not for one till he has graduated to lay his prentice fingers on a tome in the pristine _mutton_, or to endanger the maidenhood of a Clovis Eve, a Padeloup, or a Derome, which you must handle as if it were the choicest and daintiest proof medal or etching. Why, one has to bear in mind that he is not dealing with a mere ordinary source of intellectual gratification and improvement, but with a mechanical product perfect in all its parts. Let him come gloved, and his friend the owner will bless him.

Between a book bound in its original cloth or paper boards, and one in its rich vesture of morocco or russia, there is a contrast similar to that between a woodland and a park. In the one case, at a distance, perhaps, of fifty or even a hundred years from the period of publication, we hold in our hand a volume precisely in the state in which it passed from that of the contemporary salesman to the contemporary buyer; and not a stain nor a finger-mark save the mellowing touch of time is upon it anywhere. Let us look at the description in a sale catalogue of such a rarity as Lamb's _Poetry for Children_, 1807, "in the original grey boards, with red labels," or a copy of the first edition of Fielding's _Tom Jones_, absolutely uncut, and in the bookseller's pristine covers, or, better still, of the first part of the first edition of Spenser's *Faëry Queen*, 1590, in the Elizabethan wrapper! It is not the mere circumstance, let it be understood, of untrimmed edges which makes the charm; many a book or pamphlet occurs as innocent of the binder's knife as the lamb unborn, and highly desirable it is too; but to render an example of this class complete, its authentic outward integument in blameless preservation is as essential to its repute and its marketable worth as the presence of the claws is held to be in the original valuation of a fur of fox or beaver.

No educated eye can regard with indifference a more or less interesting volume clothed in a becoming livery by an accomplished artist either of other times or of these. If it is an ancient vesture, with the credentials in the form of a coat of arms, an *ex libris*, or a signature, or all of these, handed down with it to us, we appear to be able to disregard time, and feel ourselves brought within touch of the individual who owned it, of him who encased it in its lavishly gilt leathern coat, and of the circle to which it was long a familiar object, as it reposed unmolested in a corner of some *petite bibliothèque* or study during generations—if the subject of which it treated had to be handled, a vicarious copy in working raiment doing duty for it. For it is not a book in the ordinary acceptation of the word; it is a *souvenir* of the past, a message and a voice from remote times, ever growing remoter, or an *objet de luxe*, a piece of literary, or rather bibliographical, dandyism. In any case, its identity is to be preserved and held sacred.

FOOTNOTES

[3] Hazlitt's edition, 1871, iii. 193.

CHAPTER XIII

English and other national binders—Anonymous bindings—List of binders—The Scotish School—Mr. Quaritch out-bidden—The vellum copy of Boece's *Chronicles of Scotland*—Most familiar names in England—Embroidered bindings ascribed to the Nuns of Little Gidding—Provincial binders—Edwards of Halifax—Fashion of edge-painting—Amateur binding—Forwarding and finishing—A Baronet-binder—French liveries for English books—Bedford's French style—Incongruity of the Parisian *goût* with our literature—List of French binders—Ancient stamped leather bindings of Italy, Flanders, and Germany copied in France—Ludovicus Bloc of Bruges—Judocus de Lede—Rarity of early signed examples in France—André Boule (1508)—Enhancement of the estimation of old books in France by special bindings—The New Collector counselled and admonished—What he is to do, and where he is to go.

THE English School of Binding brings before us a roll of names borne by artists of successive periods and of varying merit, from the last quarter of the fifteenth century to the present time. That it is by no means exhaustive is due to the circumstance that in the case of many of the older, and some of the more recent, masters, there is no clue to the origin in the shape of an external inscription on the cover, as we find on foreign works, or in that of a ticket or a signature. As it so frequently happens with old pictures, the style of a binder was often, indeed generally, imitated by his pupils or successors, and we are apt to mistake the original productions for the copies, unless we engage in a very close study of minute details.

In the English, Scotish, and Irish series it is equally true that the preponderance of bindings are unidentified. The monastic liveries, in which so many venerable tomes have come down to us, were executed within the walls of the buildings which held the books, and had perhaps produced them; and analogously most of our early printers were binders of their own stocks, as well as of any other works brought to them. We may incidentally remind the reader that one practice on their part was to utilise waste as end-papers or pasteboard, and to that circumstance we are indebted for the recovery of numerous typographical fragments belonging to publications not otherwise known. That Pynson, Julian Notary, John Reynes, and others executed book-binding outside their own productions seems to be proved by the existence of much early literature of foreign origin with English end-papers and covers. In fact, till the Stationers' Company made the sale of books or printed matter a separate industry, the typographer was his own binder and vendor.

The bibliopegist, as an independent artificer whom we are able to identify, dates from the seventeenth century. We have already mentioned Francis Rea or Read of Worcester as flourishing in 1660. John Evelyn seems to have employed some one who executed good work in morocco, and in better taste than that done for royalty at the same period; yet we cannot be sure that he did not carry the books abroad for the purpose. Pepys had in his service a binder named Richardson, whom he mentions in the *Diary*, and who is otherwise known. A copy of Stow's *Survey*, 1633, passed through his hands; it is in the original calf; and he was merely engaged to repair it, as appears from a memorandum inside the cover.

Of authentic names of later English binders, considering the incalculable amount of work done, the number is extremely limited. If we tabulate, we find only:—

Samuel Mearne.	Charles Lewis the Younger.
∴ Bookbinder to Charles II.	Charles the Younger.
Elliot & Chapman.	J. Mackenzie.
∴ The Harleian binders.	C. Murton.
Robert Black.	Charles Smith.
∴ About 1760.	F. & T. Aitken.
Edwards of Halifax.	Wickwar.
Richard and Mrs. Wier.	J. Wright.
Roger Payne.	Hayday.
Roger Payne and R. Wier.	Hayday & Co.
Baumgarten.	J. Clarke.
Staggemeier.	Clarke & Bedford.
∴ The binder of the Psalter of 1459, formerly in the	Francis Bedford.
	Roger De Coverly.

Sykes collection, and bought by Quaritch at the Perkins sale for £4900.	Grieve.
	Henderson & Bissett.
	McLehose of Glasgow.
Charles Hering.	Holloway.
Benedict.	Robert Riviere.
H. Walther.	∴ The business is carried on by grandsons.
Fargher & Lindner.	Zaehnsdorf.
H. Faulkner.	Cobden Sanderson.
C. Kalthoeber.	R. Montague (1730-40).

This represents not only the entire assemblage and succession, so far as England is concerned, but covers Scotland and Ireland; and several of the names are obviously those of foreigners. The Scotish artists, if, as there is no absolute reason to doubt, a large number of early books were clothed on the spot, possessed much taste and originality, and some of them have descended to us in a pristine state of preservation with the lavish gilding as fresh and brilliant as when they left the workshop. We may fairly consider, looking at the intimate relationship between Scotland and France in former times, that a certain proportion of volumes of Scotish origin were bound abroad, just as Americans at present send over their books to England. Coming down to more recent days, the two names chiefly associated with Scotland are C. Murton and J. Mackenzie, neither of whom attained special celebrity.

But it is to be more than suspected that all important work in this direction was long executed out of Scotland—either in London or in Paris. The time came, however, when the Scots acquired a school and style of their own, and all that can be pleaded for it is, that it is manneristic and peculiar. Of recent years heavy prices have been paid for first-class examples, which are of unusual rarity. Messrs. Kerr & Richardson, of Glasgow, bought over Mr. Quaritch at the Laing sale in London at a preposterous figure (£295) a copy of one of Sir George Mackenzie's legal works simply for the covers; it was offered by the purchasers afterward to the underbidder, who quietly informed them that he had come to his senses again.

There is no reason why the magnificent copy on vellum of Boece's *Chronicles of Scotland* (1536), which occurred at the Hamilton sale in 1884, should not have received its clothing of oaken boards covered with gilt calf at home.

The most familiar names to English ears are perhaps those of Roger Payne, Charles Hering, C. Kalthoeber, Charles Lewis, Francis Bedford, Robert Riviere, and Zaehnsdorf. The genuine Roger Paynes in good state are very scarce and equally desirable. Hering excelled in russia and half-binding. Lewis bound with equal excellence in brown calf and Venetian morocco, and was largely employed by Heber. Bedford had two or three periods, of which the last was, on the whole, the best; he was famous for his brown calf, but made it too dark at first, instead of allowing it to deepen in colour with time. Riviere could do good work when he took pains; but he was unequal and uncertain.

Charles Lewis had been preceded by another person of his name, who is noticed in Nichols's *Anecdotes* (iii. 465) as dying in 1783, and as of Chelsea. This personage was held in high esteem by his clients, and was very intimate with Smollett the novelist, who is said to have had Lewis in his mind, when he drew the character of Strap in *Roderick Random*.

Fashions in binding, which occupy a distinct position, are the embroidered covers in gold, silver, and variegated threads, executed both abroad and in England, and of which many examples are ascribed to the Nuns of Little Gidding in Huntingdonshire; and velvet, silk, and metal bindings, which exist in sufficient abundance, and usually occur with marks of original ownership, lending to them a special value. Much depends in all these instances on the character of the work and the preservation of the copy; and each book has to be judged on its own merits. A considerable proportion of indifferent specimens are constantly in the market.

The Little Gidding bindings are made additionally interesting by the apparent connection between them and John Farrer of Little Gidding, who had a principal hand in producing a volume on Virginia entitled *Virgo Triumphans*, of which there were three issues, 1650-51, the last of which has the map by Goddard in two states, one bearing the inscription: *John Farrer, Esq., Collegit.* And the other: *Domina Virginia Farrer Collegit.* It is highly probable that the material for the book-covers worked by the Nunnery were obtained by the Farrers direct from Virginia. But it may be well questioned whether the holy ladies did more than the decorative and finishing stages.

The early provincial school of English binding is chiefly remarkable for the productions of Edwards of Halifax, who, with his two sons, James and Thomas, held a prominent rank in the book-trade at Halifax and in London in the last and present century, and whose name is also recognised as that of an enthusiastic amateur. It was at the sale of the private library of James Edwards in 1815 that the celebrated *Bedford Missal* occurred. The bindings of

Edwards present nothing very extraordinary; but many of them have painted edges or sides, sometimes executed with great care and skill. A copy of the *History of Halifax*, with a view of the place thus given on the leaves, is a favourable illustration of a practice which was formerly carried out on an extensive scale, and of course with very unequal results. A brisk demand arose a short time since for this branch of ingenuity; but it has probably ere now subsided, having been in response to a call for the artist by one or two collectors. Of course, the prices advanced instantaneously to high-water mark, from the certainty that the craze was ephemeral.

But the school of Edwards of Halifax probably borrowed the idea from earlier men, who had occasionally decorated the edges of books in this way, and we may instance Samuel Mearne, bookbinder to Charles II., by whom a copy of North's *Plutarch*, 1657, was clothed in a richly gilt morocco vesture, the leaves gilt and painted with flowers. Mearne also introduced what is known as the cottage-roof pattern.

There are two fashions in the costlier department of binding which have recommended themselves to adoption by some connoisseurs in this country, and to which we do not find it easy to reconcile our taste: the investiture of old English books in Parisian liveries and their treatment by our own binders in the French style. Both courses of proceeding strike us, we have to confess, as equally unsatisfactory. There is an absence of harmony and accord between the book and its cover, like dissonant notes in music. At the same time, Bedford was fairly successful in copying the French manner for foreign works, and his productions of this class are very numerous.

The practice of clothing English volumes in foreign liveries was occasionally followed in early times. Messrs. Pearson & Co. bought at Paris some years ago a lovely copy of Queen Elizabeth's Prayer-Book, 1590, in a richly gilt contemporary French, perhaps Lyonnese, calf binding. The work was executed for an Englishman resident abroad, more probably than for a local collector. But these instances are rare. One of a different character occurred to our notice in a copy of Whitney's *Choice of Emblems*, printed at Leyden in 1586, and still preserved in the old Dutch boards—old, but not coeval.

Of amateur binding all countries have had their examples to show, and here we do not intend the limitation of the artist to a particular pattern and material chosen by his employer, such as the Hollis plain red morocco, or the Duke of Roxburghe's half-morocco with marbled paper sides for his old plays, but the conduct of the whole process under the owner's roof, as in the case of Robert Southey, whose first wife attired many of her husband's books in cotton raiment, and led him to speak of them as his Cottonian library; or, nearer to us, in that of Sir Edward Sullivan, who devotes himself to the finishing stages of any volumes belonging to friends or otherwise, when the article has been "forwarded" in an ordinary workshop. Sir Edward tools, gilds, decorates, and letters, and subscribes or inscribes himself *E. S. Aurifex*. Specimens of his handicraft occur fairly often in the market; as to their merit, opinions differ. But after all, there is a *soupçon* of gratification in having a Baronet to your binder; and we understand that Sir Edward is complaisant enough to accept commissions outside his personal acquaintance.

A second essayist in the same way, who has become almost a member of the vocation, is Cobden Sanderson, who bound several books of ordinary character and moderate value for William Morris, and whose merit, if the prices realised for the lots in the auction be any sort of a criterion, must be extremely high. The present writer and many others carefully examined the volumes, and failed to see any justification for the enthusiasm awakened in at least two competitors.

Specimens occur also now and then in the market of the beautiful morocco bindings executed by another and (as some think) superior amateur, Mrs. Prideaux. A copy of Arnold's edition of Wordsworth's *Select Poems*, 1893, bound by this lady in Levant morocco, with elaborate gold tooling on back and sides—only one small octavo volume—is priced in a catalogue of 1898 at £12, 12s.

The Parisian differs from us islanders in these particulars *toto cælo*. There is an utter and hopeless incompatibility. His predilection is for morocco *in genere*; he estimates it not only above russia (*calf* is hardly in his dictionary), but above even the choicest vellum encasement to be procured or conceived; but on *maroquin rouge dentellé* or *aux petits fers* from some pre-revolutionary workshop he is hobbyhorsical to a pathetic extent.

The most celebrated French binders are carefully enumerated by the latest authorities in their chronological order, but there is a difficulty in respect to many of them analogous to that encountered by the inquirer on English ground, since the names of several even of the best period are unknown, and the productions are accordingly classable only under their styles or their early owners.

A good deal of the finest French work is attributed to the two Eves, whose *chefs d'œuvre* must, and can easily, be distinguished from the tolerably frequent imitations put into the market from time to time, some probably nearly coeval with the original examples. Prior to the Eves, however, France had more or less skilful artists in this line of industry. In the Frere sale at Sotheby's in 1896 occurred a copy of Philelphus *De Liberorum Educatione*, printed by Gilles Gourmont in 1508, in the original stamped leather covers, with the name of André Boule on the sides. Under Francis I. we find the names of Estienne Roffet, *dit le Faulcheur*, as "Relieur du Roy," and also with that of Pignolet. The initials *G. G.* occur on a volume of 1523 in Messrs. Pearson &

Co.'s catalogue, 1897-98, No. 679; they are probably those of Gilles Gourmont above mentioned. In 1528, according to his edition of *Meliadus de Leonnois*, Galliot du Pré was sworn binder to the University of Paris. In the imprint of his edition of *Lancelot du Lac*, Paris, 1533, Philippe le Noir describes himself as one of the two sworn binders of the same University; and we gather elsewhere that François Regnault was then the other.

When we reach the seventeenth century, greater facilities naturally arise for identification of artists. One of the earliest directly associated with his own labours was Le Gascon (1620-60), followed by the Boyets (1650-1725), Louis de Bois (1725-28), Augustin du Seuil, (1728-46), and Andreau (binder to the queen of Louis XV.). From the commencing years of the eighteenth century, in addition to the binders just enumerated, there is a fairly consecutive series, who worked for the court and the public: Padeloup, the two Deromes, Douceur (who was much employed by Madame de Pompadour), the two Bozérians, Le Monnier, Tessier, Dubuisson (famous for his gilding), Simier, Thompson of Paris, Capé, Duru, Chambolle, Lesne (who printed in 1827 a didactic poem on his craft), Trautz, Bauzonnet, Marius-Michel, and Lortic.

Agreeably to the experience in every other department of skilled labour connected with book-production, the French obeyed here the early influence of Italian and German taste, and the germ was Teutonic, as in Spain it was Moorish. The stamped leather bindings, mainly common to Germany, the Netherlands, Spain, &c., were largely copied in England for the royal and noble libraries of the Tudor era. In some of those executed abroad, the artificer, as we have seen, was accustomed to place his name or initials very conspicuously outside the cover. Ludovicus or Lodewijk Bloc, for instance, who flourished at Ghent or Bruges at the close of the fifteenth century, usually signs and claims his work in an elaborate inscription. Two specimens bear: *Ludovicus Bloc ob Amorem Christi librum hunc recté ligavi.* Jodocus de Lede adopted a similar method of commemoration.

In the case of foreign books, especially those of French origin, the presence of a pure and unblemished morocco binding by a recognised artist, coupled with the armorial cognisance or *ex libris* of some famous amateur and the binder's ticket, which is equally *de rigueur*, enhances the commercial importance of a volume or set of volumes beyond calculation, and has its only analogue in the stupendous figures paid for the Sèvres soft paste porcelain of the true epoch, when all the necessary conditions are happily united and fulfilled. Nothing is more striking than the immense disparity between a book in the right sort of garniture and in the wrong one, or, again, in the true covers with some ulterior sophistication in the shape of added arms, restored joints, renovated gilding, and a hundred other subtleties difficult to detect. The case is on all fours with a specimen of unimpeachable Sèvres contrasted with another of which the porcelain dates back beyond the painting and the gold. A French book in old morocco by Derome, Le Gascon, or some other esteemed artist, with its credentials and pedigree above suspicion, may fetch £50 or double; the identical production in old calf or in modern morocco or russia will not bring the price of the binding; all the magic is in the leather and the ticket. It is not a literary object, but an article of *vertu*. There is probably no description of Continental books which has so greatly risen in value during the last thirty years as the illustrated publications of the last century, provided always that they conform to the very exacting requirements of a Parisian exquisite. Above all, they must be of the statutory tallness and breadth, and in the livery by bibliographical injunction and usage prescribed.

No more impressive exemplification of the difference between a book or set of books in the French series, in the *right* and in the *wrong* state, could be afforded or desired than the edition of Molière, 1773, which in contemporary morocco may be worth £100, and in calf or any other ordinary dress a five-pound note. But after all, a still more signal case is that of Laborde's *Chansons mises en Musique*, published in the same year, which, even in thoroughly preserved contemporary calf, brings under the hammer in proof state nearly £200, while in modern morocco it is rather dear at a quarter of that amount.

The extreme rarity of pure and genuine specimens of the work of the earliest foreign binders—nay, of our own—has naturally produced a large inheritance of imitations of varied character and degree. There is nothing to save the amateur from deception but the same kind of training which qualifies collectors in other departments to distinguish what is true from what is false. A man who proposes to himself to make Bindings a speciality, cannot do better than graduate by studying the most trustworthy and contemporary guides on the subject in different literatures, and then we should send him on a tour round the great public and private libraries of Great Britain and the Continent. This, of course, applies only where the undertaker is in thorough earnest, and wishes to spare himself a good deal of expense and a good deal of mortification. Illustrated catalogues are of very indifferent value, especially those of auctioneers, which too often offer the result of sophistication so cleverly disguised that to an inexperienced eye the repair is not palpable. If one goes in search of *desiderata* to the trade, let it be to the dealer who knows his business and charges his price, but who supplies the article, and not to the empiric, who charges a price and does not supply it, for the excellent reason (among others) that this party does not know a fine binding when he sees it—or a spurious one.

In curiosities generally it is the safest plan for a private collector to place himself more or less in the hands of the highest firms in the particular line which he selects, provided that he is not one of a hundred thousand, and is a mile or two ahead even of professional experts. Then, wherever he goes and whatever he buys, he is always armed *cap-à-pie*. To him, to him solely, are the lots almost as precious as the purse of Fortunatus; he alone it is who may fall in with Caxtons, Clovis Eves, Rembrandts, Syracusan medallions, for a song, and carry them home without a qualm.

A curious case, unique in its way, of what may be characterised as perverted ingenuity, occurred at a public sale in November 1897 at Sotheby's rooms. It was, in the words of the catalogue, "A Remarkable Collection of Magnificent Modern Bindings, Formed by an Amateur;" but the salient feature was—in fact, the ruling one, with one exception—that the whole of the specimens represented imitations of ancient work and of historical copies of early books. The interiors were authentic; they had simply served as the medium for carrying out a rather whimsical, not to say foolish, project, and the hundred and ten lots, destitute of any conspicuous or genuine interest, probably yielded very much less than the cost of their counterfeit liveries.

The present volume is not a treatise on Binding, and we can merely indicate the general bearings of this branch and aspect of Book-Collecting, on which several useful, and some very sumptuous and beautiful, monographs have appeared of recent years. An amateur cannot do better, for purposes of reference, than secure a copy of Mr. Quaritch's *Catalogue of Bindings*, 1888, which includes particulars of all the principal works on the subject, English and foreign, and one of Zaehnsdorf's *Short History of Bookbinding*, 1895, with illustrations of processes, and a glossary of styles and terms used in the art. Mr. Wheatley and Mr. Brassington have also produced monographs upon it.

In America, during many years past, there has been a laudable effort to establish a national taste and feeling in this direction; for collectors in the States formerly made a general rule of sending their books either to London or to Paris for treatment. The institution of the Grolier Club of New York nearly twenty years since was a step in the direction of independence, and its *Transactions* form an interesting and creditable series. The Club printed a catalogue of its library of early typographical examples in 1895, with facsimiles of bindings.

The modern French school of literary architecture unites in the type, the paper, the illustrations such a remarkable degree of taste and feeling, combined with economy of production, that in England there is no present approach to what may be termed the *ensemble* of a volume placed in the market by our neighbours. This style of book-making asks of course age to mellow it, and perchance the materials employed may not bear the test of time and manipulation by successive owners, like the old eighteenth-century work. But as they emerge from the workshop, and stand upon the shelves or in the case, their aspect is decidedly agreeable, while half a roomful of them are to be had for the price of a Clovis Eve or even a first-rate Padeloup. Very much, on the contrary, we are apt to conceive a dislike for that unwieldy imperial *format* which some of the Parisian *libraires editeurs* affect, and which perhaps occupy the same place in French literature of the day as our detestable English *editions de luxe*.

CHAPTER XIV

Aids to the formation of a library: (i.) Personal observation; (ii.) Works of reference—Rarity of taste and judgment—Dependence of some booksellers on want of knowledge in their clients—Trade catalogues—Principal modern books of reference criticised—Those for the (i.) Bibliography; (ii.) for the Prices—Unsatisfactory execution of *Book Prices Current*, &c.—The British Museum Catalogue of Early English books—Obsolete authorities—Their unequal demerit—British Museum *General Catalogue* and Mr. Quaritch's *New General Catalogue*—The former not implicitly trustworthy—Source of the value of the latter—The labours of Sir Egerton Brydges, Joseph Haslewood, and others—Tribute to their worth—*Bibliotheca Anglo-Poetica*—The Heber Catalogue—Its magnitude and immense value and interest—Where Heber obtained his treasures—His library the most splendid ever formed in any country—Its absorption of all preceding collections—And the vital obligations of every succeeding collection to it—The Grenville Catalogue— George Daniel—His fly-leaf *canards*—Collier's *Bibliographical Catalogue*— Corser's *Collectanea*—Unequal value of the posthumous parts—The Huth Catalogue—Testimony to its character—Several monographs—Lord Crawford's Broadsides—Lists of the College libraries at Oxford and Cambridge—Catalogues of the Dyce and Forster Bequests to South Kensington—Halliwell-Phillipps's *Shakespeariana*—Blades's *Caxton*— Botfield's *Cathedral Libraries*—A new catalogue of the Althorp-Rylands books in preparation—Mr. Wheatley's scheme for cataloguing a library— Redundant cataloguing exemplified—Differences in copies of the same book and edition—French books of reference—Brunet, Cohen, Gay— Special treatises on Playing-cards, Angling, Tobacco: Bewick, Bartolozzi: Tokens, Coins and Medals, and Americana—Tracts relating to Popery—The Printing Clubs and Societies—Errors in books of reference liable to perpetuation—Heads of advice to collectors of books with supplements, extra leaves, &c.

THE two principal aids to the formation of a library, great or small, general or special, are Personal Observation and Works of Reference. The first is obviously an uncertain quantity, and may be restricted to an ordinary mechanical experience, or may comprise the finest commercial and literary instinct. We have had among us ere now amateurs who possessed the highest qualifications for assembling round them gratifying and valuable monuments of their taste and judgment, with the harmless satisfaction of feeling tolerably sure that the investment, if not a source of profit, would not form one of serious loss. This is a fair and legitimate demand and expectation; but such characters are far rarer than the books which they collect; and if it were otherwise, the large industry which lies in the purchase and re-sale of literary property could not exist. The buyer whose knowledge is in advance of that of the salesman is a party whom Mr. —— and Mr. —— and the remainder of the alphabet pharisaically admire, while they privily harbour toward him sadly unchristian feelings and views.

The second and remaining auxiliary, the Book of Reference, has become a wide term, since it has so enormously developed itself, and formed branches, so as to constitute a library within a library, and to call for its own bibliographer. So far as the current value and general character of literary works are concerned, all the older authorities are more or less untrustworthy, and the same is to be predicated of a heavy proportion of auctioneers' and booksellers' catalogues, where the first and sole object is to realise the maximum price for an article. The system pursued by the former class of vendors of late years renders it far more hazardous to bid on the faith of the printed descriptions, and there is, in fact, greater danger for the novice in the elaborate rehearsal of the title and the accompanying fillip in the shape of a note (usually erroneous) than the good old-fashioned plan of setting out the particulars briefly—even illiterately; for in the latter case the burden of discovering the exact truth is thrown on the customer or acquirer. We must say that few things are less satisfactory than trade-catalogues with certain honourable exceptions, which it might be invidious to particularise; and the book-buyer has to depend almost exclusively on his own discernment and the bibliographers. Of what he reads in the catalogues he may believe as much or as little as he likes.

Nothing could be more ungracious than to speak disrespectfully of the publications of those laborious and earnest workers who have preceded us, and who for that very sufficient reason did not know quite so much as we do. We admire their industry, on the contrary, their taste and their devotion; we buy their volumes because it is pleasant to have them at our side; and ever and anon we dip into this one or that, and meet with something which had escaped us. Seriously, however, they are, on the whole, not merely of slight use, but of a misleading tendency. For the gods of our forefathers, Ware, Tanner, Ames, Herbert, Oldys, Dibdin, Brydges, Watt, Park, Haslewood, the compilers of the *Bibliotheca Grenvillana, Bibliotheca Anglo-Poetica*, and *Biographia Dramatica*, and scores besides, before and even since, we have substituted others, assuredly more complete, perhaps constructed on truer and more lasting principles. We have on our shelves (i.) for the *Bibliography*, the Heber, Collier, Corser, and Huth catalogues (1834-80), and the writer's own *Collections* (1867-1903), *Bibliographica* and the *Transactions of the Bibliographical Society*: (ii.) for the *Prices, Book Prices Current* and *Book Sales*. Unfortunately the two latter undertakings are little better than mechanical transcripts from the auctioneers' extremely treacherous catalogues by outsiders. The peculiar class of information purporting to be supplied by such catalogues is often in need of some qualifying criticism or admonition, which it is not easy, if possible, for any one not on the spot and behind the scenes to offer. No mere reference to the catalogue after the event is capable of initiating one into these *arcana*; and the same has to be said of the quotations in the ordinary periodicals. This is a species of employment for which there must be either a long training or a unique instinct.

Book Prices Current and *Book Sales* cannot be trusted as an authority or a guide by any person who does not approach them with a certain measure of experience. Where an editor cites a common and comparatively worthless volume as selling for a high sum, and omits to mention that on the title there is a valuable autograph, the mischief is obvious; and this and allied forms of error are habitual. Such empirical attempts do more harm than good.

The Account printed by the Trustees of the Early English books in the British Museum is not without its value, although it is almost everything that it ought not to have been; and there are several monographs of importance dealing with special items in public or private collections. It is to be hoped that in course of time we may see a creditable catalogue of the Britwell Library, and that the Spencer books at Manchester will be done over again by a competent hand. If money is expended on these objects, it is distressing to find that the task has been confided to a gentleman whose best credentials are his personal acquaintance with the owner.

We do not add to existing authorities: (i.) for the printers, Ames, Herbert, and Dibdin, or (ii.) for general information Lowndes's *Manual* by Bohn and his coadjutors, because we are afraid that there is almost greater danger of being misled by them than being helped or enlightened. Both Ames and Herbert, however, we emphatically pronounce conscientious, and accurate in the highest degree in their respective days; but these days were long ago, and the present state of knowledge has rendered a considerable proportion of their texts obsolete and unreliable. Dibdin has certainly added to Herbert, but he has not, on the contrary, in all cases faithfully reprinted him; if his book had been as great an advance on his predecessor as Herbert's was on Ames, it would have been a treasure indeed. A new Lowndes is said to be in the hands of a syndicate. I know nothing about it; but I shall rejoice if it should prove worthy of the subject, and as unlike Lowndes or Lowndes by Bohn as possible. I labour, however, under the gravest apprehension that it will prove one of those undertakings which will just be advanced enough to block the right book without being relatively anything approaching even to an English Brunet. At least five-and-twenty annotated copies of Lowndes must exist. Will the promoters deem it necessary to acquire or to borrow them? Probably not. There must be thousands of additions and corrections in the writer's alone. It is estimated that the enlarged Lowndes contains about

10 per cent. of the literature which ought to find a place, not reckoning the earlier English books, tracts, or broadsides, and that of that proportion about 7½ per cent. are misdescribed. The anecdote of Pope and the wag who retorted to his habitual exclamation, "*God mend me!*" "It would take less to make a new one," appears to apply in the present case.

The original Lowndes in 1834 was a poor affair; but Bohn's recension twenty years or so later was by comparison a still poorer one, for there was the opportunity, in the presence of innumerable discoveries and a large body of new bibliographical material in various shapes, of rendering the new edition a really creditable performance. The name of the publisher, however, was a sufficient guarantee for this not being the case, and where the second impression is superior to the first, is where Bohn happened to have an interest in mentioning certain works, or information was communicated to him by others.

The sole comfort for us is, that Brunet has passed through five editions, and yet remains deplorably imperfect and inaccurate.

There are three prominent publications, each in its way of signal value and merit: the British Museum and Bodleian Catalogues of Printed Books, and Mr. Quaritch's New General Catalogue. The two former, of course confine themselves to the contents of the respective libraries; they are consequently far from exhaustive. They have been compiled by human beings; they are consequently far indeed from faultless. They express, as a rule, no opinions, and of commercial estimation very properly take no cognisance. But the Oxford collection has always been differently situated from the National Library in not having any adequate means of purchasing deficiencies, while it is rich in its own very interesting way by reason of bequests of unique value, making it the possessor of numerous priceless volumes not to be found in Great Russell Street or anywhere else. The Quaritch Catalogue (including the *Typographical Supplement*, 1897), a noble monument to the energy and courage of the *grand marchand* whose name it bears, is a good deal more than even a bookseller's advertising medium on a large or the largest scale. It is, in fact, a literary performance; and it is an open secret to whom we owe it. The collector, apart from the question of purchase, will find it replete with useful, instructive, and trustworthy information, so far as bibliography is concerned.

The highly honourable and equally laborious publications of Sir Egerton Brydges, Joseph Haslewood, Thomas Park, E. V. Utterson, and others, if they are of minor substantial value to us at present, demonstrate the keen appetite for bibliographical information and anecdote in the first quarter of this century. The *Censura Literaria*, extending to ten octavo volumes, passed through two editions, and, in common with other similar works, till recently commanded a heavy price. That they have fallen into neglect is due to the necessity, on the part of buyers and sellers of early literature, of studying only the latest authorities.

At the same time, from a literary point of view, the *Restituta* and *Censura Literaria* (2nd edit. 1815) of Brydges, and many members of the same group and period, will always be worth consulting, and will be found to yield a vast store of interesting and instructive matter.

Such works may at present be sterile enough, but yet we are bound to recollect on their behalf that on their first appearance they were revelations and pioneers. It is where a book at the outset is behind the knowledge of the day, or indeed rather not in advance of it, that it seems to be disentitled to respect.

Not only have more modern labours superseded the Brydges, Park, Haslewood, and other series, which till of late years held the market firmly enough, but the Rev. Dr. Dibdin, whose sumptuously printed and illustrated productions long remained such prime favourites at heavy prices, both at home and in the United States, has been overtaken by a general neglect, and the Americans, who were once so enthusiastic and generous as bidders for these books, will at present scarcely agree to acquire them at a fifth of their appreciation in the height of the Dibdinomania.

Many of the gems which have passed through the hands of successive owners are known to have once formed part of the *Bibliotheca Anglo-Poetica*, a famous—almost historical catalogue of old literature on sale in 1815 by Longmans, when that firm dealt in such commodities, and imported largely from the Continent in response to the keen and hungry demand on the part of the school created by the Roxburghe sale and the Roxburghe Club, Heber its greatest disciple and ornament, Heber a colossus in himself. Many are the traditional anecdotes of the wonderful bargains which Longmans' agent secured for his principals in all sorts of places, whither he resorted in quest of prey—of the romances in folio in the virgin stamped Spanish bindings, which they might have worn since they lay on the shelves of Don Quixote or the Licentiate, brought for sale, as it were haphazard, to some market-place in Seville or Valladolid in wine-skins. But the contents of the above-mentioned *Bibliotheca* were purely English. It was a small but choice assemblage of old poetry formed by Mr. Thomas Hill, otherwise Tommy Hill, otherwise Paul Pry, which he offered to Longmans on the plea of failing health, and for which the purchasers elected, looking prophetically at his moribund aspect, to grant him an annuity in preference to a round sum. Mr. Hill's apprehensions, however, were premature, as the transaction had the effect of restoring his spirits; and the booksellers scored rather indifferently. How pleased they must have been to see him coming for his pension year after year!

Even the outrageous prices asked for the articles, of which the condition was ordinarily poor, could not have brought Longmans anywhere near home; and the catalogue was expensively printed. Yet one would like, very much indeed like, to put down thirty golden sovereigns for *Shakespeare's Sonnets never before imprinted*, 1609, and fifty for Anthony Munday's *Banquet of Dainty Conceits*, 1588. The Rev. J. M. Rice obtained the latter in 1815; it was sold at his auction in 1834 for eighteen guineas, and when it next occurred among George Daniel's books in 1864, was bought by Mr. Huth against Sir William Tite for £225. The *Sonnets* of 1609 would at present be worth £250. As regards the bulk of the lots, however, one might almost read shillings for pounds. Sir Francis Freeling had an interleaved copy, in which he entered acquisitions. Through his official connection with the Post-Office he procured many prizes from the country districts. Dick of Bury St. Edmunds stood him in good stead. What Dibdin euphemistically christened the *Lincoln Nosegay* was a second pair of bellows applied about the same date to the reddening flame of bibliographical ardour. It was a descriptive list of certain books which the Doctor had prevailed on the Dean and Chapter of the Cathedral to sell to him for five hundred guineas, and which he divided between Mr. Heber and Lord Spencer. The collection was part of the benefaction of Dean Honeywood, and it was a shameful betrayal of trust. Our cathedral libraries still retain a host of treasures, notwithstanding all this sort of pillage; and the dim religious light which is shed around lends an air of sanctity to the spot sufficient, one might have thought, to arrest the hand of the marauder.

This was the height of the Bibliomania. Dibdin had in 1811 brought out his work so called. Perhaps it was hardly wise so to accentuate the passion on paper. He lived to publish the *Bibliophobia*.

The *Bibliotheca Heberiana*, in thirteen parts, 1834-36, which in its realisation showed a strong revulsion, or at least a marked decline, from the cometary period, 1812-25, is the most stupendous assemblage of literary treasures and curiosities ever brought together by an individual in this country. Heber was a scholar and a reader of his books; he has made memoranda on a large number of the fly-leaves; and these have been occasionally transferred to the catalogue, of which the Early English poetical portion, a singularly rich one, was edited and annotated by John Payne Collier. In using the Heber Catalogue, its mere extent and diversity ought to suffice as a warning that the prices are not in the least degree trustworthy; the classics and some of the early typography went pretty high; and the Early English books were only saved from being given away by the active competition of Mr W. H. Miller, who secured nearly everything of account at very moderate figures, and by the commissions held by Collier for the Duke of Devonshire, who bought the rarest of the old plays. The British Museum was scarcely in evidence there. It was enjoying one of its periodical slumbers.

The poetical section of the library embraced not only the lion's share of all the rarest books of the class offered for public sale in Heber's time, but an immense assortment of articles which he acquired privately from Thorpe, Rodd, and others, of whom he was the infallible resource whenever they fell in with books or tracts or broadsides which he did not possess, or of which he perhaps possessed *only one copy*.

It was not merely that Heber distanced all that went before him or have succeeded him, so far as the extent and variety of his collections go, but that with his insatiable acquisitiveness he combined so much of the bibliographer and *litterateur*. It was fairly easy for certain men with more limited means and views, such as Malone, Steevens, Douce, Brand, Chalmers, Bright, Bliss, Laing, Bandinel, Turner, Locker, Corser, and a legion more, to pose as judges of the merits of their possessions; but how comparatively little was theirs to grasp! In the case of Heber the range of knowledge was immense; and he was equally at home with all departments and all periods. He had his modern side and his interest in current affairs, and a scholarly insight into the vast literary and bibliographical accumulations which it was his bent and pride to form, beyond any one whom we can call to mind. We do not include in this sort of category the Harley, Roxburghe, Grenville, Spencer, Blandford, Ashburnham, and Huth libraries, whose owners were collectors pure and simple.

Of the Grenville Catalogue, as an independent work, it is less usual to think and speak, because the library which it describes has long formed part of the British Museum, and very few are now living who can remember it under the roof of its excellent founder in Hamilton Place. The books have now during some years constituted an integral part of the New General Museum Catalogue; there is scarcely any department of literature in which they did not contribute importantly to enrich and complete the national stores. But Mr. Grenville was particularly strong in early typography and Irish and English history.

The catalogue of Mr. George Daniel's singular and precious collection, disposed of in 1864, was an ordinary auctioneer's compilation; except that many of the owner's MSS. notes written on the fly-leaves were introduced by way of whetting the appetites of competitors; and to say that a vein of hyperbole pervaded these remarks is a mild expression; they emanated, we have to remember, from an accountant. The books, however, spoke for themselves. The printed account of them, viewed as a work of reference, must be read *cum grano salis—cum multis granis*. The sale was the starting-point of a new epoch and school in prices. Nothing of the kind on so extended a scale in that particular way had so far been seen before.

Collier's *Bibliographical Catalogue*, 1865, is an enlargement of his Bridgewater House Catalogue, 1837, without the illustrations. The two volumes are full of curious and readable matter, and as they usually deal with the *libri rarissimi*, we have to accept the accounts and extracts in the absence of the originals. To many this may be indifferent; to a few it may be a serious drawback, since, rightly or wrongly, the fidelity and accuracy of the editor have been more than once called in question. Mr Collier's book, however, is merely serviceable as a guide to the character of the works described; he does not offer an opinion on the selling values, nor does he always render the titles correctly. One signal fault distinguishes the undertaking from what may be regarded as a commercial point of view; and it is the refusal or failure to recognise the momentous changes in the bibliographical rank of a number of books through the discovery between 1837 and 1865 of additional copies. Like most of us when we are advanced in life, he thought more of what was true when he was young, than of what was so at the time of writing.

The *Collectanea Anglo-Poetica* of the Rev. Thomas Corser, in eleven parts, of which some were posthumous, constitutes a very proud monument to the memory of an accomplished clergyman of limited resources, who during the best part of his life devoted his thought and surplus money to the acquisition of one of the richest assemblages of Early English Poetry ever formed by any one, as he succeeded in obtaining many works in this extensive series not comprised even in the Heber Catalogue. Mr. Corser bought much privately; but he was largely indebted for his bibliographical good fortune to such sales as those of Jolley, Chalmers, Bright, and Wolfreston (1844-56). Of his catalogue as an authority and guide the value is unequal; the portions edited by himself are excellent and exhaustive, but it is not so with those which Mr. James Crossley superintended. A complete copy of the sale catalogue is a *desideratum* for the follower in this gentleman's footsteps; but he would have to spend more money than Mr. Corser did by some thousands.

Of the Huth Catalogue, 1880, we can only say that it is a splendid gathering in a comparatively short period of various classes of books obtained from the sales in London and elsewhere, and from private sources, and selected on account of condition and interest rather than with a view to completeness. In its character it is emphatically miscellaneous; but is very strong in Early English literature, owing to the opportunities which the founder enjoyed through the dispersion in his time of so many fine libraries of that class, especially those of Daniel and Corser, and perhaps we may add of George Smith the distiller. But there was scarcely any sale here or on the Continent from which Mr. Huth was not enabled to add to his stores. He was a very rich man; but he was not a book-hunter, and he was both inconsistent and capricious. He had, in fact, no definite plan, and took each purchase on its own merits. His Catalogue, which he did not live to see completed, is unusually free from errors, but not quite so much so as he anticipated and desired. Nevertheless, it will always be an useful guide and an honourable memorial.

Several monographs, dealing in a brief or cursory way with an entire library, or more fully with a section of it, may be noticed. The Ashburnham hand-list, 1864, now (1897-98) supplemented by the sale catalogue; the Chatsworth Catalogue, which does not include the books at Devonshire House, and Lord Crawford's catalogue of his Ballads and Broadsides. There are special accounts of several of the College Libraries at Oxford and Cambridge, as well as Hartshorne's *Book Rarities*, 1829, a disappointing yet suggestive volume. We ought to remind the reader that the catalogue of Trinity, Cambridge, embraces Capell's *Shakesperiana*, and that there are separate hand-lists of Malone's and Douce's books at the Bodleian, of the Dyce and Forster bequests at South Kensington, of the Society of Antiquaries' Broadsides, and of the Shakespearian treasures formerly at Hollingbury Copse. We have two editions of Blades's book on Caxton's press, Maitland's two Lambeth Catalogues, Botfield's *Cathedral Libraries*, and Edmond's Lists of the Aberdeen printers, 1886.

It is eminently likely that of the Rylands-Spencer library we shall have in the fulness of time a new catalogue, superseding Dibdin's publications, and of course embracing all the personal acquisitions of Mrs. Rylands, apart from the grand Althorp lot. In the capable hands of Mr. Duff it ought to turn out well.

In the *Book Lover's Library*, Mr. H. B. Wheatley has dedicated two or three volumes to the topic of forming and cataloguing a library. The object of these technical undertakings is clearer, perhaps, than their general utility; for, as a rule, a man likes to follow his own plan, and scarcely two normal collections of the average kind resemble one another, or are susceptible of similar treatment. The idea broached by Mr. Wheatley was, of course, not a new one. Gabriel Naude, librarian to Cardinal Mazarin, and subsequently keeper of the Royal Collection, printed a sketch of what in his opinion was necessary to constitute a library, and this our Evelyn put into an English dress in 1661, and dedicated to Lord Clarendon. The plan of Naude was naturally that of a Frenchman accustomed to extensive assemblages of literary monuments, and was not suited to the English taste, unless it might be in the case of a rich nobleman, to whom space and cost were alike indifferent. It was not likely to meet with adoption even by Evelyn himself, of whose acquisitions we know enough to judge that he followed his own personal sentiments rather than professional or technical advice. It rarely occurs that in the less ambitious types of library there are any bibliographical details likely to prove serviceable to the public; and the extent of knowledge gained by the owner in the course of his own experience should suffice to qualify him to become, where time is presumably not an object, his own cataloguer. For all that can be required is a hand-list on the scale of the Douce or Malone separate catalogues, where a title seldom occupies more than a single line. Plentiful illustrations of our meaning will be found by any one who opens the Grenville or Huth Catalogue, and perceives the wide discrepancy between the essential information and the descriptive and critical accounts. The primary motive in drawing up a view of the contents of ninety-nine libraries out of a hundred is the facilitation of reference, combined with an excusable personal pride; but a great deal of repetition and redundancy and useless expense are incurred by the literal transcript of the titles of books more or less familiar to all who are interested in them.

A very heavy proportion of the Early English entries in the Huth Catalogue are duplicates of those in the writer's *Collections*, and the same would be the case if the long-expected book on the Britwell heirlooms were to make its appearance. It would be, to a large extent, *bis cocta*.

In a private catalogue detailed explanation is required in the interest of bibliography, only where (i.) the owner happens to possess an unrecorded book; or (ii.) an unknown impression; or (iii.) a variant copy. Defects in important items should be particularised; in others the word *imperfect* is sufficient; and it is best to indicate from what source they have come to the immediate repository. Take a few instances:—

Reynard the Fox, 1st edit. The Inglis copy. Folio, W. Caxton, Westminster, 1481.

Hannay (Patrick), Poems. The Huth copy. 8vo, London, 1622.

Holinshed (Raphael), Chronicles, 2 vols. The Sunderland copy. Wants the plan of Edinburgh Castle. Folio, London, 1577.

Shakespeare (W.), Plays, 1st edit. The Napier copy, wanting the verses. Folio, London, 1623.

The notation of differences in copies of the same book, even if it is not one of supreme value, is always apt to be useful. Of literary comment the supply is discretionary, so long as it is new, pertinent, and interesting. The transfer to the catalogue of any inedited manuscript matter on the fly-leaves or margins, or of any proprietary marks, is eminently desirable.

For French literature, which is so largely collected in England, the *Manuel du Libraire*, &c., of Brunet, 7 vols. 8vo, 1860-78, with the works of Cohen and Gay, is the standard authority. The two latter, so far as they go, are more exhaustive than the *Manuel*, which is nearly as incomplete as our Lowndes, and not much more accurate. A new edition has been mooted; it is a clear *desideratum*. For value Brunet is scarcely more serviceable than its English analogue, and the book is, curiously enough, particularly unsafe in such a field as the French books of former times, where so much depends on factitious conditions barely intelligible to an ordinary English or American consulter.

Two books which perhaps equally appeal to the English and Continental collectors are those just mentioned: Cohen, *Guide de l'Amateur de Livres à Gravures du XVIII*th *siècle*, 5me ed. 8o, 1886-90, and Gay, *Bibliographie des Ouvrages relatifs à l'Amour, aux Femmes, au Mariage, et des Livres Facétieux*, 3me ed. 12o, 1871, 6 vols. Both, but especially the first, are essential for guidance in the choice of a class of publication of which the innumerable variations and the artificial prices necessitate the utmost caution on the part of an intending buyer.

There are, in fact, no topics to which an amateur or student can direct his notice or limit himself where he will not have been preceded, so to speak, by a path-finder; nor does the narrowness of the range always ensure brevity or compactness of treatment, since the Schreiber *Playing Cards of all Countries and Periods*, which to a certain extent enter into the literary category, occupy in the Account by Sir A. W. Franks three folio volumes; but a satisfactory view of the subject is to be gained from the works by Singer and Chatto, 1816-48. As a rule, editors of this class of publication are more modest and compressed. There are the bibliographies on Angling by J. R. Smith and Westwood; on Tobacco, by Bragge (1880); on Dialect books, by J. R. Smith (at present capable of great expansion); on Bewick, by Hugo; on Bartolozzi, by Tuer; on Tokens, by Williamson and by Atkins; on Coins and Medals, by a numerous body of gentlemen specified in a section of the writer's *Coin Collector*, 1896. In the English and American series are the well-known volumes by Henry Stevens and by Sabin, and the sumptuous catalogue of the early Laws and Statutes by Mr. Charlemagne Tower. In the Chetham Society's series, Mr. Jones, late Chetham's Librarian, printed an elaborate list of all the old English books and tracts relating to Popery.

There are many ways in which compilers of works of reference are in danger of perpetuating mistakes as to books, where they rely on secondary authorities. No account of an old book is, in the first place, entitled to credence unless it has been drawn up by the describer with the book itself before him; and when it is considered that not one individual in ten thousand can even then be trusted to copy what is under his eyes, and that there are, and always have been, those who have thought fit to exercise their ingenuity by falsifying dates and other particulars, there cannot be much room for surprise that our bibliographies, and those of every other people, are partly made up of material which never existed. Errors are heirlooms, of which it is hard to get rid.

The extent to which rare books are multiplied, as regards varieties of impression, by misdescriptions in catalogues, is remarkable and serious, and the bibliographer is not unfrequently confronted with statements of his ignorance of copies in sales of which he has not thought it worth while to indicate the true facts. But it is our individual experience that it is impossible to be too minute in pointing out snares for the unwary, and indeed for all who work at second-hand.

The Club or Society for the communication to members, and through them to the public generally, of literary and archæological material previously existing only in MS. or in unique printed copies, was at the outset very restricted in its zone and its scope; but, in spite of the circumscribed interest felt by general readers in the more abstruse or obscure provinces of research, the movement, at first confined to scholars and patrons of literature, at length became universal in its range and distribution. There is no country pretending to culture without several of these institutions. In Great Britain, France, Italy, the Netherlands, Germany, and Switzerland, they have long abounded. They have rendered accessible an enormous body of inedited or unknown material for history, archæology, and biography; and after all deductions for indiscretion and dilettantism, they may be pronounced the medium for having shed new and precious light on well-nigh all branches of human science. To the book-collector they appeal less in a possessory sense than as works of reference. Where they enter into his plan is in the practice, which some of them have followed, of striking off on vellum or other special substance half a dozen copies, which from their *presqu' uniquity* (this is as good a phrase as *rarissime*) have ere now bred unchristian sentiments among competitors for the *bijoux* in the *belles lettres*. The book-hunter's motto is *Pulchra quæ difficilia*; he reverses the common saying.

There is so far no exhaustive Guide to the Club literature, but the supplementary volume to Bohn's *Lowndes* contains a fairly complete view of it down to 1869. The additions since that date have been incessant and almost innumerable. The British Museum General Catalogue registers them all under the mediæval heading of *Academies*.

It is right and necessary that the inexperienced collector should be put on his guard against the reprehensible and dishonest practice of some professional vendors in advertising or offering for disposal books of which the leaves are not entirely genuine, which are deficient in supplemental matter recognised as part of the work, or whose bindings are sophisticated in a manner only capable of detection by a connoisseur or a specialist. There are wily persons who systematically and habitually insert in their catalogues items which they have acquired with the distinct proviso that they were defective, and have naturally acquired at a proportionate price. The forms of deception are infinitely various; but the leading points demanding attention and verification are apt to be:—

- The Frontispiece.
- The Portrait.
- The Half-title.
- The Errata.
- Supplement or Postscript.
- Starred pages.
- Extra sheets inserted.
- Plates.
- Extra Plates.

The intending purchaser must take care to satisfy himself that there are no facsimile or reprinted leaves, no catchword erased to cancel a deficiency, no mixture of editions, and no wrong or re-engraved portrait or frontispiece, or false date inserted or inconvenient one erased; and that the copy has not been unskilfully cleaned. It is *caveat emptor* indeed.

The most surprising pains are undertaken by certain persons to mislead the collector who is not very much indeed on his guard, and who yearns for the possession of some current prize. A case lately occurred in which the well-known copy of the scarce portrait of Milton, with the famous verses beneath it, attached to the first edition of the *Poems* in 1645, had been actually split and laid down on old paper to make it resemble the original print, and in the same way a plate belonging to Lovelace's *Lucasta*, 1649, representing Lucy Sacheverell, being frequently deficient, and making a good deal of the value of the book, has been ere this soaked off from the modern reproduction in Singer's *Select Poets*, and "lined" to communicate to it the aspect of a genuine impression mounted.

Other forms of deception and danger lie in the exact reproduction of ancient or early books, not always with any mischievous or fraudulent intention. Such a piece of *supercherie* as the *History of Prince Radamanthus*, professedly re-printed from a unique copy by Wynkyn de Worde, or the *Life and Death of Mother Shipton*, dated 1687, and actually issued in the latter half of the last century, are scarcely apt to impose on any but the most unobservant. It stands differently, however, with the *Declaratioun of the Kings maiesties intention and meaning toward the lait acts of parliament*, 1585, republished in 1646 in facsimile: with Marlowe's *Ovid*, originally printed in 1596, and repeatedly brought out without any change in the text down to 1630: with Sir John Hayward's *Life of*

Henry IV., 1599, similarly reproduced, and (in French literature) with the eighteenth-century edition of the works of Rabelais, purporting to have come from the Lyons press in 1558. These difficulties require on the part of buyers one of two things: an experienced eye or a trustworthy counsellor. The version of Ovid's *Elegies* by Marlowe in a re-issue of no value is constantly sold for the right one, suppressed by authority, although Dyce, in his edition of the poet, 1850, points out the differences. One has to study not merely the external characteristics of an old book, but the paper, water-mark, type. It is scarcely conceivable that the reprint by Pepys of the *Order of the Hospital of St. Bartholomew*, 1557, could be mistaken for the genuine impression; the paper and type alike betray it.

A curious and long-lived misapprehension prevails respecting certain works from the press of Thomas Berthelet, at the foot of the title-pages of which we find the date 1534; but the latter forms part of the woodcut in which the letterpress is enclosed, and was retained in publications posterior to the year named, and the same is, to a slighter extent, the case with Robinson's *Reward of Wickedness*, where the figures 1573 occur at the end within an engraved border employed for other purposes, the particular production by one of the guards set over Mary, Queen of Scots, having probably appeared some years after.

CHAPTER XV

Fluctuations in the value of books—The prices of books comparative—Low prices adverse to the sale of books in certain cases—Great difficulty in arriving at the market-price of very rare volumes—Influence of the atmosphere—Reflections on the utility and prudence of collecting—The collector, as a rule, pays for his amusement—The classes which chiefly buy the dearer books—Bookselling a speculation—The question of investment—Runs on particular kinds of books or particular subjects—Quotations of prices realised to be read between the lines—Careful consideration of certain problems essential to security of buyers—The bookseller's point of view—Books which are wanted, and why—Capital publications and universally known authors—Tendency to estimate earlier and middle period literature by its literary or artistic qualities—Collectors in the future—Interest in prices current—Some notable figures—The most precious books of all countries—Two imperfect copies of Chaucer's *Canterbury Tales* bring £2900—Henry VIII.'s own copy on vellum of a volume of Prayers, 1544, with MSS. notes by him and his family—Lady Elizabeth Tirrwhyt's *Prayers*, 1574, bound in gold—*Book of St. Alban's*, 1486, and *Chronicles of England*, printed at St. Alban's—The *Lincoln Nosegay*—American buyers and their agents—Composition of an average auction-room—An early example of a book-lottery.

THE fluctuations and revolutions in the mercantile value of old English books present phenomena to our consideration of an instructive and occasionally of a tantalising character. No one has the power to foresee what future changes time may bring forth. It is the fashion with the vendor to force a purchase on his client, because, says he, this book cannot recur for sale, or this class of books is rising; but that is a *façon de parler*, nothing more. We are apt to sigh over the times when unique Caxtons could be had—ay, in our grandsires' time—for less than £20. In the sixteenth century twenty pence paid for them. But let us recollect that our estimation of an article depends on its cost so largely. What we acquire cheaply we hold cheaply. Should we have heard of many of our great modern collectors had old quotations survived? We have known personally one or two who would not dream of taking a volume at a low price; you had, as it were, to adjust it to their meridian. They failed to perceive how anything could be worth having if it was to be secured for a song. A hundred-dollar author might be barely admissible; a dollar man would be a disgrace to the collection.

As regards the strange vicissitudes of the tariff for second-hand books prices, there is an illustrative note from Robert Scott, the celebrated dealer, to Pepys, dated June 30, 1688, where he offers his customer four books for 34s., namely:—

Campion and Others' "History of Ireland"   12   0

Harding's "Chronicle"   6   0

Sir John Pryce's "Defensio Hist. Brit."   8   0

Barclay's "Ship of Fools" [1570]   8   0

The value set on the second and fourth items would now, if they were poor copies, be vastly in excess of the figures named by Scott; but for the other two a bookseller of the present day might not expect much more than Pepys was asked more than two hundred years ago.

The anecdotes of bargains picked up from day to day at the present time are plentiful, and (except for the fortunate finder) exasperating enough. But if we go back to a period when there were no auctions, no organised book depôts, no newspapers, no railways and other such facilities, and men lived practically in separate communities, there can be no feeling of astonishment that our own early literature, like that of all other countries, has descended to us in an almost inconceivably shrunk volume. Books, and more especially pamphlets and broadsheets, were acquired, and, after perusal, flung away. There were not only no booksellers, in our sense, but down to the seventeenth century no systematic book-buyers. The library, as we understand the term and the thing, is a comparatively modern institution. Even the products of the Caxton press, very early in the next century, had sunk in commercial value to almost nothing; they were procurable for pence, nor did they acquire any appreciation till the reign of George III. and the rise of a new school of collectors, amongst whom we have to reckon the King himself.

It is not unusual to hear cases of cheap books having been acquired by the normal buyer in the open market. A friend tells you that he has bought such or such a volume of a dealer—perhaps a specialist in that line—a positive bargain; he was not very keen on purchases just at the moment, but he could not resist this. It may be so; but it is exceedingly problematical. If we were to inquire into the facts, one might, nay, one would almost certainly, find that the specialist had secured the item over all competitors at a recent auction, and had added his own profit. If he had not been present, the item would not have brought half. He was deemed rash by his *confrères* for giving so much. Of course there were two in it; but the under-bidder was, maybe, a second private enthusiast, who had gone to the full extent of his ideas or resources. Where, then, is the bargain?

The more or less artificial quotations at first-class auctions partly arise, no doubt, from the preference of certain private buyers for dispensing with the middle-man in the person of the bookseller. They do not object to employ him as an agent, and often enable him to secure their *desiderata* against all comers; but they somehow distrust him as an independent valuer of what he may offer over the counter; and this is, we fear, usually attributable to their diffidence of their own judgment and experience. There is a prevailing idea— it may be a prejudice—that in the salerooms an article fetches its worth and no more, and that you save the relative profit. You may or you may not. In the majority of cases, where the actual purchaser has no practical knowledge, and his resources are ample, the saleroom is a dearer market than the shop, if the property offered is that of an eminent person and is of high character; and even in obscurer sales bargains of any moment are only to those who are experts and are on the spot.

The prices or market values of the older and rarer books form a debateable ground, on which those interested will probably never arrive at anything approaching unanimity; and the reason or part of the reason seems to be that the actual realised figure depends on so many considerations, of which the mere character of the article put up for sale is not invariably the most influential. There is no species of weather-glass more sensitive than the bibliographical one; it responds to the slightest change in the commercial temperature, and must be carefully watched and studied by all who either seek to sell at a profit or to buy without the risk of serious loss on eventual realisation. Two books belonging to the same edition, bound in the same style by the same person, are they not one as good as the other? By no means necessarily so. Setting aside the extrinsic features which confer arbitrary value on literary property, one of the copies may have the start of the other, if it is something then in active or general demand; one may occur when the trade has a glut of stock, or has exhausted its credit at the auctioneer's; one may belong to a "genuine" collection, while the other may labour under the suspicion of being "rigged." Place them side by side; there does not appear to be sixpence between them, yet under the hammer one lot may fetch twice as much as the other.

This, it may be fairly argued, tells against the wisdom and security of laying out money by collectors of moderate resources on such doubtful investments; but look in whatever direction you please, and you will encounter similar phenomena. The buyer of coins, china, pictures, or any other curiosities, meets with an identical experience. Immense sums are lost in these recreations by one class to provide livelihoods, and very handsome livelihoods, too, for thousands and tens of thousands year by year. Sometimes the amount is not serious to the individual, or he can afford it; occasionally it is otherwise.

Prices fluctuate, and their fluctuation is apt to be deceptive. It is not merely the article which has to be considered, but the atmosphere in which it was sold. No one can be sure that he has secured a bargain till he sells it. At the Beckford sale the Thuanus copy of Buchanan's *Poemata*, 1579, fetched £54; a year or two later it was offered at £18, and in 1897 it occurs in a catalogue at £42. A rare theatrical item in the Mackenzie sale produced £62, 10s. In another in 1897 a second copy formed part of a bundle which brought 14s. At the Laing sale Beza's *Confession of Christian Faith*, in Italian, 1560, said to have been the property of Mary Queen of Scots, was carried to £149. After being kept by the purchaser many years, it realised during the current year £52. The *éclat* which accompanied these books on their original realisation was absent, or was no more than a tradition. Some judged the Queen of Scots volume very dear even at the lower quotation. We saw it knocked down, and such was our own judgment.

These samples we adduce for the advantage of ordinary purchasers of literary property, whose estimation principally depends on its *provenance*. There is an inherent proneness to shrinkage of interest and value in the hands of any one who is not equally celebrated, or is not going to become so.

Even an approximately accurate appreciation in a commercial sense of books of various classes can only be reached by one who is behind the scenes, who can feel the pulse of the market, and who follows the incessant changes in its temperature and feeling. It is absurd for a simple amateur, who passes his time in a study or an office, to attempt or presume to instruct us on this subject. He knows what he has given for his own library, and what some of his friends have given for theirs, and he reads the accounts in the papers of periodical sales. But it is a widely different affair, when one sets about the task, intrusted to this or that individual by a friendly publisher or editor-general, in a scientific manner; and it is only under such circumstances that one realises, or can render intelligible to others, what prices actually mean and are, how much they depend on perpetually modifying and varying influences, and how little the quotations found in works of reference are to be trusted. The turns of the book-market are as sudden and strange, as delicate and mysterious, as those of a Bourse; and the steadfast and keen onlooker alone can keep pace with them—not he always; the wire-pullers are so many.

How, then, shall collectors of books, for example, protect themselves? They cannot. It is their diversion, their by-play; their time and thought are engaged elsewhere in business, where it is their turn to reap the fruit of special study and experience, and they hand over a percentage of this to the caterer for their pleasure. The whole world is, in other words, perpetually intent on gathering and distributing; we are, every one of us, buyers and sellers, not of necessaries only, but of luxuries and amusements.

Coming to the more immediate point, men nowadays, in the presence of a severe and almost homicidal competition for subsistence, have to devote their whole attention to their chosen employment, and have the most limited opportunities of ascertaining or verifying values as submitted to them by experts in the book-market; they have Lowndes, which is almost worthless, and *Book Prices Current*, which is, of course, more contemporary, but must be read between the lines; and the extreme difficulty of judging what is worth having, and how much should be given for it, has led to that frequent habit of collectors favouring a particular dealer, or, as an alternative, pursuing a policy highly unpleasant to dealers by acquiring direct from the salerooms. Fortunately for booksellers the latter plan does not suit busy men, and it is just that class, especially the merchant and the stockbroker, the solicitor and accountant, who are their best clients.

The trade has its sorrows and trials; but it cannot be a very bad one when we see how many live out of it, if they do not often make fortunes. The fact is, that the motives for buying books are almost as infinitely multifarious as the books themselves, and there exists not the volume for which the customer will not arise, if the holder can wait; and this customary incidence accounts for the familiar aphorism that booksellers accumulate stock, not money—an aphorism to which the exceedingly rare exceptions prove the rule.

Putting it differently, bookselling outside the current literature is a form of speculation which varies according to the class of investment which the stockholder selects; and it is quite necessary to bear in mind the nature and tendency of the business in order to more clearly appreciate the uncertainty of prices, and how utterly impossible it must ever be for any ordinary book-buyer to rely on his purchases as a representation of value. If he does not view the matter in that light, or chooses to let the instruction or pleasure derived from his acquisitions become a set-off against the outlay, it is very well; what he or his heirs get for the property is in that case all profit.

We dwell a little on this aspect of the matter, because we are quite aware that in purchasing books many persons look at the ulterior question, and even demand of the vendor how much the article is likely to bring when or if re-sold. Such a contingency usually limits itself to cases where a volume is secured for a special and temporary object, or where funds are restricted and the fancy is purely personal.

Apart from these considerations, there are other influences always at work to render the book-market uncertain and insecure. Collectors who have no fixed plan or aim are apt to follow the precedent set by such as have, or are supposed to have, one, and this obviously tends to create a run on particular subjects or authors, till the call is satisfied, or the *coterie* grows sensible of the inexpediency of proceeding any further. A revolt from a fad naturally gluts the market with the discarded copies, and the latest vendors have to bear the brunt. Such is not an occasional incidence, but one continually in progress among a certain *quota*, and a large *quota*, too, of the book-buying public, who let others judge for them, instead of judging for themselves.

It cannot be treated as otherwise than an ordinary and reasonable *sequitur* that prices which are purely artificial are also arbitrary and precarious. The quotations which are to be found in such a publication as *Book Prices Current* are at best a bare record of facts; but with such a record at his elbow no man who does not possess a fair amount of knowledge and judgment would be safe in his figures. It would be little better than plunging. Still less is it of any use to rely on the reports in the press, which are frequently inaccurate, and in nine cases out of ten are the work of inexperienced persons.

The careful and discerning observer of these problems (for such they indeed are) discovers that the high prices for books, which the trade is never tired of citing as an encouragement to its connections, are almost invariably associated with conditions which are adventitious or accidental, and which scarcely ever comprise benefit to a living individual. A man must be truly exceptional, phenomenally above suspicion, bedridden with an incurable complaint, to disarm the scepticism of the wary buyer under the hammer; it is the property of the departed which is preferred; for the result cannot help him, and he is not at hand to reserve lots. So recently as 1896, there was an exception to the prevailing rule; but it was one rather in appearance than in reality. We allude to the FRERE sale at Sotheby's. Now, we repeat that this was merely an ostensible departure from ordinary experience; and what we mean is that the most valuable portion of the library was that which once belonged to another and antecedent person, Sir John Fenn, and that these items had been long known to exist, and were *desiderata* for which public and private collections had hitherto thirsted in vain. No wonder, then, that there was a dead set at them, the living owner *maulgre*.

The booksellers are apt to complain nowadays of their inability to move or place items with which they cannot give a certificate of character. It will not always suffice to allege that they have realised a great deal of money heretofore, as vouched by Lowndes; they must carry with them some definite recommendation; they must exhibit remarkable allusions; they may be written by an ancestor or namesake of the buyer in view; at all events, if they are not by a good author, they must be on a good subject. Their interest must be (1) personal; (2) local; or (3) topical. There is a drift on the part of collectors of the purer type toward accredited and certified securities— toward recognised writers. Established character goes for more than mere rarity. The trade can always place fine copies of authors who have made their personality standard: Chaucer, Spenser, Shakespeare, Sydney, Jonson, Milton, Butler, Swift, Thomson, Goldsmith, Miss Burney, Dr. Johnson,

Wordsworth, Coleridge, Sir Walter Scott, Charles Lamb, Shelley, Keats, Thackeray, George Eliot. If to the more fastidious or self-diffident amateur an excessively rare item is introduced without credentials, it is in danger of being rejected; the same principle applies to certain foreign writers, such as Cervantes, Montaigne, Molière, Corneille, La Fontaine. But in almost all these cases the demand is not for collected or library editions, or even for first copies of everything coming from the pens of those writers. Chaucer has to be served up in the types of Caxton or De Worde or Pynson; Spenser is only sought in quarto and octavo; Shakespeare means the four folios and certain quartos, and the Poems in octavo; the leading aim in Sydney is the *Arcadia* of 1590; Jonson is just admissible in folio (the right one), but is preferred in quarto; by Milton we mean the *Comus, Lycidas, Poems, Paradise Lost* and *Paradise Regained* in the original issues. Butler is only represented by his *Hudibras*; Swift by his *Gulliver*; Defoe by his *Crusoe* (some must have all three volumes, although the first is worth nearly all the money); Thomson by the *Seasons*; Goldsmith by the *Vicar of Wakefield*; Miss Burney by one or two of her Novels in boards; Dr. Johnson by his *Rasselas*; Scott by the *Waverley* series with uncut edges, and so forth.

The actual current appreciation of old books seems to be, to a large and increasing extent, in the ratio of their literary or artistic attraction; and under the second head we comprise typography and wood-engraving; and we think that we could establish that, as a rule, the highest bids in modern days are for something of which the reputation or importance, or both, are a matter of tacit acknowledgment and acceptance. A merely *curious* volume may fetch money; but it must be something beyond that to make the pulse beat more quickly and form a record.

Two considerations govern and recommend such a course—those of commercial expediency and of space. There is not much probability that in the time to come book-buyers will arise to renew the traditions of the Harleian and Heber libraries, or even of such vast heterogeneous assemblages of literary monuments as those formed by Sir Thomas Phillipps, James Crossley, Joseph Tasker, Gibson-Craig, and a few others. The feeling is more in favour of the French view—small and choice; and there is no doubt that, as a rule, the sale of a collection should not occupy more than three days. Beyond that time the interest flags and prices are apt to recede.

At the same time there has always been, and will be, a powerful curiosity in the direction of knowing or hearing what certain rare or superlatively important books occasionally bring. The feeling is rather more general than might be imagined, for it extends to those who are not collectors, yet like to see how foolish other people are, or, again, store up the information, in case they should have the good fortune to meet with similar things in their travels. When one thinks of the extraordinary casualties which have brought to light undescribed works or editions, and continue to do so year by year, there is no reason to despair of completing ourselves in due course in many and many a direction. The tendency in prices of late has certainly been favourable to books which are at once rare and admittedly important; and we have said that the latter feature and quality appear to be weightier than mere unfrequency of occurrence. For instance, any given number of copies of such comparatively common volumes as the first folio Shakespeare, the first *Faëry Queen*, the first *Paradise Lost*, Herrick, Beaumont and Fletcher, will present themselves in the market and command steadily advancing figures; it is the same with Pope and Dryden in a measure, and with some of the more eminent moderns. The literary *éclat* stimulates the biddings.

Those works which represent the maximum value during recent years have been:—

(i.) The earliest examples of printing, at all events in book-form; *Missæ Speciales*, and other smaller books executed by Gutenberg previous to 1455, or at all events to the Bible ascribed to that date; Gutenberg's Bible, otherwise known as the Mazarin Bible, 1455, re-issued by Fust and Schoeffer in 1456; the Psalters of 1457 and 1459, designed for the Cathedral and Benedictine monastery of Mainz respectively; the *Chronicles* of Monstrelet on vellum; *Lancelot du Lac* on vellum, 1488; the Sarum *Missal*, 1492, 1497, 1504; Caxton's two *Troy-Books*, two *Jasons*, *Arthur*, *Speculum Vitæ Christi* and *Doctrinal of Sapience* on vellum, *Canterbury Tales* and other separate works of Chaucer, *Paris and Vienne*, &c.; *Book of St. Albans*, 1486, and other works printed there, 1480-1534; Tyndale's *New Testament*, 1526; Coverdale's *Bible*, 1535; Boece's *Chronicles of Scotland* on vellum, 1536; the Huth Ballads; Montaigne's *Essais*, 1580; the same in English, 1603, 1613; Spenser's *Faëry Queen*, 1590-96; Constable's *Diana*, 1592; Bacon's *Essays*, 1597, 1598; Shakespeare's *Venus and Adonis*, *Lucrece*, 1st quartos, *Sonnets*, and the collected *Plays*, 1593-1623. (ii.) Shelton's *Don Quixote*, 1612-20; first editions of Daniel, Drayton, Lodge, Watson, Barnfield, Breton, &c.; Milton's *Comus*, 1637, *Lycidas*, 1638, *Paradise Lost*, 1667; Walton's *Complete Angler*, 1653, Bunyan's *Pilgrim's Progress*, 1678, and any other capital or standard authors of the seventeenth century, particularly Lovelace, Carew, Suckling, down to Locke's *Essay on the Human Understanding*, which, though a common book, has lately grown a dear one by sheer force of companionship.

There seems a disposition to look more indifferently on volumes which have no certificate or passport. Secondarily, as in the case of Florio's version of Montaigne, items are admitted as hangers-on and interpreters of great authors.

The last copy of the *Faëry Queen*, 1590-96, offered for sale, an extraordinarily fine one, brought £84, of *Robinson Crusoe*, £75. The British Museum paid for the *Book of Common Prayer*, 1603, a year earlier than any edition so far described, £175. It was obtained by the vendor from a sale at Sotheby's, where its liturgical interest was overlooked.

The question of prices in all these cases is involved in equal uncertainty and difficulty. The second Psalter of 1459 brought at the Syston Park sale £4950. Mr. Quaritch still holds it (1897), and asks £5250. The British Museum possesses both impressions. This was the highest figure ever reached by a single lot in this country. Gutenberg's Bible follows, copies on vellum and paper having produced from £1500 to £4000; the vellum copies are deemed more valuable, but of those issued by Gutenberg himself we seem to have only examples on paper. The Huth copy of the latter type, from the Sykes and H. Perkins libraries cost its late owner £3650. Mr. Grenville for his gave £500. As we have already remarked, the book has a tendency to become commoner. The Ashburnham Fust and Schoeffer Bible of 1462 brought £1500; at the Comte de Brienne's sale in 1724, where Hearne refers to the "vast prices," the Earl of Oxford gave for the same book £112.

The *History of King Arthur*, printed by Caxton, 1485, for which Lord Jersey's ancestor gave £2, 12s. 6d. about 1750 to Osborne, was carried at the Osterley Park sale in 1885 to £1950, the British Museum underbidding; while the *Troy-Book* in English from the same press fetched £1820; and at the dispersion of a curious lot of miscellanies, apparently derived from Darlaston Hall, near Stone, Staffordshire, an imperfect, but very large and clean, copy of the first edition of the *Canterbury Tales*, by Caxton, was adjudged to Mr. Quaritch at £1020, a second one, by an unparalleled coincidence presenting itself at the same place of sale a few months later, only four leaves wanting, but not so fine, and being knocked down at £1800 to the same buyer. The Asburnham Chaucers and other works from the same press were (with one or two exceptions) so poor, that it was surprising that they sold even so well as they did.

We descend to relatively moderate quotations when we come to the Daniel (now Huth) Ballads in 1864 (£750); the £670 and £810 bidden for the Caxton's *Gower* at the Selsey sale in 1871 and the Osterley Park sale in 1885 respectively; the £600 paid for the *Book of St. Albans*, 1486, wanting two leaves, in 1882; and the £420 at which Mr. Quaritch estimated the *Troy-Book* of 1503. The price asked for the original MS. of the *Towneley Mysteries* in 1892, £820, strikes one as reasonable by comparison.

But amounts which we venture to think unduly extravagant have of late years been obtained at Christies's rooms for certain books, such as Lady Elizabeth Tirrwhyt's *Prayers*, 1574, bound in gold, and said to have belonged to Queen Elizabeth (1220 guineas);[4] Henry VIII.'s *Prayers*, 1544, printed on vellum,[5] and enriched with notes by the King, the Queen, Prince Edward, and

Princess Mary (610 guineas, as above mentioned); and a third folio Shakespeare, 1663-64, with both titles, but represented as being almost unique in that state, £435. What a contrast to the old prices! Even in our time and memory, the first folio could be had in fine state for £50 or £60, the second for £5, 5s., the third for £50, and the fourth for £5, 5s. George Daniel, we are informed by his representatives, gave about £220 for his first Shakespeare to William Pickering, and Mr. Corser kept his 1632 book in his dining-room at Stand Rectory among the commoner volumes, although it was a fine copy. A middling set now fetches £600 or thereabout.

The earlier standard both for English and foreign rarities was undoubtedly much lower. In Osborne's Catalogue for 1751, the *Toledo Missal*, described as the scarcest volume in the world, was valued only at £35. In the Heber, and even in the Bright sale, from £10 to £25 secured some of the greatest gems in ancient English literature.

At the Frere auction at Sotheby's, 1896, however, the realisation of the Fenn books beat every record, considering that the copies were generally so poor; and it was hard indeed to see where the value was in a Herbert's Ames accompanied by an extra volume of typographical fragments, of which many were mutilated and many were worthless (£255).

The *Book of St. Albans*, 1486, as it is usually designated, has descended a little from its original rank as a first-class rarity owing to the successive discovery of unknown copies. The romance connected with the acquisition of the Grenville one has been more than once printed; but the *Chronicles of England*, from the same press, especially on vellum, maintains its reputation for the utmost rarity, although there were two impressions; and the same may be said of the issues by William of Mecklin, Caxton, and Gerard de Leeu, all and any of which could not, if complete, fail to command very high prices even on paper.

£4900 for the second edition of the Mainz Psalter, 1459, appears (as we have observed) to be the largest sum ever paid in this country for a single work; and the vellum copy of the Gutenberg Bible follows, £900 behind; at least at the price of £4000 it fell to Mr. Quaritch at the Ashburnham sale in 1897. But for the *Manesse Liederbuch*, a thirteenth-century MS. of national ballads, carried away by the French from Heidelberg in 1656, and found among the Ashburnham MSS., the German Government practically paid in 1887 £18,000. What may be termed a bad second was the Duke of Hamilton's Missal, sold to the German Government in 1887 for £10,000; but that also belongs to the manuscript class.

It must be an absolute truism to state that at the present moment the American is a material factor in influencing the book-market. He is less so, perhaps, in the sort of way in which he assisted the booksellers of a bygone generation in reducing or realising their stocks; but he has come to the front more than ever as a competitor for the prizes. There was a day when countless Transatlantic libraries were in course of formation; but they are now fairly complete, and, moreover, they have the means at hand, not formerly available, of filling up the gaps at home.

Our American kinsfolk have undoubtedly become masters of an almost countless number of bibliographical gems, and have been content to pay handsomely for them. We do not hear of any sensible reflux of old books from the States, but that might happen hereafter under the influence of financial depression. At the same time, there is perhaps nothing on the other side of the Atlantic which is not represented in duplicate here, unless it be in an instance or two, as, for example, the perfect Caxton *Morte Arthur*, 1485; and even those volumes, which are of signal rarity, are almost without exception in repositories accessible to all.

Returning for a moment to the commercial aspect of our present topic, the Transatlantic acquirer at any cost makes the fixture of high, even ridiculous, prices for certain books impossible. Beyond the *maximum* there is a higher *maximum* still. Who would have dreamed of a first edition of Burns, although uncut, bringing, as it did just lately (February 1898) in an Edinburgh auction-room, £572, or a sixpenny volume on Ploughs by one Small, £30, because it bore on the title, *Robt. Burns, Poet*, in the great man's own hand, as well as a holograph memorandum attached to flyleaf? In the case of the Kilmarnock Burns of 1786 the sole excuse of the purchaser was its uncut state, for it is a comparatively common book. It was acquired by Mr. Lamb of Dundee, a hotel-keeper, of one Mr. Braidwood for £60. A second copy in paper covers, also uncut, exists; but the general condition is not so good.

There are in London and other English centres, however, American export and commission agents, independently of those houses which make shipments to the States a collateral branch of their business. It has been the cry, ever since we can recollect, that our cousins were draining the old country of its books, and yet the movement continues—continues with this difference, that the Americans have now plenty of ordinary stock, and are more anxious to limit their acquisitions to rarities. The number of public and private libraries has become very considerable; the most familiar names are Lenox, Carter-Brown, Tower, and Pope, the last the purchaser of the *King Arthur* printed by Caxton in 1485, and formerly in the Harleian and Osterley Park collections. There is an occasional reflux of exportations, and we should like to hear one day of the *Arthur* being among them.

One not very pleasant aspect of American and other plutocratic competition has been to convert most of the *capital* old English books from literature into *vertu*. What else is it, when two imperfect Chaucers bring £2900, and a

Walton's *Angler*, £415, and where for the second and third folio Shakespeares persons are found willing to give a profit on £500 or £600?

The Transatlantic buyer, or indeed the buyer at a distance anywhere, has no option in employing an agent on the spot to acquire his *desiderata*, and he is practically in his hands. So long as your representative is competent it is well enough, and on the whole the American agencies in London are, we think, both that and conscientious. But the frequenter of the salerooms cannot fail to note a very unsatisfactory aspect of this business by proxy, where an inexperienced amateur with a well-lined purse employs an almost equally inexperienced person to act on his behalf—that is to say, one who is a bookseller by vocation, but who enjoys no conversance with bibliographical niceties. His principal consequently scores very poorly by buying *wrong* things at the *right* prices; but if he is satisfied, who need be otherwise? And his error, if his property is not realised in his lifetime, never comes home to him! Nevertheless, to buy with other people's eyes and judgment is not, after all, the best form; all that can be pleaded for it is, that it is the sole resource of the individual who has no time to devote to the practical side, or who, if he has, distrusts his own knowledge; and as everything has its compensation, such are the customers on whom the trade mainly leans. If the amateur expert were to be too much multiplied, the professional bookseller would inevitably be a grave sufferer.

Those are in the safest hands, perhaps, who are in their own. But in the case of books, as of all analogous property, the next best thing to acting for oneself is to employ a high-class dealer, or, if the line is very special, one who enjoys a reputation for conversance with the particular branch of inquiry. Where a collector who does not possess personal knowledge, and takes into his service a bookseller who is not much more informed, or who has not studied certain classes of literature, it is bound to be an exemplification of the blind leading the blind, and one, at all events, unless he has a very long purse, falling into the ditch.

Under any circumstances, it is unquestionably beneficial to any private buyer to take some pains to arrive at at least a general knowledge of values, as well as of the bearings and extent of the field which he may choose. He should not be a puppet in the hands of his representative, if he can help it. Where he cannot, he is apt to buy in one sort of market and to sell in another. Not the worst policy is to hand a commission to one's strongest opponent, if he will or can take it. It disarms him. But some firms dislike agency, as the profit, though sure, is often so narrow, particularly where the person employed is a specialist in the line, and would have given for purposes of re-sale in the ordinary way twice or thrice as much as the item fetches, his personal opposition withdrawn. Hence it is not unusual among commission-agents at book-sales to charge, not on the price realised, but on the figure given by the client. The latter authorises his representative to bid up to £10 for this or that lot; it drops at £2; the fee for buying it is a percentage, not on the lower, but the higher amount. A commission of £6 was given by the present writer for a volume of John Leland's Tracts; it dropped at 2s.; his agent charged him 10s. brokerage.

Some hand their orders direct to the auctioneer, and this may be done within certain limits; but if the practice becomes too habitual, the dealers retaliate by bidding against the rostrum. "All is fair in love and war."

FOOTNOTES

[4] Now in the British Museum by the munificence of the late Sir Wollaston Franks (Department of Antiquities).

[5] Said to have been purchased for Lord Amherst.

CHAPTER XVI

Foundations of bibliography—Commencement of advertising books through catalogues and lists at end of other publications—Classes of literature principally in demand—Origin of sales by public competition—A book-lottery in 1661—The book-auction in London makes a beginning—The practice extends to the provinces and Scotland (1680-95)—First sale-catalogue where Caxtons were separately lotted (1682)—Catalogue of a private library appended to a posthumous publication (1704)—Mystery surrounding the sources whence the Harleian Library was supplied with its early English rarities—An explanation—Indebtedness of the Heber Collection to private purchasers on a large scale—Vast additions to our knowledge since Heber's time—The modern auction-marts—Penny and other biddings at auctions—An average auction-room—Watching the Ashburnham sale—The collector behind the scenes—Key to certain prices—The Frost and the Boom—Difficulty of gauging quotations without practical experience—The *Court of Appeal*—The Duke of Wellington pays £105 for a shilling pamphlet—A few more words about the Frere sale in illustration of the Boom and something else—The Rig.

THE earliest method of communication between holders and vendors of books and probable buyers of them related to the issue of new works, or, at most, to such as were not out of date. Maunsell's celebrated folio, of which he was not apparently encouraged to proceed with more than certain sections, and which did not comprise the subjects most interesting to us, came out in 1595 in two parts, and was, notwithstanding its imperfect fulfilment, the most comprehensive enterprise of the kind in our language down to comparatively recent times. These matters usually took the form of notices, accompanying a published volume, of others already in print or in preparation by the same firm. No possessor or observer of old English books can fail to have met with such advertisements; but, as we have said, they limit themselves, as a rule, to current literature and the ventures of the immediate stationer or printer. To some copies of Marmion's *Antiquary*, 1641, we find attached a slip containing an announcement by Thomas Dring of old plays on sale by him at the White Lion in Chancery Lane, and inserted posterior to the issue of this particular drama, which does not bear Dring's name; and we all know the list of dramatic performances appended to *Tom Tyler and his Wife*, 1661, and probably emanating from Kirkman the bookseller, where we discern items belonging to an earlier period—of some of which we know nothing further. This catalogue, the material for which Kirkman had personally brought together by the expenditure of considerable time and labour, was re-issued in 1671, and from about that time Clavell and other members of the trade circulated periodical accounts of all the novelties of the season, but almost entirely in those classes which seem to have then appealed to the public: Law, Science, and Divinity—just the sections with which Maunsell in 1595 began and ended.

The absence of the machinery supplied by the auction long necessitated a practice which not only survived sales by inch of candle and under the hammer, but which still prevails, of disposing of libraries and small collections *en bloc* to the trade, and the dedication by the particular buyer of a serial catalogue to his purchase. Executors and others long possessed no other means of realisation; the Harleian printed books were thus dispersed; and even those of Heber, almost within our own memory, engrossed the resources of two or three firms of salesmen. The conditions under which a library was accumulated in former days were not less different than those under which it passed into other hands; the possibilities of profit were infinitesimal; a heavy loss was almost a certainty. But then men bought more generally for the mere love of the objects or for purposes of study. The speculative element had yet to arise.

Evelyn, in his famous letter to Pepys, August 12, 1689, speaks of Lord Maitland's library as certainly the noblest, most substantial, and accomplished, that ever passed *under the spear*. This was within two decades or so of the commencement of the system of selling literary effects by auction. We are aware that in the Bristol records of the fourteenth century the trumpet, introduced from France, is mentioned as a medium for the realisation of property in the same way; and there was the much later *inch-of-candle* principle—a perhaps unconscious loan from King Alfred's alleged time-candles, which are referred to by his biographer Asser—a work suspected of being unauthentic, yet on that account may have none the less suggested the idea to some one.

Abroad the *trumpet* or the *cry* appear among the commercial states of the Middle Ages to have been the usual forms. In the particulars of a sale of galleys by auction at Venice in 1332,[6] the property was cried beforehand on behalf of the Government, and the buyer, till he paid the price reached, furnished a surety. This process was known as the *incanto*; and it is curious enough that in the sale-catalogue of Francis Hawes, Esq., a South Sea Company director, in 1722, the goods are said to be on sale *by cant* or auction. But the modern Italian still speaks of an auction as an *asta* (the Roman *hasta*). Some of these types are illustrated by Lacroix in his *Mœurs et Usages*. In France they anciently had the bell and the crier (the Roman *præco*).

In London, firms of commercial brokers long continued to hold their sales of goods by inch of candle; but the Roman practice seems to have survived down to comparatively modern days in Spain and Portugal, if not in France and Italy. In 1554, Junius Rabirius, a French jurist, published at Paris, with a metrical inscription to Henry II. of France, a Latin treatise on the origin of *Hastæ and Auctions*, in which he enters at some length into the system pursued by the ancients, and still retained in the sixteenth century by the Latin communities of Europe. This is probably the earliest monograph which we possess on the present branch of the subject. It is a tolerably dull and uninforming one.

Some of us are aware by practical experience how deplorably tedious a normal modern auction under the hammer is, although it extends only at the utmost from one to five or six in the afternoon. But, like some of the Continental sales of to-day, the old-fashioned affair spread, with a break for refreshment, over twice the space of time, and was conducted, previous to the introduction of the hammer, by *inch of candle*. This system was somewhat less inconvenient than it at first sight strikes us as being, since the property was lotted to a much larger extent in parcels and bundles, and the biddings were apt to be comparatively fewer. Another way of saying that the early auction appealed less to private than to professional buyers, and not merely in that, but in every aspect. The same remark still applies to the dispersion of all miscellaneous collections of secondary importance, unless an amateur chooses to compete for a dozen articles, which he does not want, for the sake of one, which he does.

The steadily accumulating volume of literary production in the seventeenth century inspired two successive movements, which we regard to-day as peremptory necessities and matters of course, but which, so long as books were scarcer, and the demand for them correspondingly restricted, failed to strike any one as likely to prove popular and advantageous. These movements were the second-hand department and the auction-room. It is a sufficiently familiar fact that during the reign of Charles II. both sprang into existence, although among the Hollanders the usage of putting up books to public competition had commenced three-quarters of a century prior; but in 1661 there do not appear to have been any facilities for disposing of libraries or collections, as in that year John Ogilby, the historian, arranged to sell his books—the remainder of his own publications—through the medium of a lottery. It was within a very brief interval, however, that the sale by auction is shown to have become an accomplished fact. The earliest of which an actual catalogue has come down to us is that of Dr. Lazarus Seaman, sold by Cooper in 1676; but there were in all probability anterior experiments, and side by side with the auctioneer grew up the professional ancestor of the Thorpes and the Rodds—the men who supplied Burton, Drummond, Evelyn, Pepys, Selden, and many more, with the rarities which are yet associated with their names. The system of selling under the hammer in its various stages of development and different ramifications is not an unimportant factor in our modern social and commercial life; it did not require many years from its introduction into the metropolis to recommend it to the provinces and to Scotland; and we possess catalogues of libraries or properties dispersed in this manner at Leeds, Sheffield, Nottingham, Cambridge, Edinburgh, and elsewhere in the last quarter of the last but one century; and in one case at least of this kind of property being offered at a fair.[7] Occasionally, as in the case of Secondary Smith, 1682, a precocious feeling for the early English school reveals itself; but, for the most part, the articles accentuated by the old-fashioned auctioneer are foreign classics, history, and theology—the literary wares, in fact, in vogue. Annexed to the *Memoirs of Thomas* (or *Tom*) *Brown*, 1704, is a very unusual feature—a catalogue of his library.

Within about five-and-twenty years of the supposed starting-point of the auction, the modern practice of the London auctioneer being engaged to conduct sales in the country, even in important provincial towns, seems to have fairly commenced, for in 1700 Edward Millington of Little Britain sold at Cambridge the library of Dr. Cornwall of Clapton in Northamptonshire. In the preliminary matter attached to the catalogue, Millington remarks that "he always esteems it a privilege to exercise his lungs amongst his friends."

A glimpse of the method of collecting by the Hon. John North, one of the sons of Lord North of Kirtling, and born in 1645, is afforded by his brother and biographer, Roger North, who says that he gradually accumulated, commencing about 1666, a large collection of books, principally Greek, and generally bought them himself, spending much time in company with his relation in booksellers' shops, and not objecting to possess duplicates, if other copies in better condition were found or were presented to him by friends. Mr. North flourished during the halcyon days of the classics. The literature of his own country probably interested him little. North, however, was so far a true book-lover, inasmuch as he sought what pleased himself.

It affords a pleasanter impression of the pursuit when one perceives individuals of all ranks and callings buying themselves personally, either at the book-shop or the saleroom, in the selection of their periodical acquisitions. The marked copies of the older auction catalogues are distinguished by the names of some of our most eminent collectors, but at present gentlemen prefer to give their commissions to their booksellers from want of leisure or other motives.

I have alluded to the sale by auction of Dr. Seaman's library in 1676, which took place at his house in Warwick Court, Warwick Lane. The address to the reader, presumably by Cooper, commences:—

"It hath not been usual here in England to make sale of Books by way of Auction, or who will give most for them: But it having been practised in other Countreys to the Advantage both of Buyers and Sellers; It was therefore conceived (for the Encouragement of Learning) to publish the Sale of these Books this manner of way." The Catalogue is not divided into days, but the fifth condition says, "That the Auction will begin the 31st of October, punctually at Nine of the Clock in the Morning, and Two in the afternoon, and this to continue daily until all the Books be Sold; Wherefore it is desired, that the Gentlemen, or those deputed by them, may be there precisely the Hours appointed, lest they should miss the opportunity of Buying those Books, which either themselves or their Friends desire."

In 1682 Thomas Parkhurst, in offering for sale the libraries of several eminent men, announces that the catalogues might be had *gratis* at the Bible on London Bridge (his place of business as a bookseller), and he takes occasion to introduce (perhaps for the first time) that courageous form of statement so popular to this day among the fraternity as to the collection being the finest ever sold or to be sold, and the opportunity by consequence being one which would never probably recur.

But the present writer does not enter minutely into this branch of the subject, which Mr. Lawler has made his own.

It has always been, and must always remain, a mystery whence the Harleian exemplars of a large number of unique or almost unique volumes belonging to the early vernacular literature of Great Britain were obtained. In some cases they are traceable to anterior owners and catalogues; but a considerable residue first come to the front here, and the explanation seems to be that the practice of registering unregarded trifles, as they were then deemed to be, in large parcels was necessarily fatal to individuality and to the survival of clues. To a certain extent the same disappointment awaits us in more recent days, till, in fact, the demand for old poetry, romances, and plays made the few extant copies objects of interest to the trade sufficient to entitle them to prominence in their lists and in those published by the auctioneers. It may have been the catalogue of Joseph Ames, 1760, which was among the earliest to raise such items to the dignity of separate lots, thought by the purchasers at the time worth a shilling or two; but the noted sale of Mr. West in 1773 is entitled to rank as the foremost in those days, where the books and tracts, long since discovered to be represented by one or two accidental survivors, and grown dearer than gold a hundredfold, began to draw figures indicative of increased curiosity and appreciation.

The most eminent of the earlier race of auctioneers in London, who confined their attention to properties belonging to the fine arts, were William Cooper, a man of considerable literary taste and culture, whom we have seen disposing of Dr. Seaman's books in 1676; Edward Millington, Robert Scott, and John Dunton, of whom we know more than of his predecessors and contemporaries through his publications, and especially his *Life and Errors*. Commercial rivalry and jealousy arose among the members of the fraternity before the institution had grown at all old, and complaints were also made against gentlemen-bidders. In the preface to the catalogue of a French library, where he takes occasion to animadvert severely on his contemporary and confrère Scott, Millington refers to the third condition of sale, requiring all buyers to give in their place of abode, "to prevent the inconveniences that have more or less hitherto attended the Undertakers, and also the Purchasers, by reason that several persons, out of Vanity and Ostentation, have appeared and bought, to the damage and disappointment of the Parties they outbid, and have not been so kind to their own Reputation, or just to the Proprietors, as to pay for and fetch them away." This was in 1687.

It seems to have been a considerable time after the first institution of the auction before a fixed place of business was appointed for the sale of literary and artistic properties consigned to a particular party for realisation. We find taverns and coffee-houses much in request for this purpose during the former half of the last century. The library of printed books and MSS. belonging to Thomas Britton, "small-coal man," were sold about 1720 at Tom's Coffee-House, and about the same date portions of Thomas Rawlinson's stupendous collections, of which the dispersion extended over a dozen years, came to the hammer at the Paul's Head Tavern in Carter Lane.

It is improbable that any early auction catalogue of consequence has disappeared, and looking at those which we have, say, from the outset to 1700, we at once perceive the comparatively limited business transacted in this direction during a lengthened term of years, and the numerous instances where a not very considerable catalogue embraces three or four properties. Collections were, as a rule, made on a smaller scale prior to the Harley epoch.

The practice of publishing booksellers' and auctioneers' catalogues, rudimentary as it was at the outset, succeeded by the more systematic descriptive accounts of public and private collections, gradually extended the knowledge of the surviving volumes of early literature, and laid the foundation of a National Bibliography. We shall probably never fully learn our amount of obliged indebtedness to Richard Heber, who in his own person, from about 1800 to 1833, consolidated and concentrated an immense preponderance of the acquisitions of anterior collectors, and with them gained innumerable treasures, which came to him through other channels. His marvellous catalogue must have proved a revelation at the time, and to-day it is a work of reference at once instructive and agreeable.

What must strike any one who has attentively considered the Heber library, even if it is not a case of having had the catalogue at his elbow, as I have, in a manner, all his life, is the presence there of so large a number of items of which no trace occurs in earlier lists, and of which no duplicates have since presented themselves. It is perfectly marvellous how Heber accumulated the vast bibliographical treasures brought to light, and of which his catalogue is the record achievement; he must have been not only indefatigable in his own person, but must have furnished encouragement to many others, who met with rare books, to afford him the first refusal.

On the other hand, hundreds of early English books and tracts which this indefatigable and munificent of collectors never succeeded in obtaining, items and authors whose titles and names were hitherto utterly unknown, have within the last two generations come piecemeal into the market, to delight alike, yet in a different way, the bibliographer and the amateur. The accidental and almost miraculous survival of literary relics of past ages is curious on account of the purely casual manner in which they present themselves from season to season, as well as from the strange hands in which many of them are found—often persons of obscure character and in humble life, who have one, two, or half-a-dozen books of which all had somehow eluded the researches of every collector. Cases are known in which a single article has come to light in this manner, a unique publication of the Plantagenet or Tudor era, maybe in sorry state, maybe just as it left the press two or three centuries ago, but anyhow a monument and a revelation.

The almost exclusive sources of intelligence on these questions are the correspondence of the period, a portion of which is printed in the volumes of 1813 devoted to Aubrey's Collections, and another in Nichols's *Anecdotes*. There we perceive that Lord Oxford was indebted for many rarities to John Bagford and other private purveyors of printed books as well as MSS. In a letter of 1731 to Hearne, his Lordship mentions his impression that he had forty-two Caxtons at that date. He seems to have possessed seventy-three examples of Wynkyn de Worde.[8]

With respect to some of the college libraries at Oxford, Cambridge, and even Dublin, it is easier to arrive at the facts, so far as they go, or, in other words, many of the rare and important acquisitions of those institutions came to them at a period anterior to what may be termed the bibliographical era, and were often contemporary gifts from the authors of the volumes or from early owners of them.

The value of the auction became manifest at a comparatively early date, when a clear demand for certain descriptions of literary property had set in, particularly when the formation of the Harleian library was in progress. In 1757 the representatives of Sir Julius Cæsar, Master of the Rolls under James I., proposed to sell his MSS., and eventually negotiated with a cheesemonger, who offered £10 for the collection as waste paper. Paterson, the auctioneer, fortunately heard of the affair, dissuaded the family from it, and prepared a careful catalogue of the articles, by which he realised to the owners £356. Take another case. In 1856 the Wolfrestons decided on parting with a lot of old books and pamphlets which an ancestor had collected under the Stuarts, or even earlier, and would, as one of them informed us, have gladly accepted £30 for the whole. But they were sent to Sotheby's, and realised £750.

On the other hand, instances are by no means unknown, in spite of what the auctioneers may assert, where it has suited a bookseller to give for a library or a parcel of books a sum at all events sufficient to tempt the owner, who has always before his eyes, in the case of a sale under the hammer, a variety of risks and draw-backs, which an immediate cheque, even for a lower amount, at once removes.

After all, the book-lover must, as a rule, be satisfied with the pleasure attendant on temporary possession.

Of the houses which lend themselves in our own day, and have done so during the last hundred or hundred and fifty years, to the incessant redistribution of literary acquisitions, and have gradually reduced an originally rather rudimentary principle to a sort of fine art, so much has been written by a succession of gentlemen interested in these specialities that we could hardly add much that was new, or treat this aspect of the topic without repeating others or ourselves.

A point which merits a passing mention, however, is the history of the bidding at these scenes of competition. It has been remarked as a singular circumstance that in the seventeenth century penny biddings were usual; but it was the silver penny of those days, and we have to remember the higher purchasing value of money. Twopenny and threepenny advances succeeded, and although these have long ceased in London, they yet survive in the provinces, where the lots are less important. Some of the principal houses now decline even sixpence, a shilling being the *minimum* offer entertained. The twopenny bidding still prevailed in 1731, as a priced copy of the sale catalogue of Robert Gray, M.D.,[9] shows. An offer of threepence is still not unknown in the provinces, as we have intimated above in our notice of an episode in Lincolnshire—not the Spalding one, but a second about the same point of time.

One of the not least interesting and curious aspects of the auction system is the diversity of motives inducing owners to part with their property. A study of the title-pages or covers of catalogues admits us ostensibly to the confidence of this or that collector. We should not otherwise become aware that some fairly obscure gentleman or lady was leaving his or her actual abode, that Balbus was changing the character of his library, that his friend so-and-so, owing to a failure of health, had found it necessary to settle in a more genial climate, or that "a well-known amateur," of whom we never heard before, was selling his duplicates. What does it signify? Literary acquisitions, in common with everything else, are constantly passing from one hand to another. Of course, if the last proprietor is deceased, if it is an executor's affair, it is just as well to mention the fact, as it places the operation on a clearer footing, and there is little, if any, suspicion of nursing; but with ordinary lots of books, where the party or parties interested may be living, it seems preferable to describe the objects of competition purely and simply as so many items for sale. The reason for the step is immaterial, more especially as there is a proneness to receive the one tendered, if not with indifference, with incredulity.

A singular entry in one of the sale catalogues of Edward Jeffery, of Warwick Street, Golden Square, under 1788, is a property described as "the *lounging* books of a gentleman," in the near vicinity of which we come across "the Parliamentary and constitutional library of a man of fashion."

Of course, where a famous or capital assemblage of literary treasures is for sale, it is quite proper and expedient on every account to connect with it the name on which it confers, and which may even confer on it, distinction. But it is different when Mr. Jones is changing his lines, or Mr. Brown is removing into the country or out of it, or the executors of the late Mr. Robinson have given instructions for the submission of his effects to the hammer. *Qu'importe?* Who cares?

The composition of an average auction-room, where the property is miscellaneous, is a curious and not unedifying study. One beholds a large, closely-packed room, where the atmosphere is not too salubrious, and yet the names which the auctioneer proclaims as those of the buyers are not numerous, are not even in all cases the names of persons present. The reason is that booksellers or their representatives often attend sales for the sake of watching the market or of noting the prices, and are on the spot when a lot occurs which suits them, or for which they have a commission. It is not perhaps too much to say that if the company should be reduced by 75 per cent. the quotations would remain unaltered, for a certain proportion are dummies beyond a moderate figure, and a certain proportion never open their mouths. The latter are spectators, or proprietors, or individuals whose biddings are given from the rostrum by proxy. An experienced dealer will probably guess for whom the salesman or his clerk is acting, and will be guided by such a hint in his own course of proceeding.

Where the goods on sale are of a prevailingly low standard, the scene varies in compliance with the circumstances, and the purchasers' names in the priced catalogue are almost without exception the names of booksellers, who make their account by going in for heavy lots and rough stuff—an excellent vocation thirty years ago, but now a fairly forlorn hope and quest. The bargain is no longer to the man who can buy for a shilling and sell for a pound, but to him who has the courage and means to buy for fifty pounds what he can sell for five times fifty by virtue of his knowledge and connection.

To watch carefully and studiously a big sale such as that of the Ashburnham library, of which two out of three portions are now scattered, is a bibliographical, if not a commercial, education in little. We attended in person throughout, and observed with interest and profit the curious working, unappreciable to those not practically versed in books, and acquainted with the result only through paragraphs in the newspapers. A spectator with some preparatory training could see how and why certain lots fetched such and such abnormal figures; and a leading agency in this direction was the unfortunate employment—unfortunate for himself, not for the owner or the auctioneer—by a leading buyer of an agent who had to win his purchases from men stronger than himself. Thus the Caxton's *Jason*, instead of bringing perhaps £1000, ran up to more than twice that sum, while, if it was re-sold under different conditions, it might not even reach the lower amount. Still more striking were the offers for such things as the first English edition of More's *Utopia* (£51), a volume which has repeatedly sold for a couple of guineas; while, on the other hand, a handsomely bound copy of Bourrienne's *Memoires* in ten volumes went for 11s., and other ordinary works in proportion.

The names in the booksellers' ledgers and in the auctioneers' catalogues as buyers of old or scarce literature are not by any means necessarily always the names of collectors. They are often those of middlemen, through whose hands a volume passes before it reaches its ultimate destination—passes in many cases from one of these channels to another. This is, of course, another mode of saying that the number of actual book-holders on their own permanent account is comparatively limited, and so it is. A call on the part of two or three persons for a particular class of work or subject immediately puts the whole trade on its mettle; everything directly or indirectly connected with the new topic is bought up or competed for with extraordinary and abrupt eagerness; the entire fraternity is bent on supplying the latest demand; and prices rise with proportionate rapidity to an extravagant height. The market consists of a couple or trio of individuals, who might be insensible to the excitement which they have occasioned if it were not for the offers from all sides which pour in upon them from day to day; and in a season or so it is all over; quotations are as before; and the running is on something different. Books of Emblems, Catholic Literature, Gardening and Agriculture, Occult Sciences, Early Poetry, Old Plays, Americana, Bewick, Cruikshank, the modern novelists, have all had their day. But the cry and the want are largely artificial. The customers are few; the caterers are many. Such a criticism applies only to the rarer and costlier *desiderata*.

The characteristics and frequent surprises of auction figures largely proceed from the pressure brought to bear from without by bidders who are in the background, who often possess slight bibliographical knowledge, and whose resources enable them to furnish their representatives with generous instructions. These competitors are usually restricted to prominent sales, where the capital items are numerous, and the name of the proprietor is that of a departed celebrity, or at all events, where certain copies, whether of manuscripts or printed books, are submitted to public competition after a lengthened period of detention in the hands of the late holder. The Ashburnham sale (now completed) afforded abundant proof of the influence on the market of a collector who began to form his library before many of us were born, and who succeeded not only in securing many treasures at present almost beyond reach, but in doing so at fairly moderate prices. But even when the late Lord Ashburnham went to what was in his time considered an extreme figure, he or his estate generally gained. For example, his *Parzival and Titurell*, 1477, which cost Mr. Quaritch £30, and was sold to his Lordship for £45 or less (Lord Ashburnham did not object to a discount), was reacquired by the former for £81, and the set of Walton's *Angler*, which is understood to have cost £200, realised four times that amount.

The auction mart, where literary property of all kinds changes hands, possesses its slang vocabulary, and knows alike the *Frost* and the *Boom*—not to mention the *Fluke*. In the notices which occur in the press the public sees only one side, only the high quotations. The public are of course, as a rule, destitute of bibliographical knowledge, and so is the normal journalist. He marches into the room after some sale, asks for the priced catalogue, scans the pages, and makes notes of the highest figures, which are as often as not misprinted by him in the organ by which he is employed. He does not say that a lot which was worth £20 went for £2, or that one which would usually fetch £2, brought £20 by reason of some mentioned technicality, because he does not know. A man who has devoted his life to the study of books and prices is aware that there are occasions when very ordinary property realises silly prices, and that there are others when the rarest and most valuable articles are given away. Sometimes, again, the company is not *unanimous* enough, and a sovereign's worth may go for more than a sovereign, or, if there is perfect friendship among those present, a first folio Shakespeare may drop at a dozen pounds; but then there is, you know, *the court of appeal*, which reassesses the amount to be finally paid. Not invariably. We have our very selves not so long since, on a hot Saturday afternoon, sat at the auctioneer's table, and made nearly a clean sweep of a library of old English plays, where the maximum bid was eighteen pence, and there was a buzz through the room when one, no better than the rest, was accidentally carried to 14s.

But to the artificial inflation of prices in our salerooms there is more than one side and one key. There was not so long since an instance at Christie's, and a second at Sotheby's, where the high quotations were entirely due to the competition of a so-called interloper, who bade, as he thought, on the judgment of the room, and was signally handicapped. Again, something has ere now been carried to a prodigious figure owing to an unlimited commission inadvertently given to two agents. The old Duke of Wellington once gave £105 in this way for a shilling pamphlet, and even then the bidding was only stopped by arrangement. However, of all the miraculous surprises, the most signal on record was one of the most recent—the Frere sale at Sotheby's in 1896, already alluded to, where the prices realised for books in very secondary preservation set all records and precedents at thorough defiance. The phenomenon, if it could be referred to any cause, arose from the peculiar atmosphere and surroundings; it was a *bonâ fide* old library, formed partly by the Freres of Roydon Hall, Norfolk, and partly by their relative Sir John Fenn, editor of the *Paston Letters*, and a rather noted antiquary of the eighteenth century. It was all straight and fair, so far as one could see; there was no "rigging," and the competition was simply insane. A portion of the Paston Correspondence struck us as cheap by comparison at £400; it was that which was offered at Christie's some time since, and bought in at about the same figure.

There were one or two singular errors in the catalogue. An Elizabethan edition of Sir John Mandeville's Travels was ascribed to 1503 and the press of Wynkyn de Worde, and the Tylney Psalter, belonging to the fifteenth century, was stated in a note by a former possessor to be of the age of Richard Cœur de Lion. One of the most unaccountable blunders in an auctioneer's catalogue which we can call to mind was the description of a Sarum service book as a grammatical treatise. But solecisms of various kinds are periodical. A German book is said to be printed at Gedruckt, and a copy of Sir John Mandeville in Italian is entered as *Questo*, that being its compiler's frugal method of giving the title (*Questo e il libro*).

One striking feature in the Frere sale was that it was only a part of the library, and that not the part which the auctioneers' representative saw at Roydon. Some further instalments occurred at another saleroom a few months later; and perhaps there is yet more to come. But in a bibliographical respect the dispersion proved of interest, as many of the items, formerly Sir John Fenn's, had remained imperfectly known and described; and it was not absolutely certain that they survived.

An element in the modern auctions which is patent to all fairly conversant with such *mysteria*, and has become one not less indispensable than normal, is what is commonly known as the *Rig*. A Rig is a sale which departs or declines from the strict line of *bona fides* so far as not to be precisely what the forefront of the catalogue avouches it, and by one or two houses it is discountenanced. Nevertheless it exists, and will continue from the nature of things to do so; and we observe in the very opening decade of auctions, in the very infancy of the system, a trace or germ of this commencing impurity or abuse. For some of the catalogues, so far back as 1678, purport to register within their covers the libraries of certain noblemen or gentleman "and others" (*aliorumque*, in the Latin diction then so much in favour), and so it has been ever since. When we go to the rooms and lift up our voices, we do not always know whose property we are trying to secure; nor, if our own judgment is worth anything, does it greatly signify.

FOOTNOTES

[6] Hazlitt's *Venice*, 1860, iv. 431.

[7] The library of James Chamberlain, sold at Stourbridge Fair in 1686.

[8] See *Catalogue of Early English Miscellanies formerly in the Harleian Library*, by W. C. Hazlitt, 1862.

[9] See besides, *Hazlitt's Memoirs*, 1896, chaps. vii, viii, ix; and Hazlitt's *Confessions of a Collector*, 1897, p. 150 *et seq.*

ADDITIONAL NOTES

P. 5. Of the public collections in England, those of Humphrey, Duke of Gloucester, at Oxford, of which very little remains, and of Sir John Gyllarde, Prior of the Calendaries' Gild in Bristol (founded before 1451), appear to be the pioneers. For the latter the Bishop of Worcester is said to have provided, in 1464, a receptacle or building; but the collection was destroyed by fire in 1466.

P. 5. *Illuminated MSS.*—A great store of information is capable of being collected on the subject of the embellishing and finishing processes which MSS. underwent when the scribe had done his part. Among the Paston Letters occurs a bill from Thomas (the) Limner of Bury St. Edmunds to Sir John Howard, afterward Duke of Norfolk, in 1467, for illuminating several books, and we have also one of Antoine Verard of Paris, "Enlumineur du Roy," in 1493 for similar work executed for the Comte d'Angoulême by artists in the printer's employment.

P. 7. *Circulating Libraries.*—There was a library of this class at Dunfermline in 1711 and at Edinburgh in 1725. When Benjamin Franklin came to London, there was nothing of the kind. A bookseller named Wright established one about 1740, and it was kept up by his successors. Sion College was limited in its lending range to the London clergy.

P. 9. Add the Le Stranges of Hunstanton to the East Anglian collectors.

P. 9. *Kent as a Hunting-ground for Books in Old Days.*—Flockton of Canterbury it was who once sold Marlowe's *Dido*, 1594, for 2s. He was a contemporary of William Hutton, the Birmingham bookseller. This may have been the very copy which formerly belonged to Henry Oxinden of Barham, near Canterbury, and passed in succession into the hands of Isaac Reed, George Steevens, the Duke of Roxburghe, Sir Egerton Brydges, and Mr. Heber. The price charged by Flockton, however, was fairly extravagant in comparison with that given by John Henderson, the actor, for the copy which subsequently belonged to J. P. Kemble and the Duke of Devonshire—fourpence—probably the original published price.

P. 10. *Bristol Houses.*—Add *Strong*. Strong's catalogues for 1827-1828 are now before me, and describe 10,000 items. No such stock has been kept at Bristol since. Jefferies had in former days some very remarkable books on sale—Caxtons included; and Kerslake and George could shew you volumes worth your notice and money, whoever you might be. Now, alas! you have to leave the city as empty as you entered it.

P. 18. *Loss of Old Books.*—The fate of a heavy percentage of our earlier books—of the earlier books of every people—is curiously and mournfully readable in the illiterate bucolic scrawls, doing duty for autographs and inscriptions, which tell, only too plainly, how such property slowly but surely passed out of sight and existence.

P. 19. *Old Libraries.*—Add Fraser of Lovat, Boswell of Auchinleck, and Fountaine of Narford.

P. 25. *Rolls of Book-Collectors.*—Rather say 5000 names.

P. 29. *Spoliation of Libraries.*—A precious volume of early English tracts was not very long since offered at an auction, which had been stolen from Peterborough Cathedral, and another, which constituted one of the chief treasures of Sion College.

P. 32. The bulk of the books of Mr. Samuel Sandars were left to the University Library, Cambridge, which has since acquired those of the late Lord Acton.

P. 33. *Lincoln Cathedral Library.*—Besides the Honeywood books sold to Dibdin, the Dean and Chapter have suffered others to stray from their homes. A notice is before me of one, a large folio on vellum, containing tracts of a theological complexion, chiefly by an Oxford doctor, Robert of Leicester, which was presented, as a coeval inscription apprises us, by Thomas Driffield, formerly Chancellor of the Diocese, in 1422 to the new library of the cathedral.

P. 34. *Provincial Libraries.*—Of the books at Bamborough Castle, a catalogue was printed at Durham in 1799. Some of the books at York Minster appear to have been gifts from Archbishop Mathews. At Colchester they are fortunate in possessing the library of Archbishop Harsnet.

P. 35. Marlowe's *Edward II.*, 1594.—Possibly obtained by the Landgraf of Hesse during his visit to London in 1611. This is mentioned by me in my *Shakespear Monograph*, 1903.

P. 37. *Private Libraries.*—In the case of private collections, we have to distinguish between those of an ancestral character, insensibly accumulated from generation to generation without any fixed or preconcerted plan, and such as have been formed by or for wealthy individuals in the course of a single life, if not of a few years, on some general principle, with or without an eye to cost. Under either of these conditions the motive is usually personal, and the ultimate transfer in some instances to a public institution an accident or afterthought.

P. 38. *Harleian Library.*—The taste of the Harley family for books dated from the time of Charles I. Sir Robert Harley, of Brampton Castle, is credited with the possession of "an extraordinary library of manuscript and printed books, which had been collected from one descent to another." The house was besieged and burned in 1643, and these literary and bibliographical treasures probably perished with it. But his grandson, the first Earl of Oxford, restored the library; and we all know that the second earl, who survived till 1741, elevated it to the rank of the first private collection in England, while he unconsciously sacrificed it to the incidence of a languid and falling market.

P. 42. Mr. William Henry Miller of Craigentinny was originally a solicitor in Edinburgh.

P. 65. *Books of Emblems.*—Besides those described is the translation executed by Thomas Combe, and licensed in 1593, of the *Théâtre des Bons Engins* of Guillaume de la Perriere, of which no perfect copy of any edition had been seen till the writer met with one of 1614 among the Burton-Constable books.

P. 103. *Books Appreciable on Special Grounds.*—Among these are—Pennant's *Tour in Scotland*, 1769, and White's *Selborne*, 1785. Everybody is aware that there are better works on Scotland than Pennant's, and better accounts of birds, those of Selborne included, than White's. But we desire the two heirlooms, as their authors left them, pure and simple. We prefer not to have to disentangle the two pieces of eighteenth century workmanship from the editorial and artistic improvements which have overlaid them. A much-edited writer becomes a partner in a limited company without a vote. His pages are converted by degrees into an arena where others commend him above his deserts, or what might have been his wishes, while here and there he finds a commentator, whose aim is to convince you how superior a job he would have made of it had it been left to him.

P. 109. *Translations.*—It is remarkable that Aulus Gellius makes the same complaint as is embodied in the text, about the lame versions of Latin writers from the Greek.

P. 117. Howell's *New Sonnets and Pretty Pamphlets.*—The Huth fragment seems as if it would complete the unique, but imperfect, Capell copy.

P. 119. *A Hundred Merry Tales.*—Besides the Huth mutilated copy and the Göttingen complete one (of 1526) there is a fragment at the Birthplace Museum, Stratford. I saw it there, but did not note to what impression it belonged.

P. 122. *Four Sons of Aymon*, 1504.—A fine copy is offered at 15s. in a catalogue about 1760. Of the *Famous history of the vertuous and godly woman Judith*, 1565, all that is so far discoverable is that it is a translation in English metre by Edward Jenynges. A title-page, preserved among Ames's collections at the British Museum, is copied by me in *Bibl. Coll.*, 1903, pp. 210-11.

P. 125. *Destruction of Books.*—Untold numbers of volumes have also been sacrificed to the accumulation of material on special lines. Tons of the *Annual*

Register, Gentleman's Magazine, Notes and Queries, and the like, have been lost, if it be a loss, in this way. A few pages, maybe, are all that survive of a book, and when the library of the specialist is sold, the rest shares the same fate at the hands of an unsympathetic purchaser.

P. 126. *Unique copies.*—The play of *Orestes*, 1567, came to light at Plymouth about forty years ago with an equally unique issue of one of Drayton's pieces. Of such things the present writer has met in the course of a lengthened career with treasures which would make a small library, and has beheld no duplicates.

P. 128. *Fragments.*—The Fragment has within the last twenty or thirty years come into surprising evidence, and in my latest instalment of *Bibliographical Notes*, 1903, I have been enabled to supply numerous deficiencies in existing records even of modern date from a variety of sources not ostensibly connected with Bagford, Fenn, or any other culprit of this type, shewing that the process of disappearance was in universal operation, and that mere chance arrested it here and there just in the nick of time.

P. 128. *Capital Books.*—It is perhaps not unfair to add that although Milton's *Poems*, 1645, is not a rare book, it is eminently so in an irreproachable state, to say nothing of such a copy as the Bodleian one presented by the poet himself, which one of the earlier officials, a Dr. Hudson, thought might be thrown away without detriment to the library.

P. 171. *Early Prices of Binding.*—The books or pamphlets issued at one penny, that is, a silver penny of the day, were usually stitched or sewn.

The edition of the *Book of Common Prayer*, 1552, was sold, bound in parchment, at 3s. 4d., and in leather, paper boards, or clasps, at 4s. But in the next impression, it being in contemplation to suppress certain matter, the price was to be reduced in proportion.

P. 183. There has been recently added to Cohen's work a companion one on the French illustrated literature of the nineteenth century.

Books like Bewick's *Birds and Quadrupeds*, and indeed all works of the modern side in request, are best liked in the original boards with labels inviolate.

P. 191. *Cloister Life of Charles V.*—The Keir illustrated copy was long at Leighton's in Brewer Street, while the late Sir W. Stirling-Maxwell was known as Mr. Stirling.

P. 198. *Henry VIII., Prayers*, 1544.—This exists in later impressions in English, and of the date 1544 in Latin.

P. 200. *Special Copies.*—To the list given may be added the extraordinary volume of tracts formerly in the possession of Edmund Spenser and Gabriel

Harvey, a MS. note in which throws an entirely new light on the earlier life of Spenser, as first pointed out by me after my purchase of the book at an auction, where its importance was overlooked.

P. 205. *Shakespear's Copy of Florio's Montaigne*, 1603.—In my *Monograph on Shakespear*, 1903, I have adduced new evidence in support of the authenticity of this and other signatures of the poet.

P. 206. *Books with MSS. Notes.*—There is yet another category of remains among the older literature of all countries, and it is that, in which an acknowledged judge or master of a subject, though himself perhaps a person of no peculiar celebrity, has rendered a copy of some book the medium for preserving for future use matter overlooked by the author or editor or correcting serious errors, and the lapse of time exercises its influence in the appreciation of such *adversaria*. A living scholar may be capable of going far beyond his predecessors in enriching margins and flyleaves; but there is the caveat that he is our contemporary. The privilege of the grave appertains to the man who laid down his pen ever so long ago. We may know much more than Langbaine or Oldys about the drama, and than Johnson or Malone about Shakespear; yet, depend upon it, their notes are more wanted than ours.

P. 208. *Autographs in Books.*—In his copy of Slatyer's *Palæalbion*, 1621, the poet Earl of Westmorland wrote on a flyleaf: "Solus Deus Protector Meus. W. Ex dono Danielis Beswitch servi mei fidelis, 1654."

Among his books Robespierre possessed a MS. Account of the Glorious Achievements of Louis XIV. with illustrative drawings, and did it the honour of attaching his autograph—an operation seldom so harmless.

P. 218. *Books on Vellum.*—The *Horæ* of the Virgin in the ancient impressions on vellum are commoner than those on paper, though, as the late Mr. Huth quietly observed to me, the vellum copies may be more desirable.

The material, on which the Gwynn and Methuen copy of *Helyas*, 1512, was printed, was unusually coarse, and this criticism applies to other early English books taken off on that substance. They are a powerful contrast to the Italian productions of the same class.

P. 232. A good deal of information has gradually accumulated respecting the Venetian school of binding; but undoubted examples of early date remain singularly scarce. See my *Venetian Republic*, 1900, ii. 663, 728. The older school of French binding resembled that of the finer porcelain of Chantilly and Sèvres, where on a choice piece of the Louis XV. period are found, side by side, the separate marks of maker, painter, and gilder.

P. 244-5. *English Binders.* Add:—

- Edmond Richardson of Scalding Alley.

- Matthews. (Binder of the Hibbert, Wilkes, Gardner, and Huth copy of Shakespear, 1623.)

- Hayday. (Worked for W. Pickering.)

- Leighton.

- J. & J. Leighton. (This firm still does business in Brewer Street.)

- Douglas Cockerell.

- J. Larkins.

- Miss Prideaux.

- Sir Edward Sullivan.

R. Montague (1730-40), bookseller, publisher, and binder, had a place of business in 1732 at the corner of Great Queen Street, Drury Lane, and in 1740 in Great Wyld Street. He undertook to gild and letter books at his customers' own houses. John Bancks of Sunning was his journeyman. It was the late Mr. Huth who expressed to me the opinion that Bedford's brown calf should have been left to acquire a natural tone.

P. 248. *Books with Painted and Goffered Edges.*—I have seen volumes belonging to the first quarter of the sixteenth century with the leaves goffered and ornamentally inscribed; but the painted edge, as we know it, was then already in existence in Italy, and the most eminent artists did not disdain to execute this kind of embellishment. One family at Belluno long possessed numerous examples enriched by the hand of Cesare Vecellio. See my *Venetian Republic*, 1900, ii. 728. The major part of a sale at Sotheby's a year or so ago consisted of books treated on this principle by the owner; and the commercial result was not joyous.

P. 253. *French and other Binders.* Add:—

- Brodel Ainé et fils.

- Bisiques. (Famous for his Turkey leather.)

- Thouvenin.

- L. Muller. (Thouvenin's successor.)

The house of Marius-Michel combined binding and gilding. Among the Rothschild MSS., now in the British Museum, is a Boccaccio bound by Thomas Berthelet before 1552 for the Protector Somerset. It is in gilt calf with the motto: *Foy povr Debvoir.*

P. 263. The catalogue of the Early English Books in the British Museum was mainly the work of Mr. Eccles, a late member of the staff. A new, enlarged, and much improved edition by Mr. Pollard is in progress.

P. 271. That fairly familiar term, *Unique*, has been very badly entreated. A late eminent auctioneer, who was not shy of using it, tried to bring into vogue the variant form, *Uni Que*.

P. 274. *Huth Catalogue.*—My copy is full of corrections, the text abounding with errors, some of a very serious character. The late Mr. F. S. Ellis was the responsible editor, and omitted at his discretion much interesting matter.

P. 275. *Bibliographical Works of Reference.*—One of the best is Dickson and Edmond's *Annals of Scotish Printing*, 1890. The Rylands Catalogue proved a *fiasco*.

P. 298. Of course the notification in the press of a signally high price at an auction for a really important lot overwhelms the vendors with inquiries and offers—offers of similar treasures, which are extremely the reverse.

P. 307. Mr. Robert Hoe acquired the bulk or whole of Mr. Pope's books after his death, including the Caxton *Arthur*, 1485, and this gentleman continues to buy some of the most important items which occur for sale in London.

After all said, much as we at home here in Britain need to be better instructed in the art of Book-Collecting, our American cousins are still farther from having completed their education in this way—a few have not commenced it, I fancy. It is not generally realised in England that the American collector of loftier range is a type entirely distinct from the normal book-collector, whose limit is quickly reached. Those who buy books in the United States are by no means all Hoes and Morgans.

P. 311. *Early Catalogues of old Plays.*—I should have added the so often quoted one annexed to the *Old Law*, 1656.

P. 314. *Inch of Candle.*—This practice survived down to modern times both in France and England in the disposal or transfer of real property.

P. 315. *Lazarus Seaman.*—This gentleman was a member of the Assembly of Divines, and at one time chaplain to the Duke of Northumberland. He held the living of All Hallows, Bread Street, and became Master of Peterhouse, Cambridge. But he lost his clerical preferment at the Restoration, and chiefly resided in his later days in Warwick Lane, London, where he died in 1675.

P. 317. *Book Auctions.*—It is at present, I believe, at the discretion of the auctioneer to postpone a sale, when the company is too small to promise a satisfactory result, yet I have known one carried out when not more than two influential bidders were present. In a catalogue of 1681, however, there is a proviso that at least twenty gentlemen must attend.

P. 323. It is a powerful exemplification of the contrast between old times and ours, that Mr. Pierpont Morgan is credited with having acquired forty Caxtons at one swoop.

CPSIA information can be obtained
at www.ICGtesting.com
Printed in the USA
BVHW071519131221
623924BV00003B/365

9 789355 390271